City of Noise

STUDIES IN SENSORY HISTORY

Series Editor
Mark M. Smith, University of South Carolina

Series Editorial Board
Martin A. Berger, University of California at Santa Cruz
Constance Classen, Concordia University
William A. Cohen, University of Maryland
Gabriella M. Petrick, New York University
Richard Cullen Rath, University of Hawaiʻi at Mānoa

City of Noise

Sound and Nineteenth-Century Paris

AIMÉE BOUTIN

UNIVERSITY OF ILLINOIS PRESS

Urbana, Chicago, and Springfield

Library of Congress Cataloging-in-Publication Data
Boutin, Aimée, 1970–
City of noise: sound and nineteenth-century Paris /
Aimée Boutin.
pages cm. — (Studies in sensory history)
Includes bibliographical references and index.
ISBN 978-0-252-03921-8 (cloth: alkaline paper)
ISBN 978-0-252-08078-4 (paperback: alkaline paper)
ISBN 978-0-252-09726-3 (e-book)
1. Paris (France)—History—19th century.
2. Paris (France)—Social life and customs—19th century.
3. City noise—France—Paris—History—19th century.
4. Noise pollution—France—Paris.
5. Street vendors—France—Paris—History—19th century.
6. Urban renewal—France—Paris—History—19th century.
7. Urban policy—France—Paris—History—19th century.
8. City and town life—France—Paris—History—19th century.
I. Title.
DC733.B68   2015
944′.36106—dc23   2014037009

Contents

List of Illustrations

Acknowledgments

C ompleting this book would not have been possible without the support and assistance of my colleagues, friends, and family. I would like to thank Professors Richard Cullen Rath and Mark M. Smith as well as Dr. Regier Willis and his team at the University of Illinois Press. Jeremy Popkin gave me some helpful advice that proved formative early on in the project's development, whereas David Howes provided instrumental feedback toward its end. I thank Helen Abbott, Elizabeth Emery, Stephanie Leitch, Martin Munro, Charles Upchurch, Lauren Weingarden, and Seth Whidden for their feedback on selected chapters. I am also grateful to Priscilla Ferguson, Catherine Nesci, and Cheryl Krueger for their insights on the flâneur and the senses. Nate Johnson, Leonard Reidy, and Karen Hallman helped make the writing effective. Special thanks goes to William Cloonan for arranging research leave. Arnaud Bernadet and McGill University Library facilitated productive summer research in Montreal. This book would not have been possible without the support of the FSU Council on Research and Creativity and of my colleagues and graduate students at Florida State University. Most of all, I have my family to thank for their patience, support, and encouragement.

An early investigation into street cries appeared as "Sound Memory: Paris Street Cries in Balzac's *Père Goriot*," *French Forum* 30.2 (2005): 67–78, published by the University of Nebraska Press. Material from chapter 1 was published as "Aural Flânerie," in *Dix-Neuf: Journal of the Society of Dix-Neuviémistes* 16.2 (2012): 149–61, distributed by Maney Publishing at www.maneyonline.com/dix. I am grateful for permission to reuse this material.

Introduction

On July 4, 1835, the day John Sanderson (1783–1844) set foot in Paris for the first time, the street noise so overwhelmed him that he felt that Paris was "ahead of [his] experience":

As for the noise of the streets, I need not attempt to describe it. What idea can ears, used only to the ordinary and human noises, conceive of this unceasing racket—this rattling of the cabs and other vehicles over the rough stones, this rumbling of the omnibuses. For the street cries—one might have relief from them by a file and handsaw.—First the *prima donna* of the fish-market opens the morning: *Carpes toutes fraîches; voilà des carpes!* And then stand out of the way for the glazier: *Au vitriere!* [*sic*] quavering down the chromatic to the lowest flat upon the scale. Next the iron-monger with his rasps, and files and augers, which no human ears could withstand, but that his notes are happily mellowed by the seller of old clothes: *Marchand de drap!* in a monotone so low and spondaic, and so loud as to make Lablache die of envy. About nine is full chorus, headed by the old women and their proclamations: *Horrible attentat contre la vie du roi Louis Philippe—et la petite chienne de Madame la Marquise—égarée à dix heures—L'Archevêque de Paris—Le Sieur Lacenaire—Louis-Philippe, le Procès monstre—et tout cela pour quatre sous !* Being set loose all at the same time, tuned to different keys. All things of this earth seek, at one time or another, repose—all but the noise of Paris. The waves of the sea are sometimes still, but the chaos of these streets is perpetual from generation to generation; it is the noise that never dies.[1]

In a comic mix of French and English text, Sanderson describes the panic and disorientation produced by the onslaught of ubiquitous street sounds—"let loose all at the same time," "tuned to different keys," "perpetual," "unceasing racket." His was not a singular experience. The Paris correspondent for the *Springfield Republican* and *Boston Transcript*, Edward King (1848–1896) also recalls how "When one awakens in the morning in Paris, no matter in what quarter, far above all the other dins arise the curious cries of the street peddlers. A motley crowd indeed they are. In midsummer, the flower-seller's wagon makes a bright color-spot in many a dingy side avenue. At early morning its perfume is wafted to you, and the cry, 'Pansies! Daisies!' comes up loud, long, and shrill."[2] Some tourists found the motley assortment of cries disturbing. James Jackson Jarves (1818–1888), a native of Boston and an American expatriate, art writer, and collector, speaks dismissively of the "discordant notes" and "horrible sounds of Paris" in *Parisian Sights and French Principles, Seen through American Spectacles*.[3] When Pauline Cushing, Paris correspondent for the *Christian Advocate* in the last decade of the nineteenth century, writes about "Paris Street Life" for *Zion's Herald* in 1897, she describes how "the loud cry of [a female vendor] advertising her goods, makes the stranger shudder." Other visitors were charmed. At the turn of the century, at a time when Paris has become a modern metropolis and one might expect hawkers to have disappeared from the city, American journalists were still writing articles on Parisian street cries.[4] Rowland Strong, Paris correspondent for the *New York Times*, on the contrary, waxed nostalgically about street cries in *Sensations of Paris*, as did Bradley Gilman of the *Cosmopolitan*.[5] Gilman, who made a compilation for the magazine, found the cries of Paris the most musical he had heard.

It was not only foreign tourists who sought to characterize the ambiance of a city newly encountered. Arriving in Paris for the first time, migrants from the French provinces were frequently struck deaf by the overpowering and disorienting noise. Henry Martin (1810–1883), for example, came to Paris from Picardie at the beginning of the year 1830 and wrote with awe about what he heard his first morning in Paris:

> We will never forget our first morning waking up as a Provincial in Paris, the day after our arrival: those thousand intonations, that seize our attention by their bizarre affectation, and often resemble the monotonous chants of maniacs, have on whomever hears them for the first time, an effect that the born and bred Parisian rocked by these strange voices since birth, would never suspect.[6]

Again, the chorus of street cries rises above the clamor. They strike the ears because of their bizarreness, an incongruity this book aims to explore. Newcomers hear the cries of small-scale itinerant tradesmen that most of the residents, "born and bred Parisians," no longer pay attention to. Those who experience a place for the first time are often more sensitive to the sounds that residents take for granted; foreign tourists, visiting scholars, or new immigrants from the provinces who wrote about their move, and literary guidebooks promoted to Parisians and newcomers alike, provide important records of the ambiance of the city. Street cries were not insignificant sounds; rather they signify the economic abundance and disparities of the capital, the coexistence of old and new traditions, the vibrancy of the streets or the weariness of street noise. Peddlers circulated meaningful sounds that triggered a defining affective relationship to street life, connected and divided social classes, and disseminated popular sounds into highbrow works of literature, music, and the visual arts.

City of Noise adopts a sensory approach to understanding the city as a sonic space that orchestrates different, often conflicting sound cultures. I show how city noise heightens the significance of selective listening in the modern urban condition and argue for an aural rather than visual conception of modernity. Urban renewal in nineteenth-century Paris did not mark the beginning of a period of diminution of sound, but rather it was a time of increasing awareness of, and emphasis on, noise. By reconsidering the myth of Paris as the city of spectacle, where the flâneur's scopophilia reigns supreme, this book attends to what has been silenced by the visual paradigm that still prevails in nineteenth-century French cultural studies. Visual studies privilege the eye over the other senses, and, accordingly, see the nineteenth century as a period in which the supremacy of the visual was entrenched. New approaches to the humanities and social sciences, namely "sensory studies" and "sound studies," aim to make sense of modernism in a broader sensorial field.[7] In *Noise, Water, Meat* (1999), Douglas Kahn provocatively states that "modernism thus entails more sounds and produced a greater emphasis on listening to things, to different things, and to more of them and on listening differently."[8] In order to make sense of street noise in nineteenth-century Paris, this book draws on interdisciplinary research in "sound studies" and "soundscapes"[9] developed by cultural historians, ecologists, and anthropologists such as Alain Corbin, R. Murray Schafer, Jacques Attali, and David Howes, and extended more recently by Mark M. Smith, Steven Connor, Emily Thompson, John Picker, David Garrioch, and Karin Bijsterveld, to name just a few.[10] *City of Noise* investigates further what arrested the ears of nineteenth-century listeners in the city and, taking a cue from American tourists, provincial migrants, and Parisian residents, it listens attentively to the practice of hawking merchandise in the streets.

Noise perception is subjective and related to a specific historical context. Though our ears work the same way as they did in the nineteenth century, we do not hear things the same way: our sensitivity to city noise has changed, as I discuss in chapter 3. In the nineteenth century, prior to the development of the decibel measuring system in the late 1920s, it was not possible to accurately quantify audio levels. Noise abatement campaigns, as Emily Thompson has discussed in *The Soundscape of Modernity*, were stalled until these acoustic measures, standards, and instruments became available in the twentieth century.[11] Moreover, street noise in the nineteenth century was associated with people and the spaces they moved in, rather than with technologies. Indeed, qualitative measures of noise more widely available to researchers often underscore how perception of street noise filters other reactions to social phenomena, such as poverty, class antagonism, xenophobia, and anxieties about gender roles. These documents also accentuate the degree to which the reverberations of the streets characterized the unique sense of place, in an era in which noises remained directly related to the people and spaces that produced them. This is why literary texts are useful to researchers who seek to understand how past epochs perceived noise; guidebooks of Parisian types, verbal and visual sketches, and poetry about Paris are used in this book to ascertain the cultural significance ascribed to the networks of sonic relations that bound peddlers to their unwitting bourgeois customers and to the city in which they made their livelihoods. Poetry is an especially rich source for understanding street noise, as street cries, like poems, rely on the interdependence of medium and message, and the first *Cris de Paris* were recorded by medieval poets.

This book, however, does not give a definitive answer to the question "what did nineteenth-century Paris sound like?" or even "what did peddlers sound like?" Any fascination for the sounds of the past must confront the reality that, in the absence of objective acoustic measurements and standards, we can only describe how street noise was perceived by selected listeners. To explore perceptions of street noise in nineteenth-century Paris, I selected specific sounds from the 1830s to the 1890s—peddling sounds—that were distinctive, and sought to find out how they were perceived by the kinds of listeners who would be likely to leave detailed accounts of their impressions of street noise, namely flâneurs, journalists, and poets. Though the tense relationship between descriptions of sound perception and the historical question of how the street *really* sounded is irresolvable, it propels the research. We will never *really* know the actual levels of ambient noise produced by peddlers, but we can estimate them from the frequency with which certain traits appear in the literature: the shrillness, the incongruity, the discordance of peddlers' voices were frequently cited. There are limits to what this material can tell us about the past. Representations of peddlers were so clichéd that they sometimes obscure the reader's access to historical experience, rather than convey an unmediated account of it. Such overused descriptions block any access to "true" experience—though some might argue there is no experience other than the cliché. Throughout *City of Noise*, we hear listeners orchestrating their impressions of street noise, giving shape to their sensorial experience, figuring that experience in pre-given artistic terms, often those of the *Cris de Paris*. In fact, one of the conundrums of this book involves puzzling out the extent to which the picturesque tradition of the *Cris de Paris* modulates how bourgeois listeners heard noisy peddlers and hawkers.

Noise is a common word, but a complex phenomenon.[12] For a sound to qualify as noise, it must lack syntax and be disorderly, unregulated, unrhythmical, and discordant. Noise can be shrill or mournful, but not harmonious. Frequently, noise lacks a temporal or concrete form, because it is persistent and uncontrollable. Yet, noise is context-bound and subjective. What sounds like rhythmic, harmonious, and expressive sound to one person in a given context, may be noise to another; despite the particularity of noise perception, however, cultural meanings of noise are typically shared. Additionally, noise confounds meaning and is linked to distraction as well as nonsense. Sounds are likewise perceived as noise when they do not have use-value and seem gratuitous. The writers discussed in this book do not for instance show the same kind of distaste for traffic noise as for the shrill cries of peddlers; whereas the one is tolerated because it is inevitably linked to economic progress and bourgeois mobility, the other seems antiquated and unnecessary ear-strain. Finally, noise elicits strong affective reactions; it irritates and can drive some people mad, whereas others are revitalized by the blare.

City of Noise draws on the derivation of *noise* to argue that the loud cries of peddlers were perceived as nuisances by bourgeois listeners increasingly sensitive to sound, especially noxious sound. Peddlers, in part because of their noise, were perceived as troublemakers (*noisers*). In French, the common word for noise is *bruit*, but the word *noise* exists in both languages and means "tumult" or "quarrel." *Noise*'s etymology is instructive, if unclear: it derives either from "nausea" (from the Latin *nausea*) or from "nuisance," "noxious behavior," and "crime" (from the Latin *noxia*). The derivation of "noise" then blurs distinctions among those who make noise, and those who are subjected to and annoyed by it. Their relationship is inextricable. The power dynamic between sender and receiver is key to any historical understanding of which party is labeled noisy in a given period. With their newfound sense of entitlement to quieter private interiors, many bourgeois listeners railed against the encroachment of street noise, especially the soaring voices of small-scale itinerant tradesmen and peddlers. Indeed, there are no examples in this book of peddlers' self-identifying as noisy, because illiterate hawkers left few, if any, material records.

To control noise is to impose order or to harmonize what is perceived as formless, unrhythmical, discordant cacophony into a melodious orchestration.

As Jacques Attali reminds us in his thought-provoking book *Noise: The Political Economy of Music*, music "simulates the social order," and noise is a "simulacrum of murder" or violence because of the way it disturbs that order.[13] As attributes of power, music, and noise, according to Attali, work to "make people *forget* the general violence," to "make people *believe* in the harmony of the world," and to "*silence*" "those who oppose bureaucratic power."[14] Power exerts itself both through strategies of control as well as through ritual and representation. When the *Cris de Paris* endow street noise with harmonious form, we hear an expression of power relations. Indeed, harmony, as the attenuation of discordant sounds of conflict, makes people "believe" in a conciliatory, pleasing aesthetic experience that fosters acceptance of, even complacency toward, the bourgeois social and hierarchical order. *City of Noise* explores the ways in which poetic or pictorial representations of street criers, flâneur-writing in literary guidebooks, ethnographic, or musicological discourse on Paris, all attempted to harmonize street noise in some *form* or another. Formal harmonization was seconded by urban policies on noise abatement. Noise, however, would not be "noxious" if it did easily submit to power; instead noise frustrates attempts to control it, and that elusiveness affords it a kind of resiliency. Similarly, when noise obstructs the effectiveness of the message, sounds become playful and poetic by focusing attention on disruptions to channels of communication. The association of noise with resistance certainly helped endear it to artists such as Charles Baudelaire, Stéphane Mallarmé, and avant-garde poets, seeking to oppose their culture's dominant discourses and to provoke their complacent audiences. Through listening to the noisy streets of Paris with keen attention, avant-garde artists and writers broadened their perceptions of new tonalities and new rhythms, and they explored the relationships between lowbrow and highbrow sonic cultures.

The avant-garde explored the aesthetic potential of street vendors, but up until the mid-nineteenth century, itinerant tradesmen were considered a paltry and piddling subject. For instance, small-scale tradesmen were considered "ridiculous" and "grotesque," early modern adjectives that berate them as insignificant, nonsensical, and monstrous. Representations of hawkers and peddlers followed an age-old practice memorialized in the popular tradition of the *Cris de Paris*. Dating back to the Middle Ages, the *Cris de Paris* were a musical, textual, and graphic genre that classified tradesmen as fixed, often idealized types, identified by their cries and the accessories of their trades. In their modern incarnations, the *Cris de Paris* intersected with flâneur-writing in literary guidebooks and visual sketches. They stood for a long-standing sensory experience of the city, and they continued to fulfill that role, albeit in ways that accentuated shifting old and new sound cultures, at a time when Paris was undergoing urban transformation. Indeed, when writers such as Charles Yriarte and Victor Fournel listen to Parisian street cries with a mix of fascination and aversion, they draw on cultural memories of the sounds of medieval Paris arranged in the tradition of the *Cris de Paris*. As I discuss further in chapter 2, my approach to cultural memory is influenced less by Pierre Nora's sites of memory ("lieux de mémoire"), than by Aleida and Jan Assmann's emphasis on the constant interaction between remembering and forgetting, past and present. Equally influential has been Ann Rigney's "dynamics of remembrance," which helps explain how elements of the urban picturesque were selectively recalled and repeatedly circulated across a variety of media (musical, textual, graphic); these dynamics elucidate the mid-nineteenth-century nostalgia for the harmony of prerevolutionary epochs, and the maladjustment to the discord of the modern, urban, capitalist present.[15]

Bourgeois nostalgia and the cult of the picturesque in effect obfuscate peddlers' relationship to the economy. Historian Laurence Fontaine has shown that peddlers, as seasonal merchant migrants with elaborate credit and supply networks based on kinship, played a significant economic role in highland communities; although her focus on rural society tells us little about the impact on urban economies, Fontaine argues that peddling extended capitalism among groups (many from mountainous communities) who were not part of the lowlands' bourgeoisie or guilds, through complex commercial networks. Peddlers thus played a role in the rise of merchant capitalism, at least until peddling's decline in the mid-nineteenth century when new systems of distribution, suppliers, middlemen, and credit made their village- and kinship-based networks obsolete.[16] In the nineteenth century, the demise of the profession meant that peddlers were indeed marginal subjects because of who they were, where they worked, and how they related to the dominant economy. Guidebooks of Parisian types certainly reinforced peddlers' marginality. Peddlers were often seasonal migrants and foreigners whose provincial accents identified them as non-Parisians. Even so, their regular presence in the streets of the capital helped define Parisian urban culture. Whether they carried their merchandise on their backs (hawkers), or transported their wares in baskets, racks, or carts (peddlers), they were itinerant tradesmen. Their itinerant lifestyle set them at odds from sedentary shopkeepers, in this age of the department store and the rise of the bourgeoisie. Their techniques of advertising by crying out their wares or services differed from the marketing strategies based on silent print advertising, anonymous transaction, and in-store sales. As a resource for unskilled and migrant workers, peddling provided important conveniences and services to a growing but underserved working-class population. Peddlers worked on the margins of the formal economy, a by-product of or sometimes an illicit branch of regulated commerce. By virtue of their flexible small-scale entrepreneurial contributions to the informal economy, it could be said that they played a role in the transition from preindustrial to industrial urban society. Thus they were not simply a de facto criminal underclass. Narratives about peddlers in literary guidebooks are divided in their emphasis on the vendor's dependence or independence from the marketplace. Some praise the vendor's entrepreneurial spirit, making evidently misleading claims that peddlers appear to be emancipated from actual work. Such attributions of independence cultivate their resiliency, whereas other narratives make a point about peddlers' insecurity at a barely subsistence level. Peddling was a precarious cover for begging; in other words, not commerce but charity. Peddling and pauperism were indissociable in nineteenth-century regulatory discourse. The story of peddling's decline and impending disappearance is a vexing issue that I return to in the conclusion. Whether we choose to identify peddlers with winners or losers, the intrusiveness of their cries and call-outs insistently gets our attention.[17]

City of Noise explores different types of source material to provide a broad, multidisciplinary investigation into the impact of street noise and the tradition of the *Cris de Paris* on modernity: (i) literary guidebooks, such as *Les Français peints par eux-mêmes* and *Le Diable à Paris*; (ii) visual sketches by caricaturist Bertall (Charles Albert d'Arnoux) and illustrator Jean-François Raffaëlli; (iii) cultural history by amateur historian and *flâneur* Victor Fournel; (iv) writings by nineteenth-century music critics such as Joseph Mainzer and Jean-Georges Kastner; (v) and poetry by Charles Baudelaire, Charles Cros, Stéphane Mallarmé, and others. The different types of evidence help us reconstruct the experience of nineteenth-century Parisians. They share a connection to the type of the flâneur whose writing moves from sensual observation to introspection. Because flâneur-writing was designed to circulate descriptions of what Paris looked, sounded, smelled, and felt like (to better make sense of the vast and multiple identities of "Paris" during this period of urban transformation), they are rich material for anyone interested in understanding the history of the senses. Flâneur-writing in guidebooks and in poetry manifests the crossover in the period between journalistic writing and "high art" and places the flâneur, like the peddler, at the intersection between economic and aesthetic interests. One of the reasons this book is organized around sources rather than themes is indeed to demonstrate how texts work across disciplinary boundaries. Including musical examples, visual sketches, historical documents, and poetry in one book widens the interdisciplinary reach of the analysis commensurate with the expansive nature of sound itself, but interdisciplinarity also has its limitations. One of these is certainly the inability to delve deeply into each discipline. More is gained, however, when the disciplines work in concert to arrange a work on street noises. The *Cris* impose order onto the sensory overload of the city, either in the form of an orchestration, an iconography, or conventional versification. As the lowbrow sonic culture of the streets comes into contact with high art, street cries are transformed through idealization or parody and in turn disrupt artistic conventions with their discordant sound.

Chapter 1 establishes that scholarly approaches to flâneurs have downplayed urban experience's broader impact on the senses and underappreciated their aural acuity. From the type's early formulations by Honoré de Balzac, Auguste de Lacroix, and Victor Fournel, the flâneur is attuned to city sounds, and flâneur-writing arranges them to portray the city as concert. The art of flânerie consists of transforming the empirical confusion of city sounds into a unified musical composition. What sounds then strike the ears of the composer in the city-space with special stridency? Do all flâneurs and flâneuses perceive the street as the same harmonious concert or with the same level of interest? As the clamor of the streets promoted selective hearing, street musicians were targeted as major contributors to the city as concert. My close readings of verbal and visual sketches by Delphine de Girardin, Maria d'Anspach, Bertall, and Old Nick show that class-biased ideas about concert music influenced their often-humorous reactions to street noise; nevertheless, the neurasthenic bourgeois ear was often less than receptive to the intrusive noise of foreign street performers. In contrast, Victor Fournel waxed enthusiastic about the people's love of music. Known for its widely cited definition of flânerie, Fournel's writing is rarely examined in detail. A close reading of his *Ce qu'on voit dans les rues de Paris* makes sense of his distinctive appreciation for street music.

The city-as-concert trope in flâneur-writing draws from the long-standing tradition of the *Cris de Paris*. Chapter 2 examines how this medieval tradition that harmonized the streets thrived in nineteenth-century French music, visual arts, and above all guidebooks of Parisian types. Given the close ties between the *Cris* and what Walter Benjamin termed "panoramic literature," peddlers are generously treated in *Les Français peints par eux-mêmes* by the music critic and pedagogue Joseph Mainzer. They also flourished in visual sketches, prints, and photographs, which collectors prized because they revived childhood memories and fed the nostalgia for old Parisian soundscapes. Given their circulation in a variety of media, the transmedial *Cris* formed a cultural memory that created a sense of place for Parisians and developed a sense of the urban picturesque.

These guidebooks' accounts of changing urban soundscapes during Haussmannization (broadly conceived) show that urban renewal produced a sensory overhaul and changed how Parisians experienced city sounds and urban space. Chapter 3 investigates repeated attempts to control street noise in order to cleanse Paris of its antiquated soundscapes, which social policy makers associated with mendicancy, vagrancy, sedition, and economic parasitism. Conversely, amateur historians, preservationists, bibliophiles, collectors, and musicologists were enthralled by what Victor Fournel called the "plaintive cry of Old Paris," which stood for the resistance to modernity. In their nostalgic writings, these members of the elite circulated shared cultural memories of street cries that erased peddlers' associations with sedition and revolution and fostered the picturesque charms of urban strolling. Fournel and Mainzer repeatedly refer to the need to preserve street cries for posterity, thus anticipating future documentary recording projects, such as Ferdinand Brunot's *Archives de la parole*. Fournel's attempt to render tradesmen mutedly picturesque, however, is not completely successful, as street cries resist complete co-optation.

Shrillness of the cry, which social policy makers and nostalgic amateurs of Old Paris alike toned down, is the subject of Charles Baudelaire's prose poem "Le Mauvais Vitrier." Baudelaire's representation of glaziers and ragpickers has not gone unnoticed, but its importance and legacy should not be underestimated. It contributes to our understanding of how modern poets perceived the city-as-concert and how dissonant city noise impacted the thematic content and formal style of modern poetry. The fourth chapter compares Arsène Houssaye's "La Chanson du vitrier" and Baudelaire's "Le Mauvais Vitrier" in terms of their use of the discourse on flânerie and the picturesque, and their transposition of the cry into song. I show how Houssaye's transcriptions of the glazier's cry and his use of the cry as refrain relate to efforts by musicians such as Mainzer and Kastner to document the cry for posterity. Houssaye harmonizes the cry to exploit its pathos and, in tandem with Nerval, Gautier, or Dupont, he seeks to achieve an authenticity through the transposition of song. In contrast, Baudelaire espouses dissonance in "Le Mauvais vitrier" and evokes the sinister and demonic effects of strident noise.

Chapter 5 chronicles representations of peddlers among Baudelaire's followers, from François Coppée, Charles Cros, and Jean Richepin, to symbolists such as Stéphane Mallarmé and J. K. Huysmans. I show how poetry about peddlers addresses social concerns about the intrusiveness of lower-class noise, either by attenuation in Coppée for example, or by parodic intensification by bohemian and *fumiste* poets. After close readings of selected poems by Cros and Richepin that parody Coppée's sentimental *dizain* inspired by street scenes, I offer a close reading of Mallarmé's *Chansons bas* alongside Jean-François Raffaëlli's illustrations of types in the tradition of the *Cris de Paris* in *Types de Paris*. Poems about peddlers invite reflection on the commercialization of the word in the era of the mass market press and on the cultural associations that connected the modern poet to his alter ego, that persistent survivor who resists modernization, the street crier.

CHAPTER 1

Aural Flânerie

The Flâneur in the City as Concert

Nineteenth-century urban experience often is apprehended through the figure of the *flâneur*. The flâneur is a mythic type that emerges in the late eighteenth century in urban sketches and panoramas such as Louis-Sébastien Mercier's *Tableau de Paris* and persists in the work of nineteenth-century writers and artists examined in this book, including writers and journalists Honoré de Balzac and Victor Fournel, poets Charles Baudelaire and Stéphane Mallarmé, as well as artists Jean-François Raffaëlli and Charles-Albert d'Arnoud, better known as Bertall. The flâneur is usually a man of leisure, but in less frequent cases, a *flâneuse* strolls through the city as well. He or she saunters through Paris, on foot, unhurried, attentive to everything on offer, and familiar with all little-known attractions. In the course of his meanderings, the flâneur encounters peddlers, hawkers, acrobats, street musicians, and beggars; whereas the average bourgeois pedestrian would ignore (sometimes willfully) the social outcasts who embody their anxieties about pauperism, flâneurs are increasingly fascinated by the underside of Paris, as it exposes the precariousness of modernity. As such, the flâneur serves as a focal device for organizing the wealth of the city's sights and sounds into a *panorama* that presents the attractions in an orderly narrative.

Notwithstanding its modernity, the flâneur's panoramic approach to the city links him to earlier representations of urban types, such as the *Cris de Paris*. While predating modern configurations of poverty and social marginality, the *Cris* figure early modern class biases and sensory experiences of the city that continue to act upon nineteenth-century perceptions of urban experience.

The continuities and discontinuities between the traditional *Cris* and modern panoramic literature are one of the subjects of this book.

Attuned to the popular tradition of the *Cris de Paris*, the flâneur understood the city as a melodious space that orchestrates different, often conflicting sound cultures. The aural dimensions of flânerie have too often been ignored by the critical tradition that mythologizes the flâneur as the icon of a visually inflected modernity. The flâneur was popularized as a theoretical construct by the writings of Walter Benjamin on Charles Baudelaire in particular, and on Paris in general in the nineteenth century.[1] Following Benjamin's paradigm, much twentieth-century critical writing about the flâneur positions him above the fray rather than in the crowd, accentuates his visual mastery of the urban spectacle, and emphasizes his moral detachment from what he sees. The flâneur's superiority is predicated on the command of his visual abilities and the impassivity that keeps objects of sight at a distance. Moving beyond this visual framework forces us to rethink the flâneur's sensual immersion in the city.

What sounds emerge out of the city clamor to strike the ears of the flâneur with special stridency? How do different flâneurs and flâneuses react to these sonic encounters? Which noises are so intrusive as to undermine the flâneur's aloofness? From the type's early formulations by Honoré de Balzac, Auguste Lacroix, and Victor Fournel, the flâneur is attuned to the city as concert or as cacophony. The art of flânerie consists in transforming the empirical confusion of city sounds into a unified musical composition.

Walter Benjamin's approach to the flâneur, which has been so influential to the contemporary understanding of the type, has tuned out the aural dimensions of flânerie. This toning down of city noise follows Georg Simmel's sociology of the senses, which privileges the eye over the ear in the modern metropolis. As a result, the Benjaminian framework has restricted how we make sense of the flâneur. Prevalent visual constructs in flâneur theory, such as the city as readable book and "capital of signs," and as kaleidoscopic spectacle, have aural counterparts. Writings on the flâneur, especially Honoré de Balzac's *Physiologie du mariage* and Victor Fournel's *Ce qu'on voit dans les rues de Paris*, represent the city as a musical score, and as harmonious or cacophonous concert. As we listen to the flâneur's encounters with street musicians, we can better account for the range of reactions to street life and urban sounds. Fournel's writings offer an exceptionally rich appreciation of the aesthetic experience that can move the flâneur who can listen to the city streets. Aural flânerie[2] describes walking in the city as a multisensory embodied experience rather than a disengaged spectatorship, making the artist's contact with the sounds of the city a formative creative experience. An understanding of the flâneur conceived as bathed in a multitude of sounds and sights rather than as an untouchable mobile gaze enriches our definitions of modernity.

Walter Benjamin Gives Half an Ear to Flânerie

Though the flâneur is a nineteenth-century character type firmly anchored in his age, many students and scholars of flânerie—today—first run across this ever-popular icon of modernity in the writings of Walter Benjamin. As revisionist critics Martina Lauster and Margaret A. Rose have shown, however, Benjamin underplays the significance of the pre-1850 social caricatures and *physiologies* that originated the type by reading the flâneur in a distinctly twentieth-century analytical framework.[3] Benjamin's metaphysical concern with the flâneur's disembodied, alienated gaze is absent from the earlier material, more clearly intent on describing how the flâneur senses the city.

Critics are divided as to Benjamin's sensitivity to sound. As others have pointed out, Benjamin's autobiographical and travel writings suggest a man "finely tuned to sound,"[4] but also one for whom city sounds disrupt the free flow of the imagination. The *Berlin Chronicle* frequently evokes childhood memories about the unsettling quality of the city's constant noises—voices, cries, doors slammed shut, rattling coaches, and military bands—but as Gerhard Richter argues, noises also function as enabling mnemonic triggers in autobiographical writing.[5] Referring to passages in "One-way Street" on Seville, Marseille, and Freiburg, Fran Tonkiss remarks on how Benjamin "souvenired sounds from different places, composed urban vignettes as if they were aural postcards."[6] Of Freiburg Minster, Benjamin writes, "A town's most specific feeling of homeliness is associated . . . with the sound and the gaps between strokes of its tower clocks."[7] Given his aptitude at evoking a sense of place through sound in these texts, it is surprising that, as Lutz Koepnick notes in *Sound Matters: Essays on the Acoustics of Modern German Culture*, Benjamin "takes little notice of the fact that nineteenth-century urbanization and industrialization also resulted in an equally diverting and disruptive cacophony of sounds."[8] There are inconsistencies as well among the number of references to city sounds in his notes in *The Arcades Project*, the lack of recognition of the disruptive potential of noise in his essays on the flâneur that Koepnick signals, and the tactile ability and aural acuity he attributes to the flâneur.[9] There seems to be a tension in Benjamin between presenting flânerie as "intoxicated" embodied experience and shutting out sensory data to better focus on theory formation.

Benjamin's approach to the sensorium was influenced by Georg Simmel, whom he cites twice in the notes on the flâneur in *The Arcades Project*. Simmel's

"Sociology of the Senses" follows the traditional hierarchy of the senses by privileging the eye over the ear, and both sight and hearing above the "lower" senses (smell, taste, touch). His sociological approach is innovative in that it accounts for the role of bodies in social interaction. "That we get involved in interactions at all depends on the fact that we have a sensory effect upon one another," writes Simmel. "Every sense delivers contributions characteristic of its individual nature to the construction of sociated existence; . . . the prevalence of one or the other sense in the contact of individuals often provides this contact with a sociological nuance that could otherwise not be produced." Simmel's essays, however, present the changes to the modern urban sensorium in a largely negative light. The segmentation of the senses causes disorientation as "one who sees without hearing is generally much more confused, helpless and disturbed than one who hears without being able to see."[10] He shares this aversion for modern noise with Theodor Lessing, who wrote a full chapter on the exceptional vulnerability of the ear as compared with the eye, and who campaigned against noise pollution in his manifesto "Noise—a War Cry against the Loud Clatter of Our Lives" (1908).[11] The often-quoted claim that the modern city impairs hearing is crucial to the thesis of Simmel's most renowned essay, "Metropolis and Mental Life." The ear is figured there as a passive defenseless organ as opposed to the eye conceived of as a shield.[12] Urban overstimulation—in the form of noise, discontinuous and unexpected impressions or "shocks"—accompanied by the hypersensitivity of the city dweller results in neurasthenia. Desensitization acts as a coping mechanism, Simmel contends, and leads to a loss of sensory acuity among metropolitan inhabitants that he refers to as a blasé attitude.[13] Benjamin's ambivalence toward city noise can be directly linked to Simmel's influence, though it also resonates with a general trend among early-twentieth-century intellectuals who campaigned against noise.

In *The Arcades Project,* Benjamin adopts the theory of shock experience, but his more positive approach differs from Simmel's negative view.[14] Shock experience can reawaken the senses of the blasé, anaesthetized city dweller. Benjamin's flâneur seeks out the "intoxication" of the senses by actively drowning the senses in sensory overload. Citing Charles Baudelaire, Benjamin famously evokes the motif of the kaleidoscope to capture the rapidly changing sensations experienced by the modern stroller as a unified scene controlled by the viewer:

> Moving through this traffic involves the individual in a series of shocks and collisions. At dangerous intersections, nervous impulses flow through him in rapid succession, like the energy from a battery. Baudelaire speaks of a man who plunges into the crowd as into a reservoir of electric energy. Circumscribing the experience of the shock, he calls this man "a kaleidoscope endowed with consciousness."[15]

Benjamin remembers Baudelaire's use of the kaleidoscope in his discussion of Edgar Allan Poe's flâneur in "The Man of the Crowd"; Poe had himself referred to the flâneur's state of "electrified" intellect at the beginning of his story.[16] The kaleidoscope, an instrument invented by Scottish physicist David Brewster in 1817, which became an object of curiosity and entertainment in Europe in the 1820s, quickly acquired cultural currency and assimilated metaphorical meanings.[17] As Catherine Nesci outlines, the term connotes the shared restlessness, fragmentation, and variation of the modern metropolis and the flâneur who perceives it,[18] and, as such, the instrument is associated with other protocinematic gadgets-cum-metaphors such as the magic lantern, the daguerreotype, the diorama, and the panorama, apparatuses that are also used to connote the flâneur. Moreover, he is frequently associated with spectators at diorama and panorama expositions.[19] In fact many scholars use the flâneur as "shorthand for describing the new, mobilized gaze of the pre-cinematic spectator."[20]

The privileging of the flâneur's camera-like visual faculty enhances the myth of his intellectual detachment. The flâneur—the "unseen seer," like the detective to whom Benjamin compares him—is "partout mais nulle part" as Janin eloquently put it in *Un hiver à Paris*.[21] The visionary invisibility of the flâneur may be the result of predominantly visual paradigms that privilege the distinctive features of sight, namely spatial distance, at the expense of the other more proximate senses (a paradigm shared by some nineteenth-century writers and the critics who read them).[22] Positioned at the inception of a protocinematic genealogy that emphasizes its central role in the society of spectacle and spectatorship, the flâneur is seen as a capital player in the remapping of the sensorium, which, as Jonathan Crary examines, compartmentalized the senses and, notably, dissociated sight from touch at the beginning of the nineteenth century.[23] The separation of the senses is considered by many a defining trait of modernity. The critical success of compelling metaphors such as that of the kaleidoscope accounts for the visual-focus of studies on the flâneur, but the privileging of the eye over the other senses obscures even the references to other senses in these stock metaphors. For example, the magic of the kaleidoscope results from the interaction between hand and eye. Read in its Baudelairean context, the kaleidoscope has an added tactile dimension because of its discursive association with electric energy and shocks. Making sense of the flâneur as a man in the crowd amid a kaleidoscopic reservoir of electric energy restores the type's full sensory perception. Getting in touch with the flâneur's sensory experience can move us beyond the myth of the detached disembodiment of the flâneur.

Physiology of the Flâneur's Auditory Acuity

Knowing Benjamin's bias against noise, it makes good sense to return to the primary materials that originated the nineteenth-century type: the *physiologie*, social sketches of character types, "literary guidebooks" in this vein, whose importance Benjamin had generally dismissed.[24] In some of the early-nineteenth-century descriptions of the flâneur, such as those in *Nouveaux Tableaux de Paris* and in *Le Figaro*, the flâneur seeks out the heightened sensations offered by free urban entertainment—outdoor puppet shows, the morgue, public lectures, university courses, museums, libraries, curiosity shops, altercations and riots, fires, and floods. Huart's *Physiologie du flâneur* builds on the metaphor of the city as book: the flâneur reads the city as if it were a sensuous book. Using his sense of taste and touch as well as sight, he reads all the "delicious posters, red, yellow, white, green, poppy, that wallpaper all the walls of Paris."[25] The flâneur may be a "perspicacious"[26] close reader, but he is also an avid conversationalist, eavesdropper, and attentive listener. In Jouy's *Nouveaux Tableaux de Paris* and in *Le Figaro*, the flâneur is frequently said to engage people in conversation.[27] In *Paris ou Le Livre des Cent-et-un*, the author describes the flâneur as "[un] aimable conteur,"[28] whereas Auguste de Lacroix shows him engaged in news and gossip by listening to "commères"[29] in his portrait in *Les Français peints par eux-mêmes*. Huart characterizes him further when he adds that "One of the great pleasures of the flâneur is to learn a lot of really extraordinary news for free, that could not even be found in those gazettes most famous for their canards. There is not one journalist who is not overshadowed by men and especially women hawking the news."[30] Eavesdropper as well as observer, the flâneur has his ear to the ground, collecting news, stories, and gossip.

Frequently the flâneur's acuity is described in both visual and auditory terms. As Lacroix writes, citing zoological terms in a parodical gesture, "he moves his hare's ears and lynx's eyes incessantly around Paris."[31] "Good legs, good ears, and good eyes," adds Huart, "these are the principal physical advantages that must be held by any Frenchman truly worthy of joining the club of flâneurs when one is established."[32] That the flâneur does not merely passively hear sounds, but actively listens to his sonic environment in a focused and discriminating way distinguishes him from the *badaud* (gawker). The *badaud* "has eyes but he won't see, ears but he won't hear."[33]

Balzac offers perhaps the most eloquent example of the flâneur's auditory prowess in *Physiologie du mariage*:

> Where is the foot-soldier of Paris upon whose ear these words, out of the thousands uttered by the passers-by, have not fallen, like bullets on the day of battle?

Where is the man who has not seized one of those innumerable words, frozen in the air, of which Rabelais speaks? But most men walk about Paris as they eat and as they live, without thinking. There are but few musicians clever enough to recognize the key of those few scattered notes, few practiced readers of faces who can tell from what passion they proceed. To wander through Paris! Truly a delightful, an adorable existence! Strolling is a science, a feast of the eye. Walking is vegetating; strolling is life. A pretty woman who has long been gazed at with burning eyes will be far more worthy of claiming a reward than the cook who asked the Limousin for twenty sous, with his nose all swollen from sniffing up tasty smells.[34]

Balzac begins by comparing the flâneur on foot in the streets of Paris to an infantryman on a battlefield pummeled by a confused barrage of spoken words. Referring to François Rabelais in whose lineage he places *Physiologie du mariage*,[35] Balzac evokes the "frozen words" episode from chapter 55 in *Le Quart Livre*, in which the giant traveler Pantagruel hears sounds of a battle, frozen in the ice, emerge, as they are released in spring. The passage is remarkable for the way it evokes sight, hearing, taste, and smell, and even touch (the infantryman's walk, the sublimated possession of the desired woman). The sensual perception here is interconnected and intersensorial.[36] Balzac sums up flânerie as empirical, sensual observation followed by recognition and analysis, a science that relates manifestations back to their hidden causes ("from what passion they proceed"). As Nesci demonstrates in her exegesis of this passage in *Le Flâneur et les flâneuses*, the art and science of the flâneur, a superior physiognomist, gastronome, and musician, consists in the ability to decipher, analyze, and transform this confusion into a unified musical composition and render the city into a musical score.[37] As such, the barrage of bullet-words is transformed into reasoned science; shock experience is avoided and sublimated into intellectual reflection and literary remembrance (e.g., Rabelais's *Le Quart Livre*, Brillat-Savarin's *Physiologie du goût*).

Victor Fournel pursues the Balzacian model of sensual flânerie under the Second Empire. Writing a generation later than Balzac but fully cognizant of his debt to him, amateur historian, journalist, and flâneur Victor Fournel is often cited as one of the theorists of "the art of flânerie."[38] He defines flânerie in an often quoted passage from the second section of *Ce qu'on voit dans les rues de Paris*, "L'Odyssée d'un flâneur dans les rues de Paris." Fournel is frequently cited in definitions of flânerie but his writings are rarely explored in detail. A closer reading shows a particularly sensual temperament whose idiosyncrasies were tempered by the period's collective class biases. Like Balzac, Fournel moves from multisensory empirical perception to intellectualization, as he stresses the combination of naiveté and lightness of heart, as well as science and gravity required of the flâneur: "It is not a given that everyone can stroll naively, and yet cleverly. . . . On the contrary, for he who knows how to understand and practice it, this lifestyle is the most active and the most fecund in useful results."[39] The passage continues by performing at length, rather than theorizing, the art of flânerie:

> Have you ever reflected on all that is contained in the word flânerie, that charming word, adored by poets and humorists? To make interminable expeditions through the streets and promenades; to wander, nose in the air, both hands in one's pockets and an umbrella under one's arm, as befits any candid soul; to walk straight ahead, if peradventure, without thinking where to go and without hurrying, in the manner of Jean de La Fontaine going off to the Academy; to stop at each shop to look at the images, at each street corner to read the posters, at each stall to touch the books; to watch a group circled around a clever rabbit and to join in without a human care, fascinated, delighted, given over to the spectacle with all the senses and heart; to listen to the homily of a soap merchant here, the dithyramb of a twenty-five cent watch seller there, the elegies of a misunderstood charlatan a little farther away; to follow at will along the docks the music of a regiment passing by, or to lend an ear truly to the cooing of the prima donnas at the Café Morel; to savor the variations of an organ of Barbary; to stand in file around the outdoor jugglers, the tightrope acrobats, and magnetists; to contemplate the stone breakers with admiration; to run when one sees running; to stop when one wants; to sit when one feels like it; what pleasure, dear God! And that's the existence of a *badaud*![40]

Despite his earlier comparison of the flâneur to the mobile daguerreotype, Fournel's description of the art of flânerie appeals not just to vision, but to all five senses, such that *Ce qu'on voit dans les rues de Paris* might have more aptly been entitled *Ce qu'on sent dans les rues de Paris*. The flâneur must give himself over to the depths of the senses. He walks "nose in the air"; he looks at shop windows and billboards; he touches the books on display; hands in his pockets, he feels the swell of the crowd around him. Taste is not as prominent, but he uses the language of taste to describe how "to savor the variations of an organ of Barbary." The mobile subjective viewpoint so typical of flâneur literature is here channeled through the ear. Fournel's flâneur listens acutely to his surroundings: his roving ear records street criers, street musicians, performers in cafés and restaurants, and military parades. The aural flâneur pays close attention to sounds that other urban dwellers might dismiss as mere distractions. As in Balzac, the flâneur not only hears the street criers, but his ear transforms their sounds into musical forms such as the dithyramb, the elegy, or the homily. In his definition of flânerie, Fournel uses the musical lexicon to construct the metaphor of the city as concert and the flâneur as concert master.

The City as Concert

Before we listen to what Fournel hears as he walks about the city, let us turn to two of Balzac's contemporaries, whose reactions to the music of the streets provide a useful comparison with Fournel's. Delphine de Girardin and Bertall (Charles Albert d'Arnoud) give a sense of how the city-as-musical-concert sounded. Though less common than the motif of the panorama, descriptions of the city as concert oscillate between a cacophonous fragmentation and a totalizing harmony. Consider for instance the description of noisy Paris in journalist and *flâneuse*[41] Delphine de Girardin's *Lettres parisiennes du Vicomte de Launay* in an entry dated August 25, 1837:

> A third observation concerning the future restfulness of the capital worries us once again: the progress made by French music is frightening. In Paris today, the day is a perpetual concert, a series of uninterrupted serenades; Parisian ears have not one instant of rest. Starting in the morning, the organs of Barbary divide up the neighborhoods of the city; an implacable harmony spreads over the city. At noon—the harps begin; the harps that played at night are late to rise; but what chords! It's Saul in fury making David's harp groan. At three o'clock—eight *hunters* dressed in green and dawning grey hats go door to door with their horns; unluckily they claim to be an *ensemble* group: they are a *chorus* of *horns*. It is something unimaginable and frightful; nothing can give an idea of it. One single horn already can sound a false note; just think then what can be produced by eight horns that screech at the same time! It's awful, it's the end of the world, it's the trumpets of the Last Judgment. At four o'clock—the acrobats arrive with their tambourines, castanets, and triangles. At seven o'clock—several blindmen play the oboe. At eight o'clock—several children play the hurdy gurdy. Finally, in the evening, great serenades! Violins, *galoubets*, flutes, guitars, and Italian singers! It's a concert to die for, and there is no refuge; all this takes place under your window, it's a residential concert that you cannot possibly avoid. All your life's actions are accompanied by the obligatory violin; you discuss politics, you make a tender confession, and the orchestra that besieges you always sustains your voice. One single means, only one, is available to fend off this scourge of harmony: one can sometimes combat it homeopathically, by similar means: hurry over to your piano and there play with all your strength three sonatas one after the other without relenting; but take care to open the window, use the pedal, and pound the keys. If your piano has *depth*, if it's an offspring of *Érard*, with good resonance, you have a chance to win; the enemy, defeated by the noise, discouraged by this forceful rivalry, will perhaps end up making way for you! But the means are terrible: what can I say? Today we love music in France, and that is how we love it.[42]

With virtuoso irony, Girardin describes the "perpetual concert" in Paris from her window on rue Saint-Georges (at the time, la "Nouvelle Athènes" was a popular quarter among actors, artists, and writers in today's ninth *arrondissement*), a vantage point seemingly above the fray. Many homes of the wealthy had balconies. This type of modern bourgeois architectural feature enabled the separation of the leisured from the working classes. The detached point of view also fits the traditional characterization of the flâneur, though here the connection is more to Jouy's *L'Hermite de la Chaussée d'Antin*, or to Hoffmann's "My Cousin's Corner Window," than to the mobile stroller on the streets. As Philippe Hamon reminds us, the trope of the window from which the viewer first sees and captures the outside world and then retreats into a world of reverie prefigures the dark room of the photographer.[43] In other works, as in the novella "Le Lorgnon," Girardin's protagonist uses a magic lorgnette to penetrate society's secrets, while remaining at a safe remove. In Girardin's description of street musicians, however, the observer can no longer maintain a distanced point of view.[44] The window does not shield the ear as it does the eye; no retreat is possible.

Girardin refers to the hours of the day to structure her litany against the perpetual noise caused by street musicians. By showing the timetable governing the various sounds, she implicitly recalls the ways in which sounds, such as bells and sirens, traditionally structured the diurnal cycle and calendar. These street noises, however, have lost their ability to punctuate the day in any significant manner. They are just noise that heightens the narrator's awareness that she has no control over what she hears, given that the ear "cannot turn away or close itself, like the eye; rather, since it only takes, it is condemned to take everything that comes into its vicinity."[45] Counting the hours has the added effect of recreating the experience of duration, and conveying the narrator's exasperation, mania even, caused by lack of sleep and overstimulation. Girardin ironically evokes the Books of Samuel in the Old Testament (2 Samuel 6:5 and 6:14). Whenever Saul was tormented by evil spirits, he called on David to play the harp and soothe him. Girardin's torment, however, cannot be soothed.

The sanctuary of Girardin's private, indoor space is invaded when the street noise becomes a "concert à domicile" or residential concert. This was an age where music moved indoors, and it was common among the wealthy to host chamber musicians in their salon. The salon served as a kind of bourgeois interior that shielded against the noise outside and compensated for the ear's fragility and defenselessness. To compound the violation of the indoor/outdoor and private/public divides, the noise outside is, as the day progresses, associated with foreigners (especially Southerners), with exotic instruments (*tambours de basque* or tambourines, Spanish castanets, *galoubets* or flutes popular in Provence, Italian singers). The racket is relentless, the "perpetual concert" experienced as a series of discontinuous, invasive shocks rather than a harmonious whole. In these conditions, the narrator's use of "an implacable harmony," "a scourge of harmony" is ironic. The double-entendre, "a concert to die for" (une fête à en mourir), says it all. The narrator retakes control over her sonic environment when she fights back by playing her piano loudly, upstaging the street instruments with her more powerful and elite Erard-brand piano, beating noise with noise in a perpetual concert.

Bertall's ensembles of sketches on street music in *Le Diable à Paris* illustrate several of the social and spatial contrasts made by Girardin (figures 1a and 1b). "La Musique à Paris" consists of twenty-one comic sketches that oppose "Musique d'artistes" and "Musique d'amateurs," as well as music heard out- and indoors. Ironically, the artists are from the lower classes, and the amateurs, from among the wealthy and leisured. The "artists" are street musicians and include a clarinetist with his dog; "aboyeurs" or barkers who stand at theater entrances; a harpist and guitar duo singing a song by Frédéric Bérat; an organ grinder cranking out the popular Norman anthem "J'irai revoir ma Normandie" (also by Bérat)[46]; a trio of broom sellers; as well as a drummer, horn players, and accordionists. In contrast, the "amateurs" from the leisure class perform in their homes: tenors of dubious talent (the "Lablache de salon" who seeks his notes in the depths of his cravat cannot match the renowned Italian bass singer Luigi Lablache); society ladies attempting the very difficult final aria of Bellini's *Norma*, "Qual Cor Perdisti" (What a Heart You Have Lost) possibly losing their admirers' hearts in the process; young girls playing sentimental *romances* at the piano, such as Francesco Masini's "Petite fleur des bois" (1839–40), misspelled "boas" for effect in Bertall's vignette. Whereas the "artists" (some wearing folkloric dress) feature home-grown music from the French provinces, as the references to Bérat's *J'irai revoir ma Normandie* or to the Savoyards playing "Hé ioup, la Catarina!"[47] on the hurdy-gurdy make clear, the "amateurs" prefer imported taste (mostly Italian). The mix of repertoire ranging from easy *romances* to difficult arias gives us a sense of the evolution of musical culture among the elite class. Ironically among the "artists," none are likely professionals, as we understand the term today, namely someone whose career requires years of study.[48] The amateurs, however, are no more skillful. The division in fact draws attention to the permeability of the categories, as crossovers were not unheard of. In *La Comédie de notre temps*, Bertall observes that borrowings from popular cries are commonplace and cites as example how the cry "Belles bottes d'asperges!" inspired J. F. Halévy's air "Quand renaîtra la pâle aurore" from *Guido et Ginevra ou la Peste à Florence* (1838). Félicien David also thought that the song of the old-clothes—woman who circulated in the Faubourg Saint-Germain would make

Figures 1a and 1b. Bertall [pseud. Charles-Albert d'Arnoud (1820–82)], *La Musique à Paris,* in *Le Diable à Paris* (Paris: Hetzel, 1846), 1:266–67. Courtesy of Bibliothèque des livres rares et collections spéciales, Direction des bibliothèques, Université de Montréal.

MUSIQUE

D'AMATEURS

Aux Fenêtres

(MINUIT 25 MINUTES.)

Essai de Polka sur
la trompe.

La rifla, fla, fla ; la rifla, fla, fla ;
la rifla, fla, fla !!

Effet produit sur
l'auditeur.

A l'intérieur.

Ténor léger, inamorato,
chantour
de petites romances
mélancoliques.

Lablache de salon
occupé à chercher son *fa*
dans les profondeurs
de sa cravate.

NORMA.   POLLIONE.
« *Quale cor perdesti !* » — « *Sublime dona !* »

Bluettes sentimentales.
« *Petite fleur des Bôas* »

Effet produit sur
l'auditeur.

L'enfant prodige
et le père de l'enfant prodige

a good motif in a piece, *Les Quatre Saisons*.[49] At least one street crier became an opera singer in the nineteenth century; the countertenor Étienne Lainez, son of a Vaugirard gardener, started out as a Parisian street crier and asparagus seller. After he was discovered by the director of the French Royal Academy of Music, he embarked on a career in opera from 1773 to 1812.[50] Organ grinders also frequently appropriated pieces by established composers such as Auber, Grétry, Rossini, Halévy, and even Wagner. In Bertall's caricature "Musique d'artistes," a timpanist and his daughter play Beethoven's Symphony no. 6 in F major (also known as the Pastoral Symphony). The vignette of the "musical caravan" could also refer to the Overture of Grétry's *La Caravane du Caire*, which music critic Édouard Fétis remembered hearing as a youth on the streets of Paris.[51]

The "Musique d'amateurs" is divided in two; in the upper half, three vignettes under the heading "Aux fenêtres (minuit 25 minutes)" illustrate bohemian revelers sitting in windows right before midnight. These recall some of Girardin's complaints. One vignette, for example, portrays a sleepless man in a night cap sitting up in bed vociferating and pounding the ceiling with a stick. Much legislation from the period attests, indeed, to new levels of intolerance for noises that trouble the sleep of city residents.[52] The other scenes also represent the effects of the music on the listener in vignettes strategically positioned in the center at the bottom; a dog is shown running and barking in "Musique d'artistes," whereas the listener in "Musique d'amateur" is a young man who has fallen asleep. Bertall does not hesitate to satirize the pretentious and soporific qualities of the bourgeois amateur music scene, but by depicting a dog's rather than a human's reaction, it is up to the viewer to decide whether street musicians are so noisy that even a dog cannot bear to listen.

These representations of street musicians tell us a great deal about how the middle class perceived the "city-as-concert." While we cannot definitively say that the modern city was simply louder than the provincial village, we can conclude that new urban-middle-class expectations that their interior spaces not be invaded by sounds from the street indicate a shift in social and spatial relations that diverge from what would have been typical in the countryside, where church bells were the common sonic denominator of community spirit and shared social space.[53] Moreover, two sound cultures developed that, if they were not mutually impermeable, were at the very least distinctive. Whereas in the street one heard music that satisfied nationalist taste, foreign music dominated in the salons. Whereas the middle class developed a taste for indoor, controlled, ordered sound,[54] the lower classes reveled in outdoor, spontaneous, untimed, uncontrolled street performances. When writers talk of the city-as-concert, it is the street noise that they hear, but they conceive it in relation to the auditory salon culture that they increasingly find more appealing.

The Flâneur and Street Music

While Girardin and Bertall contrast indoor and outdoor music cultures, other flâneurs-writers, such as Victor Fournel, encountered itinerant musicians at street-level. Fournel makes his standpoint clear in *Ce qu'on voit dans les rues de Paris*:

> I would like to present to you today the unsung heroes of popular music and literature. I can discuss them knowingly, if not dignifiedly, because I have seen them up close; I have followed their sessions with the avid curiosity of an adept, and I have rarely repented. The reader can be certain that I have more often congregated around a street singer than taken a box at the Opera: it costs less and it is often just as amusing.[55]

Fournel presents himself, rather iconoclastically, as a fan of popular street entertainment. Accordingly, his book has two sections; the first, "Les artistes nomades et l'art populaire" is less often discussed than the second, "L'Odyssée d'un flâneur dans les rues de Paris." The first section, in fact, takes the reader on a tour of the haunts of street musicians, orators, and street poets. The "odyssey" in the title of the second section connotes a journey, though here the flâneur remains within the city of Paris (Paris being a world onto itself), but the title, with its reference to Homer, also evokes time travel. Walking nurtures introspective thinking and reminiscence, and the narrator's travels through space are projected in time. Fournel enjoys historicizing, contrasting Old and New Paris, and expressing his nostalgia for disappearing practices, sounds, or sights.

If the "Odyssey" begins by sketching a theory of flânerie and *badauderie*, the narrator abandons such an impossible task (by definition, there can be no *theory* of flânerie) in favor of showing and telling us the observations of a flâneur as he had done in the first section. The narrator begins his flânerie at the Place des Écoles, observing, listening to all the city has to offer. On his odyssey through the streets of Paris, he stops to dine at a restaurant where more performers can be heard. We meet a boy whose youthful singing enchants his audience, picturesque bohemians with mandolins, a virtuoso with a wooden leg.

> I dine out every night, me who speaks to you; a privilege that does not make me conceited, even though there would be cause, as you will see in an instant; because my feasts, like those of Homer's heroes, take place at the sounds of an enchanting harmony, that as it intoxicates the senses, gently enables the laborious work of digestion. I do not ignore the thirty-two cent restaurants, Edens where I sometimes penetrate, and of which I have kept a most tender and most respectful memory. But I invite you to sit at the same table as me, if you like music and the study of social mores. What can be more curious than all these nomadic artists, singers, violin players, harpists and guitar players, crooners of *romances* and barcaroles,

Rubini in an oversized jacket, Jenny Lind in a tartan shawl who come to show their famished faces at mealtimes, a strange people, in rags, picturesque, coming from nowhere, a bizarre family that seems composed of characters resuscitated from the *Roman Comique*.[56]

The passage appeals to sight, hearing, taste, smell, and even touch in order to connect with the reader. Reminiscent of Balzac's Rabelaisian "gastronomy of the eye" (*Physiology of Marriage*) in its combination of empiricism and intellectualization, the descriptions of the surrounding sounds trigger personal memories and evoke literary recollections of Homer's *Odyssey* and Paul Scarron's picaresque novel (Fournel wrote a preface to Scarron's *Virgile travesti* in 1858). The street becomes an interior for the flâneur, as Benjamin describes, when Fournel compares street performers to famous opera singers he remembers, such as Giovanni Battista Rubini and Jenny Lind. As in Odysseus's encounter with the Sirens, the flâneur is intoxicated by the songs, but transforms his desire into aesthetic experience and intellectual reflection.

At the Pont des Arts, the flâneur joins a crowd listening to a blind man play the accordion. Later, he enjoys the "gigantic, cyclopean, titanic concert" of blind musicians at the Café des Aveugles located underground at the Palais-Royal. He encounters "L'homme-orchestre," a one-man-orchestra and a street celebrity chronicled in Charles Yriarte's *Paris grotesque: Les Célébrités de la rue* and depicted in Bertall's vignette "Musique d'artistes." Despite his cymbals, Fournel describes him as "homme-harmonie."[57]

Organs of Barbarie are ubiquitous; one in particular captivates his ear: "One especially! . . . Once I stayed twenty minutes dreaming at the window just listening to him. When he left his post, I went down into the street and followed him from station to station. He had a dapper tune, braided with bells that transported me in ecstasy and that would have made me dance in the middle of the street, as King David did before the Ark of God."[58] Following a paradigm set in Poe's "The Man of the Crowd," Fournel is first completely absorbed by the musical scene and then leaves the window to follow the musician into the streets. The reference to King David bringing the Ark of God into Jerusalem recalls Girardin's use of the same biblical allusion (2 Samuel 6:5 and 6:14); the reference distinguishes different audience expectations as David's music pleased his followers but not God. Whereas the flâneuse perceives the invasion of indoor space with anxiety, the flâneur who steps out of doors into the shared urban spaces of terraces and cafés is transported in ecstasy.

Such a haphazard journey among the streets and their noisy occupants is not uncommon in flâneur literature, though it is tempting to identify what makes Fournel's writing distinctive. Consider works such as *Voyage d'un flâneur dans les rues de Paris, album biographique grotesque contenant les portraits en miniature de toutes les célébrités en plein vent recueillis et saisis à la volée par le petit fils de M. Muzard*[59] (1839) or Charles Yriarte's *Paris grotesque: Les Célébrités de la rue* (1864). These portray street musicians, hawkers, and peddlers too, but lack the appeal to the senses that characterizes the rich impressionistic writing of Fournel, who would later publish *Esquisses et Croquis parisiens* under the pseudonym Bernadille.[60] *Voyage d'un flâneur* and the very similar *Paris grotesque* delve into the biographies of the characters habitually encountered on the streets, but leave it to the reader to imagine the full range of the street musician's effect on the flâneur. Yriarte discusses "l'homme à la vielle" and "l'homme-orchestre," some of the same celebrities as Fournel, whom he credits as an influence. Yet Muzard and Yriarte subordinate sensory description to the dramatic or narrative impulse, whereas for Fournel, plot remains a secondary consideration. He even draws attention to the jerky movement of flânerie when he begs the reader's indulgence for the lack of smooth transitions.[61] Fournel's individual sensibility as a flâneur and talent as a writer might explain his rare ability to make sense fully of his experiences of city sounds, yet he denies any musicological schooling and chalks up his aptitude to basic receptivity:

> I am not an expert concerning complicated harmonics, I can't fathom the arcane rules of the fugue and of counterpoint, and I confidently admire those men capable of discovering, at first glance, how many sharps there are in a key. I love and understand music as do rats attracted by grand organ melodies, which one sees peering out of their holes and stepping out timidly, delighted, fascinated, ecstatic, yet without the slightest clue as to the key of the piece that enchants them.[62]

Fournel's ear is receptive to popular music and traditional arts. In an unexpected turn of phrase, he compares himself to a *rat d'église* or a church mouse with an unusual passion for music, to underscore street music's appeal to base instincts; but, in practice, Fournel's responses are far from spontaneous or dirty. As a flâneur, he brings the attentive listening skills of a middle-class concert-goer to the streets; indeed, this passage, in which Fournel eschews technical music appreciation in favor of a subjective description of his absorption and emotional reaction, seems to reference the new romantic paradigm for attentive listening to concert music identified by James Johnson.[63] A member of the educated elite with many pseudonymous identities, Fournel was among other things a seventeenth-century theater scholar and Molière specialist. As such, his sensory appreciation is informed by knowledge of classical French popular humor, social satire, and the traditions of the picturesque and the grotesque (also prized by the French Romantics). This taste for and knowledge of popular traditions make Fournel, as compared with some of his contemporaries, better able to perceive, digest, and compose the city-as-concert, a soundscape he knows warrants attentive listening. He can experience the intoxication of and let himself be transported in ecstasy by the music of the streets.[64]

Let us now follow Fournel and some of his contemporaries onto the Champs Élysées, a well-established destination for the flâneur mapped out in chapter 14 of Huart's *Physiologie du flâneur*. Usually thought of as the place to see and be seen, here, the avenue is where strollers enjoy musical entertainment and musicians find avid audiences.[65] Street performers had historically congregated on the Pont Neuf, making Paris's oldest bridge the original center of their activities, as Fournel discusses in *Les Rues du vieux Paris*. The Second Empire flâneur, however, strolls on the boulevards. "The Champs-Élysées especially," writes Fournel in *Ce qu'on voit dans les rues de Paris*, "are at the center of that *deluge of harmony* which, in the nice summer weather, overflows onto Paris's streets. One can't even take a step, from the roundabout until the Place de la Concorde, without receiving full on something like a *discharge of artillery*, here a romance, there a song, a little farther a grand air or the overture of an opera."[66] Evoking Balzac's military metaphor, Fournel describes an unyielding experience of shock as the musical sounds in the street pummel him like a "discharge of artillery," but these produce a feeling of release and spring tide. Similarly, a group performance at the Carré Marigny sounds like "an arresting concert of *jerky harmony*, strange, original, which strikes a different chord than pale ceremonial concerts and forces the most indifferent to pay attention."[67] Rather than bore, annoy, or deafen the listener, an unexpected harmony whose dissonance enchants, jars the listener out of his blasé attitude. The metaphor of the city-as-concert as a staccato and a "deluge of harmony" evokes positive connotations, rather than what we might find elsewhere, in Girardin's description of a sonorous plague ("fléau d'harmonie") or in Old Nick's and Grandville's comical vignette "Ne pas être sourd" for example.

Neurasthenia is targeted in P. D. Forgues's (a.k.a. Old Nick's) and J. J. Grandville's tongue-in-cheek sketch about two friends who are besieged by a "frightful charivari," while seated at the Brasserie Anglaise on the Champs Élysées. The narrator's companion states up front the premise, that it would be preferable to be deaf: "That's the way things are, accordingly, our eyes, ears, palate, etc. . . . transmit more disagreeable impressions—more deadly in their consequences— than profitable and benign sensations." By way of illustration, we follow the narrator and his friend Maurice as they are seated:

> all of a sudden we saw with desperation one of the itinerant orchestras that, deplorably, have multiplied with the growing bad taste in music here. The troupe's three players—two women and one man—had inscribed on their goodly physi-

ognomies the premeditated smile of the pleasure they would infallibly bestow upon us. Our fearful stares did not deceive them and instantly they started their frightful charivari.[68]

Their eyes announce the presence of the performers whom they recognize as well-intentioned yet simple-minded and persistent, but it is their ears that are assaulted. In the illustration by Grandville accompanying the verbal sketch, a group of three street musicians, on the left of the image, crowd the two friends seated at a table at an outdoor café (figure 2). All the well-to-do strollers are confined to less than half of the space on the right of the image (the background includes a man with a take charge stance looking in the direction of the musicians, and a man who appears to be yelling at a single female stroller). The musicians, a male harpist, a female guitarist, and a female violinist, look unattractive, especially the women whose exaggerated facial features masculinize their faces. They are indeed "frightful" (*effrayant*) because their appearance and discordance instill fear in the listeners. The flâneurs lean uncomfortably to the right as the musicians step into their space. The flâneur with the top hat and the hand on his waist adopts an aggressive pose, whereas his hatless friend looks resigned. The image humorously shows the neurasthenia caused by street musicians and the flâneur's inability to control the charivari imposed upon him.

Indeed, Grandville's image evokes the custom of the charivari that subjected offenders to rough music as a means of public derision and chastisement. A group of young people would assemble to serenade by loud noise-making: banging pots and pans, blowing horns, shaking rattles and bells, and shouting cries and insults. As a well-established plebeian right, the ritual was used by the community (especially its youth) for its own self-regulation outside a bureaucratized justice system.[69] Scholars' opinions vary as to the charivari's significance as a carnivalesque means to mock authority with a potential for subversion, or as a "safety valve" to defend social custom and re-establish order. Nathalie Zemon Davis states it succinctly when she writes that "misrule always implies the rule." The custom of the charivari was still practiced in the nineteenth century, especially in rural villages and urban *faubourgs*, although the penal code of 1810 made disturbances of the peace ("bruit et tapages injurieux et nocturnes"), including charivari, illegal (articles 479–80). In post-Revolutionary France, the charivari acquired new political expressions, making it an antecedent to other modern forms of collective protest, such as the rally or the demonstration (*manifestation*).[70]

The reference to charivari in Old Nick and Grandville flaunts many of the traits of the traditional ritual,[71] but it draws out the tradition's ambivalence toward misrule. As is clear from the narrative point of view of Old Nick's story,

Ils commencèrent à l'instant même leur effrayant charivari.

Figure 2. J. J. Grandville, *Ils commencèrent à l'instant même leur affreux charivari* from *Petites Misères de la vie humaine* (Paris: Fournier, 1846), 330, Courtesy of McGill University Library, Rare Books and Special Collections, Montreal.

the leisured characters sitting in a public space use the word "charivari" to disparage the racket made by the musicians, without conceding their plebeian right to rabble-rouse. The scene evokes the class boundary between elites and underclass that the ritual delineates and transgresses. The musicians apparently knowingly inflict the charivari onto the two gentlemen (for an offense that remains unstated), thus aggravating their ear-splitting pain. The gentlemen are thus victims of a charivari that may be enacted to put them on the spot as elites, but at the same time, they reverse the offense by insulting the musicians as lower-class noisemakers. The class conflict is humorously muffled in this "frightful" scene, where a return to order is implied, but not at all guaranteed.

A similar aversion to street noise on the boulevards speaks volumes about Maria d'Anspach's fear of class boundary incursions in her portrayal of itinerant musicians in *Le Prisme* from the series of *Les Français peints par eux-mêmes*.[72] Flâneuse, she complains of not being able to walk down the street without encountering "[des] lambeaux d'harmonie" [tatters of harmony].[73] The metaphor aptly conflates misery, mendicancy, and street music. Flâneurs during the July Monarchy commonly complained about their encounters with paupers and vendors. Honoré de Balzac had earlier written a similar diatribe against beggar-musicians in 1831 in *La Caricature*: in Paris "one cannot take one step without being assailed . . . by nimble beggars, who flay the ears with their noisy songs and their barbaric instruments; by street vendors who exchange a packet of toothpicks, or give you a swipe of the broom in the legs, for alms."[74] Have things changed ten years later? Not according to Anspach: "Paris is prey to an invasion of itinerant musicians," she writes, "so that if we are not careful, the noise from their instruments will soon dominate the sound of carriages, and foreigners, already little convinced of the dignity of our customs, will rightly take us for a nation of quacks."[75] Whereas during the Restoration, street entertainers could be found in almost every Parisian neighborhood, the circulation of travelling acrobats and buskers was severely restricted in Paris in several ordinances during the July Monarchy.[76] The ordinance of December 1831, for instance, regulated street musicians on the premise that they obstructed circulation and amassed crowds that disrupted order and disturbed the public peace. Moreover authorities feared that their music spread salacious, antigovernment content.[77] The ordinance restricted their circulation to specific boulevards and squares (but not public gardens, bridges, or courtyards). Ordinances multiplied attempts to crack down on street performers because law enforcement could not easily identify those targeted by the complaints.[78] Noise can be elusive precisely because it is pervasive. Not all street musicians were treated the same. For example until 1853 (when the legislation was standardized), organ players were allowed to play anywhere until 10:00 P.M. (ordinance of December 14, 1831, article 9), whereas other musicians and singers were restricted to specific zones and schedules.[79]

Like Girardin who expressed anxiety over the sonic permeability of the bourgeois interior space, the more virulent xenophobe Anspach lamented that the intrusion of unwelcome foreign voices—accents from Italy (Parma), Savoy, Alsace, and Germany that were more audible than others—threatened her sense of place and national pride. The author's concern over how the city would be perceived by foreign tourists bespeaks an awareness of how the sonic environment creates a sense of the local, but also how its ties to national and international contexts affect that very sense of place. The local, informal economy is pitted against the global, formal economy that the author considers more significant (for instance the presence of the World's Fair in Paris in 1839). Seasonal migrants came to Paris from the French provinces, particularly Savoy (musicians) and Auvergne (peddlers), to supplement their incomes in winter after the harvest and before the sowing season. Whether they peddled or performed in the street, their activities were equated with begging. Since begging was illegal, street musicians were in an ambiguous position. Amid the general alarm and fear caused by mendicancy and migration in the mid-1830s, recent immigrants were perceived as morally "undisciplined" and potential criminals.[80] Thus, what a listener sympathetic to the cause of the people heard as "these raucous cries of workers and these lifeless voices of paupers," a more bigoted listener invested in class distinctions heard as threatening sounds of lawlessness and dissolution. Intolerance for the "noise" of street musicians is commensurate with these social concerns, rather than with health issues, as was the case with the period's growing intolerance for stench. In fact, the perceived dissonance of the street performers' charivari metaphorically figures their impossible social integration.[81]

As in Old Nick's sketch, the urban stroller is subject to neurasthenia: "Your ears ring and your frustrated nerves contort."[82] The ear, which cannot turn away or close like the eye, necessarily elicits physiological and emotional responses, either painful ringing in the ears in Anspach or "ecstasy" in Fournel's case. Unlike seeing, hearing forces social engagement and participation so that the unwilling listener confronts the limits of their auditory freedom. Flâneurs cannot remain disengaged, though their perception of street noise as intoxicating harmony or neurasthenic charivari depends on their comfort level with the urban crowd and their tolerance for class interaction. Either way, they are touched by the streets and cannot remain unmoved by the sensations they experience strolling.

While he feels pathos for street musicians, Fournel aligns with the intolerance expressed in Anspach and Old Nick when he disdains members of the lumpenproletariat. Contrary to Anspach, however, Fournel clearly distinguishes street musicians from beggars:

> I call beggars, not those workers in public squares, those street artists, who ask for a penny in exchange for their songs, feats and tricks—ah! Poor folks, my good friends, God save me from treating you with such indignity, I who have contemplated you for so long, have listened so much, have even admired you!—but these

parasites without shame, these hideous and sterile superfetations that one stumbles over at each step. . . . [83]

Whereas Fournel treats street performers as artists and dignified peers, he consigns beggars to a parasitic, excessive, and shameful subcategory by comparing them to "superfetations" or the secondary fertilization of a womb already containing an established fetus. When describing the Paris Temple "pandemonium," he cannot hide his revulsion at the "Tower of Babel" spoken there: "That fetid bazaar, that resembles a lair, full of some sort of tenebrous and repulsive mystery, where a sinister and subterranean slang is spoken, where merchants exchange amongst themselves strange monikers that do not belong to any known language, frightens the inoffensive flâneur."[84] As Dietmar Rieger has shown, Fournel manifests no social solidarity toward ragpickers, who are among the lowest members of the working class. He sees no affinities with this type that Baudelaire and Benjamin famously associated with the flâneur. Fournel concludes his odyssey of a flâneur by evoking his "tranquil consciousness" and by imagining the sweet dreams he will have despite the misery he has seen while strolling in the streets of Paris.[85] Why then is his treatment of street musicians so different? Perhaps his flâneur-like shifts from the sensory to the reflective and literary plane avoid the confrontation with the realities of social marginalization and pauperism. To be sure, Fournel exoticizes the street performers and captures their "bizarre," "fantastic," and "picturesque" qualities. Though he turns them into freaks, he nevertheless feels the poignancy of the sounds they make: "I have never felt, as when I listened to this old man, what fantastical effects and picturesque charm an already trembling and withered voice could sometimes add to a melody." Or, "What a warm, frank, colorful language, soaking by its roots in this picturesque and vigorous idiom, speaks the people!" Street music resonates with an authentic Gallic spirit ("l'esprit gaulois"), a waning melody frozen in time and in space, traces of which Fournel's ear can still decipher. Like him, "the people are essentially melomanic [mélomane]."[86]

Leaving the crowd, the flâneur takes a carriage or omnibus to observe the "typographical eloquence"[87] of city signs and posters, and to listen to street criers, while moving about the city both in space and in time:

> What does one do in a carriage, when one is bored of looking at the billboards and signage through the carriage-window, if one doesn't listen, half-squatting in a corner, to the symphony so monotonous in its variety, so varied in its monotony, which rises incessantly from each street of the capital? Lend an ear, and you will at first hear only the disagreeable rumbling of the carriages on the pavement; but then soon will rise next to this noise the discordant and screeching melopoeia of the thousand Cries of Paris.[88]

The billboards representing the industrialized arts are juxtaposed with the traditional cries of hawkers. Countering the more usual statements about the never-boring urban spectacle, street cries distract from the lassitude of looking at street signage, though, as we shall explore, street cries and posters share a common purpose. The flâneur listens attentively to the city streets, tuning into the soaring melopœia ("mélopée") of the Cries of Paris set against the background of the carriage wheels on the pavement.[89] Fournel finds the sound of human voices more meaningful than the mechanical sound of the moving wheels. Street cries, whose sounds and history Fournel took a special interest in, resonate loudly within the literature on flânerie and thus deserve closer attention.

CHAPTER 2

Blason Sonore

Street Cries in the City

For nineteenth-century ears, street cries had always defined the ambiance of Paris. From the Middle Ages through to the nineteenth and early twentieth centuries, street cries were used by hawkers to publicize announcements or news and to sell merchandise of all kinds. Peddlers could be male or female itinerant, small-scale merchants. Whereas wagon vendors such as flower peddlers used a cart to transport their merchandise, pack peddlers such as glaziers or ragpickers carried their supplies on their body. Some made their rounds in the early morning hours, whereas others worked at night. Food vendors and some tradesmen performed "useful" services, while other peddlers entertained. Peddlers could have an official status or a more marginal one and could end their days, if successful, rivaling resident shopkeepers, or if not, subsisting as quasi beggars at the periphery of the law. Despite such diversity, the use of cries united these trades. Each trade had a distinctive cry, a combination of words and a characteristic tune, such that buyers could identify each peddler by a sound marker. Nevertheless, street criers were frequently conflated into a broad, if heterogeneous, category of itinerant tradesmen: the "petits métiers," also known as "industriels en plein vent," "gagne-petits," "camelots," or "colporteurs." These different comprehensive terms variously emphasize their lowly status ("*petits* métiers" or small-scale tradesmen), their tenuous relationship to productive labor ("métiers" or "industriels"), their meager earnings ("gagne-petits" or small-wage earners), the outdoor location where they exercise their trades ("en plein vent" or in the open air), or the low quality of their wares ("camelots" sell "camelote" or junk).[1] Although originally *colporteur* signified the official profession of the itinerant vendor of broadsheets (*papiers volants*) and images, the word came to designate all hawkers.[2] Street musicians for example were also *colporteurs* who sold song sheets. The collapse of distinctions among the small-scale tradesmen reflects bourgeois perceptions of street vending's marginal status. In a word, the category of "petits métiers" was a catch-all grouping that unified disparate types of peddlers, much like the *Cris de Paris* attempted to harmonize a cacophony of street cries.

Street cries did not undergo substantial change until the Industrial Revolution in France in the 1830s, but overall it is difficult to measure accurately any timeline of the decline of peddling. French writers bemoaned the slow disappearance of the practice of hawking merchandise or street crying throughout the mid– and late nineteenth century, but there is conflicting evidence about whether or not the practice was in fact disappearing. Georges Kastner can on the same page quote a journalist stating "the cries of Paris are receding, but the street vendors remain; that's our gain," and write "the streets of Paris have therefore not lost their criers. Nevertheless these nomadic vendors are not quite what they used to be."[3] American visitors, such as art collector James Jackson Jarves, also remark upon the obsolescence of peddlers who are faced with the "tide of improvement." The Paris correspondent for the *New York Times*, American journalist Rowland Strong acknowledges that the cries are disappearing, but that a few survive in the early twentieth century. After describing a few of them, he writes that "the charm of these old cries is that they are the echoes of a Paris which in nearly every detail, whether of architecture or the customs and costumes of its inhabitants, has vanished or is vanishing."[4] The journalist Bradley Gilman, however, still hears these echoes loudly and clearly in 1905 and precisely records several Parisian street cries in an essay in the *Cosmopolitan, a Monthly Illustrated Magazine*.[5] These Americans presume that cries belong to a premodern economy that will necessarily and inevitably fade with the development of modern capitalism.[6] Since these accounts report the decline as gradual—perhaps even a desired or willed, rather than an observed phenomena—narratives about street cries' disappearance often express ambivalent feelings toward modernity.

Irrespective of their disappearance or endurance, literary and artistic representations of the *Cris de Paris* (in various media including music, theater, prose fiction, poetry, journalistic writing, or graphic works) persisted and arguably *increased* over the course of the nineteenth century. As Brigitte Diaz has suggested, the doubt cast around the disappearance can be tied to the perception of an acceleration of time in the modern city—"la forme d'une ville / Change plus vite, hélas! que le coeur d'un mortel" ("the form a city takes / More quickly shifts, alas, than does the mortal heart").[7] From Balzac's "Ce qui disparaît de Paris" to Janin's introduction to *Les Français peints par eux-mêmes*, writings about Paris present a new self-awareness of urban change and attempt to record the city's transformation. As commentators recognized that it was only a matter of time before earwitnesses of their era would die out, they worked to preserve the memory of fading sound cultures by collecting, adapting, and recirculating the *Cris de Paris*. Renewed interest in the transmedial and multimodal genres of the *Cris de Paris* in the nineteenth century shows the extent to which this long-standing tradition continued to be relevant in the present. The peddling sounds of the streets constituted shared memories that evoked childhood and that fostered a sense of place for Parisians. A nostalgic longing for better days combined with the antiquarian's interest in Old Paris also motivated efforts to document and preserve traces of sounds perceived as having survived through the ages, but now at risk of disappearing. We have heard how the cries of ped-dlers joined with the sounds of street musicians to create a sensuous urban space, the city-as-concert that the flâneur could orchestrate. Subsequent chap-ters demonstrate how street cries offer especially resonant material to sound out the process of social and urban transformation, class conflict, and the inter-relation between high and low art. This chapter traces street criers' functions as noisemakers, place-makers, and "sound souvenirs,"[8] in the musical, graphic, and textual traditions of the *Cris de Paris*.

The Multimodal Genres of the *Cris de Paris*: Musical, Graphic, Textual

The *Cris de Paris* refer both to the historical practice of peddling and to transme-dial art forms (textual, graphic, or musical) originating in the Middle Ages. The *Cris de Paris* record street noise in various media so that peddlers' cries can be replayed and thus remembered. The discourse of the Cries thus constitutes a cultural memory[9] that is shared and transferred through the generations. The history of how this medieval tradition was actively remembered, adapted, and circulated in nineteenth-century France, as I survey here, richly demonstrates how they were invested with new ideological meanings and values (related for instance to a modern consciousness of historical change or to the develop-ment of group identities based on sonic relations between middle and working classes) that sustained their relevance in modern times. The *Cris de Paris* date back to "Les Crieries de Paris," a thirteenth-century poem by Guillaume de la Villeneuve, republished in the nineteenth century by printer Georges-Adrien Crapelet and later by archivist Alfred Franklin.[10] Both these connoisseurs were intent on making sources on medieval street sounds available to their contemporaries. Villeneuve's catch-all enumeration of approximately 130 street cries (194 lines of octosyllabic rhyming couplets) is narrated in the first person by a self-described poverty-stricken Villeneuve, who records the sounds of criers advertising a bounty of things he cannot afford to buy, but can barely resist. From morning until nightfall, the speaker roams the streets hearing the taunts of peddlers trying to sell him fresh herring, watercress, cheeses, nuts, pears, chestnuts, figs, and much more. The cries in the poem are not necessarily an accurate index of what one might hear in medieval streets. Even in the Middle Ages, the *Cris* were a literary topos, used widely in medieval *dits* and farce. Debates about the cries' authenticity as a record of daily life continue. Rather than consider Villeneuve's poetry as mere factual transcriptions, Laurent Vissière argues that "Les Crieries de Paris" use word play for effect. According to Vissière, humorous features connote "l'esprit de la rue," namely the truculence and "esprit gaulois" or ribald humor that amuse and attract customers. Vissière, therefore, reproves the suggestion that the Cries directly represent medieval clerks' mocking condescension toward the lower classes, an attitude nevertheless manifest in many nineteenth-century bibliophiles' descriptions of what they call "burlesque" and "ridiculous" Paris.[11] Musicologist Emma Dillon is also skeptical about placing the "Crieries" "in a tradition of realistic reportage," but she is equally cautious about "the assumption that contrivance and artistry were the defining aspect of the cries." She argues instead that the narrator's poverty is a clue to the significance of the excess evoked in the "Crieries." Villeneuve comments on the city as marketplace where perishable consumer goods are continually replenished; using a polyphonic form in which sound overtakes sense, he lauds the grandeur of the protean city, constantly exhausting and renewing its supply of pleasures.[12] Villeneuve's poem, therefore, inaugurates a rich legacy whose questions about authenticity as a sonic record, social class, linguistic play, the marketplace, and the very identity of the city of Paris will capture readers' attention for centuries.

The *Cris* spawned both musical and iconographic traditions. A motet for three voices in *The Montpellier Codex*, similar to Villeneuve's poem, "musicalizes" the hubbub of the street cries to convey the vitality of the city.[13] One of the better known early modern musical compositions influenced by the Cries is a polyphonic composition of 1528, "Voulez ouir les Cris de Paris" by Clément Janequin, a contemporary of François Rabelais, well-known for *Le Chant des oiseaux* and *La Bataille*, his musical imitation of the Battle of Marignano of 1515 in which the army of Francis I was victorious over the Swiss. Fifty years later, Jean Servin composed the even more dizzying *La Fricassée des Cris de Paris* in which he trumps Janequin's 50 with 120 cries. Both Janequin and Servin use polyphony, onomatopoeia, and *quodlibet* (patchwork quotation) to convey, with humor, but also with virtuosity, the soundscape of the city in which the volume of sound exceeds anyone's ability to make sense of it all. There was a revival of interest in Janequin's programmatic music on profane themes in the nineteenth century. Championed by Alexandre Choron, Janequin's secular music was performed widely beginning in the 1830s.[14]

Janequin's composition also influenced Georges Kastner, who produced a symphony adapting the *Cris*, the score of which is included in his book-length essay of musical ethnography, *Les Voix de Paris* (1857).[15] Like the composer Choron, who introduced the French to music history under the Restoration, Kastner was a conservatoire-trained composer and music scholar, who took an interest in early music. His chronicle of the tradition of the *Cris de Paris* in *Les Voix de Paris* is further evidence of the cultural salience in the nineteenth century of this long-standing representation of street noise. Kastner catalogs no less than ten compositions from the first half of the century inspired by the *Cris*, including works by Daniel-François Auber, Victor Parisot, and Félicien David.[16]

Over the course of the century, the "tableau" or soundscape of Cries made its way into every venue, from the popular vaudeville stage to the more elite Paris opera houses. Many works such as the "coarse panorama" *Les Cris de Paris: Tableau poissard en un acte, mêlé de couplets* by Francis, Simonin, and d'Artois (Théâtre des Variétés, 1822), or the musical sketch-panorama titled *Les Cris de la rue. Saynète-panorama* by Baumaine, Blondelet, and Déransart (1881) ostensibly sought to recreate the noisy soundscape of street criers as a musical spectacle, for popular amusement. Significantly, the appearance of the words "tableau" and "panorama" in their titles suggests a desire to orchestrate the music of the streets into a pleasing composition and thus to harmonize the city noise. Other popular works, instead, probed the sinister connotations of small-scale tradesmen; a case in point is a pantomime on the old-clothes–man performed at the Funambules in 1842, in which the mime Pierrot kills the peddler and is later haunted by his ghostly and strident cry: "marrrchand d'habits!" (any clo-o-othes?).[17] The cries of small-scale tradesmen filled the popular stage.[18]

The Cries were also adapted in elite productions such as Gustave Charpentier's *Louise*, performed at the Opéra-Comique in 1900. Charpentier allegedly was inspired to include street cries in his opera by the street noise he heard one evening: "There came to me through the open door the cries of the street-sellers of the old faubourgs: and so I could confront these far away music(s) with my young efforts. After a hard night of labor, while the dawn threw its blue light on my paper, the songs were like the smiling 'good-day' of friends who cared about my task, knowing that I was trying to write their story, and so wishing to encourage me."[19] Charpentier's appropriation of the popular "panorama" of street cries into the naturalist opera is more complex than these reminiscences of the circumstances of inspiration suggest. Street scenes of waking and working Paris are integrated into *Louise;* as a result, the *Cris de Paris* are not merely used for the purpose of sound realism, but rather reinterpreted and transformed into musical and symbolic motifs according to the needs of the composer.[20]

Similarly, the realist, dramatic, and musical potential of street cries was exploited in fictional works, notably Honoré de Balzac's *Le Père Goriot.*[21] At a critical turning point in the narrative, right before he is unmasked and arrested, the criminal mastermind Vautrin conducts a "veritable opera" of the *Cris de Paris* at Madame Vauquer's boarding house. Although the museum employee initiates the singing in the passage, Vautrin prepares the scene by getting the dinner guests roiled up and providing "a glass or two of Bordeauxrama":

> Imitations of the cries of various animals mingled with the loud laughter; the Museum official having taken it into his head to mimic a cat-call rather like the caterwauling of the animal in question, eight voices simultaneously struck up with the following variations: "Scissors to grind!" "Chick-weeds for singing birds!" "Brandy-snaps, ladies!" "China to mend!" "Boat ahoy!" "Sticks to beat your wives or your clothes!" "Old clo!" "Cherries all ripe!"[22]

Raucous animality and incoherence, as well as playful bantering, characterize the random series of bellowing and meowing noises made by the boarders. The Balzacian narrator's attention then shifts to Vautrin, and the "head-splitting racket in the room" acquires form, musicality, and coherence as it is transformed into the "veritable opera" conducted by Vautrin. Vautrin, the outsider, stands apart from the boarders' hilarity and the general disorder induced by their drunken revelry. Thus Vautrin takes lower-class "noise" and turns it into "music," in a manner parallel to Balzac's own aesthetic appropriation of street cries in the novel. The *Cris* scene not only acts as a dramatic plot device that heightens Vautrin's skills as a concertmaster just prior to his fall, but also structures relationships among the novel's characters in aural terms. Balzac, who opposes the noisy lower class and quiet-seeking bourgeoisie in several writings, alternately accentuates peddlers as hideous noisemakers in *Illusions perdues* or tuneful fixtures of picturesque Paris in "Ce qui disparaît de Paris." *Le Père Goriot*, however, complicates the use of sound to define class identity by comparing the protean Vautrin to a shrewd peddler (a *marchande à la toilette* or old-clothes-woman). The novel also draws extensively on vaudeville airs to characterize the protagonists' relationships and to signify the indomitable nature of popular sonic culture. The musical tradition of street cries is therefore full of examples of reciprocal appropriations between high and low sound cultures, as street criers (like the street musicians in Bertall's caricature discussed in the previous chapter) appropriated popular airs and *bel canto* arias to better demarcate their cry from the city drone, and composers or novelists sought inspiration in the city streets.[23]

We have seen how the musical Cries were reprised, adapted, and recirculated in the nineteenth century by archivists, composers, music theorists, vaudevillists, and writers. In addition to musical compositions, the *Cris de Paris,* like the *Cries of London,* also refers to series of prints, which became popular in the sixteenth century. Depictions of street criers were especially prominent in France, as Karen Beall remarks, where the earliest and latest series known are found, and where more prints were published than anywhere else.[24] Typical of the genre, figure 3 represents a woodcut of a distinctly French type, an itinerant pastry

Figure 3. Anon., *Le Marchand de gâteaux: Anciens Cris de Paris,* ca. 1500, colored engraving (woodcut). Reprinted by permission of Bibliothèque Nationale de France, Paris.

merchant wearing an apron and carrying a tray of *oublies* (a type of round, wafer-thin, crisp pastry), who cries out "Échaudés, gâteaux, petits choux chauds."[25]

A modern revival of interest in the *Cris de Paris* took place from as early as the mid– to late eighteenth century with series of prints by Edmé Bouchardon, François Boucher, and others,[26] but peaked especially during the French Restoration with extensive series of lithographs by Carle Vernet.[27] In addition to cheap broadsheets with serial types, original drawings of single types by masters such as Boucher or Bouchardon were frequently engraved and sold as fine prints. Graphic works on the *Cris* were propelled by the development of printmaking with print runs in the thousands.[28] This practice accounts for the existence of low and high quality images that sold at different price points and appealed to different markets.[29] Antiquarians and collectors prized fine engravings of the *Cris de Paris* that were advertised in elite periodicals.[30] As can be seen in the eighteenth-century frontispiece for a suite of twelve engravings of street vendors by Jean Duplessi-Bertaux, prints sold on the street were also accessible to a range of buyers. The frontispiece represents the *colporteur* or image vendor's outdoor booth and prominently includes a street sign that identifies the title of the set of prints it introduces, *Suite des Cris des marchands ambulants*. The *Suite* therefore depicts the context of its own distribution. Print vendors sold a wide selection of subject matter, including religious prints, portraits, mythological nudes, and street scenes, to well-to-do collectors. According to the frontispiece, those who bought the prints had little need of the services offered by street criers, but appreciated the picturesque quality of their artistic renderings (figure 4). The *Cris* were also made available as collector's items, such as the luxury facsimile edition of the series of woodcuts from which figure 3 derives, produced jointly in 1885 by the archivist at the Bibliothèque de l'Arsenal, Jules Cousin, and the engraver Adam Pilinski.[31] Collectors were interested in prints of street criers for their quaint and naïve qualities. Realist writer and critic Champfleury spelled out his appreciation for the naïveté of popular arts, sensing in them an unmediated representation of plebeian life.[32] Such views were widely held, especially among realists and other writers sympathetic to the working class. The naturalist novelist Edmond de Goncourt, for instance, owned no less than twelve *Cris* by Boucher, a suite of sixty Bouchardon as well as the rare *Cris de Paris dessiné d'après nature par M. Poisson*, as he catalogs in *La Maison d'un artiste* (1881).[33]

As prints depicting laborers for the benefit of elite buyers, the *Cris de Paris* raise questions about how labor is represented. In the woodcut in figure 3, the earth tones chosen (not necessarily by the block cutter) to color the pastry vendor's costume suggest his lowly status. The figure is in profile, a pose frequently used in subsequent images of criers. Boucher's drawings in the eighteenth cen-

Figure 4. Jean Duplessi-Bertaux (1750–1818), frontispiece for *Suite des Cris des marchands ambulants de Paris,* engraving and etching; sheet: 4 × 3 in. (10.16 × 7.62 cm). Courtesy of Minneapolis Institute of Arts (The Minnich Collection, The Ethel Morrison Van Derlip Fund, 1966, p.17, 507).

tury were anything but crude; instead, the *petits métiers* are idealized, their labor unacknowledged.[34] The *chaudronnier*'s clothes and pots are represented in detail, with a sophisticated use of shading, in the engraving after Boucher (figure 5). The figure's ragged and baggy clothes, floppy hat, and ungroomed hair accentuate the lowly status of the boilermaker, but the print evacuates signs of physical labor: the *chaudronnier*'s posture is as upright as a nobleman's, and his pots and

CHAUDRONIER CHAUDRONIER

Paris, chez Huquier Avec privilège du Roi

Figure 5. François Boucher (after), *Chaudronier Chaudronier* (*Boilermaker*), ca. 1737, engraving by Simon Francis Ravenet the Elder (1706–74), 25.2 × 16.9 cm, Inv.: 18983LR. Rothschild Collection. Photo: Thierry Le Mage. Musée du Louvre, Paris, France. © RMN-Grand Palais/Art Resource, New York.

pans seem weightless. The profile of the face, though hidden from view, suggests neither exhaustion nor strain.[35] It is not typical of the *Cris de Paris* for the scene to include relations between buyers and sellers, or wholesalers and retailers. Rather, the types are usually isolated on the page in a blank or timeless setting and defined solely by their accessories and clothes, instead of their emotions

Figure 6. Paul Gavarni (French, 1804–66), *Marchand de casseroles,* 1814–66. Lithograph on paper, image: 10 1/16 × 7 3/4 in. (25.5 × 19.7 cm); sheet: 15 11/16 × 10 7/8 in. (39.9 × 27.7 cm). Sterling and Francine Clark Art Institute, Williamstown, Massachusetts, 1955.2304 (Photo by Michael Agee).

or human relationships. Although Boucher breaks convention and alludes to a narrative by including a young woman, whose curiosity is triggered by the cry, the boilermaker's eyes and ears do not engage her. (Could he be deaf? Boilermakers often were.)

Marchand de casseroles by Paul Gavarni, among his works made in England,[36] attempts to match Boucher's level of detail in *The Boilermaker.* The figure stands stiff and upright, unencumbered by his merchandise, which overwhelms the image (figure 6). Although the idealized posture has not changed, the cloth-

LES GENS DE PARIS.   Petit commerce. — 2.

Machine à pleurer la Bretagne ou la Normandie — de la force d'un Auvergnat.

Par Gavarni.   Gravé par Brevière.

Figure 7. Paul Gavarni, *Machine à pleurer la Bretagne ou la Normandie—de la force d'un Auvergnat,* from *Le Petit Commerce* (2 plates) in *Le Diable à Paris,* 1:239, 241. Courtesy of Bibliothèque des livres rares et collections spéciales, Direction des bibliothèques, Université de Montréal.

ing however has. Unlike the peddler in Boucher's print, this one is abstracted from the context of his labor, and he carries many more pots and rags than his model. Shabbier looking, he also wears the kind of modern top hat and dark jacket worn by city dwellers in contrast to the provincial clothing and hat of Boucher's type. Gavarni, like his contemporaries Honoré Daumier or Bertall, would later sketch street types in the press and in literary guidebooks. In the

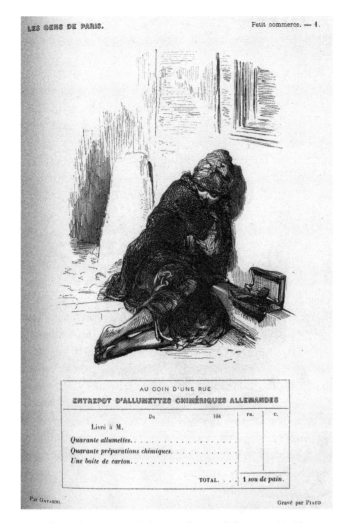

Figure 8. Paul Gavarni, *Au coin d'une rue. Entrepôt d'allumettes chimériques allemandes,* from *Le Petit Commerce* (2 plates) in *Le Diable à Paris*, 1:239, 241. Courtesy of Bibliothèque des livres rares et collections spéciales, Direction des bibliothèques, Université de Montréal.

series "Petit Commerce" (figures 7 and 8), Gavarni abandons the traditional concealment of criers' labor and instead emphasizes the laborer's physical exertion and exhaustion. In "Machine à pleurer la Bretagne ou la Normandie—de la force d'un Auvergnat," the organ grinder is bent over under the weight of the organ and his wide stride shows the physical force needed to move forward with the bulky instrument. The second plate in the series, "Au coin d'une rue.

Entrepôt d'allumettes chimériques allemandes," shows a dirty-looking child huddled up on a street corner, with a box of—chimerical rather than chemical—matches for sale.

I discuss how Jean-François Raffaëlli accentuates the miserable conditions of the chestnut seller's labor in the last chapter, but perhaps the most extreme revision of the idealization of labor in the *Cris* can be found in Fernand Pelez de Cordova's "Un martyr ou le marchand de violettes," exhibited at the Salon in 1885, representing a sleeping child street vendor (a violet seller) collapsed from exhaustion on the street. The iconography of the *Cris de Paris*, like that of *images d'Épinal*, remains a reference point and even a source of renewal for avant-garde artists such as Edouard Manet, Henri de Toulouse-Lautrec, and Eugène Atget (figure 9).[37]

Atget's basket seller stands tall, still, and mute on the street, like Boucher's and Gavarni's figures. Rather than actively hawking his wares, he is posing silently for the photograph. It is easy to conceive how musical or theatrical compositions imitated street cries, but much harder to imagine how they were evoked in silent prints. How might images of peddlers record their cries? The *Cris* would not be true-to-life representations of street cries. Since the *Cris* iconography codified vendors as visual types, often generalizing and enhancing their appearance rather than providing a realistic rendering, there is no reason to assume that sounds evoked by the images would be authentic rather than representational. They reflect how sonic relations were imagined. Representing peddlers one to a sheet against a vacant background has the effect of muting street trades; the images suggest they worked in silence.[38] In contrast, assembling suites of prints would be the equivalent of evoking the multiplicity of overlapping urban cries, not so much as an accurate historical record, but rather as a polyphonic orchestration of the city imagined or remembered as concert rather than cacophony.[39]

Images of street vendors certainly triggered memories of past experiences of hearing noisy streets. The print collector Edmond de Goncourt makes this point clearly in *La Maison d'un artiste:*

> With these three volumes, not only do you have the representation of all small-scale itinerant trades, but you hold in your ear the noise of the streets of former times, as if an extension of the echo of sonorous voices whirring from dawn until dusk in the big city. And first here is the beautiful and original cry, resurrecting for a moment the man and woman of the streets out of their mortal exhaustion: *Eau-de-vie, vie,* and all the others: *Mend your old bellows.—Brooms, brooms.—Chickweed, groundsel for littl' birds.—Sweep your chimney, up and down.*[40]

Figure 9. Eugène Atget, *Marchand de paniers, Paris pittoresque, 1e série*, 1898, albumen photograph. Reprinted by permission of the Bibliothèque nationale de France, Paris.

Goncourt states evocatively that the prints resurrect and prolong into the present the echo of street noises that are no longer heard in late-nineteenth-century Paris. Recognizing but not really weighing the exertion of labor, the collector can listen at a remove to the "exhausted" voices of peddlers in the tranquility of his home. The safe distance from actual peddlers gives nostalgia free reign. Like a sea shell you hold to your ear, the *Cris* bring back to life not Goncourt's individual lived memories, but shared collective memories of sounds of the past that have been silenced. Untethered from the dominance of the visual, the *Cris* multiply the bodily impressions in nineteenth-century viewers and appeal to their sensuous imaginations.[41] The sensualization of the *Cris* is furthermore evident in attempts to record the cry in musical scores accompanying traditional images of vendors. If Boucher's engraving *Chaudronier Chaudronier* merely suggests a cry by representing the boilermaker's open mouth, some prints such as Édouard Wattier's 1822 series of twelve engravings or Bertall's *La Comédie de notre temps* include a musical score.[42] It is, however, in literary guidebooks that we find the most thorough attempt to account for the aural dimensions of the *Cris de Paris*.

The subject of peddlers was a favorite of contributors to "literary guidebooks"[43] from Louis-Sébastien Mercier's *Tableau de Paris* to Léon Curmer's *Les Français peints par eux-mêmes* and Jules Hetzel's *Le Diable à Paris*. Meticulous attention to the soundscape of the city is from the outset an integral part of panoramic literature as set out in the model of the genre, Mercier's *Tableau de Paris*: "No other work offers as complete a panorama of the noises and sounds of the big city as Mercier."[44] Moreover, connecting modern physiological types to early modern typologies of criers is one instance of the interplay between the ancient and the modern that characterizes Curmer's project as outlined by Jules Janin in the introduction. Janin explains that the city and its inhabitants have changed; "if the theater is more or less the same, the actors on the stage have changed." That is why, he adds, *Les Français peints par eux-mêmes* will borrow from typologies of old—the works of moralists Theophrastus and La Bruyère—but depict contemporary society in word and image.[45] Visual and verbal interrelations are essential to both *Les Français* and the *Cris de Paris*; in both cases, word and image relations facilitate neophyte readers' access to the content.[46] As Ségolène Le Men has shown, the *Cris de Paris* iconography had a profound influence on panoramic literature; for example, the serial and diagrammatic presentation of types in the table of contents of *Les Français peints par eux-mêmes* (figure 11), or in Bertall's *Les Petits Métiers de Paris* (figure 12) was likely influenced by the checkerboard format typical of prints and *images d'Épinal* representing the *Cris de Paris* (figure 10).[47]

Some *Cris* especially those published in a frieze format, such as the *image d'Épinal* image in figure 10 make manifest their ties to other pictorial traditions, such as the veduta, the painted or engraved cityscapes that were popular in earlier centuries. They also could be interpreted as a graphic version of the polyphony of early modern compositions. Both correspond to an attempt at a composition that orders, even harmonizes, the fragmentary sounds of the city. The serial graphic presentation reflects the fact that many of the Parisian types would be seen and heard on the street by passersby and flâneurs.[48] Both

Figure 10. Daguerre-Pellerin, *Les Cris de Paris, marchands ambulants*, print (image d'Épinal), ca. 1856. Reprinted by permission of the Bibliothèque nationale de France, Paris.

the collective sketches and the *Cris* classify types, using sound and sartorial markers to identify them, but neither the sketches nor the *Cris* impose an organizational structure onto the street scenes, sounds, and types; rather the serial presentation represents the happenstance order and equal standing of those who walk by, as the random series of types in figures 10 and 11 show.[49] Bertall's

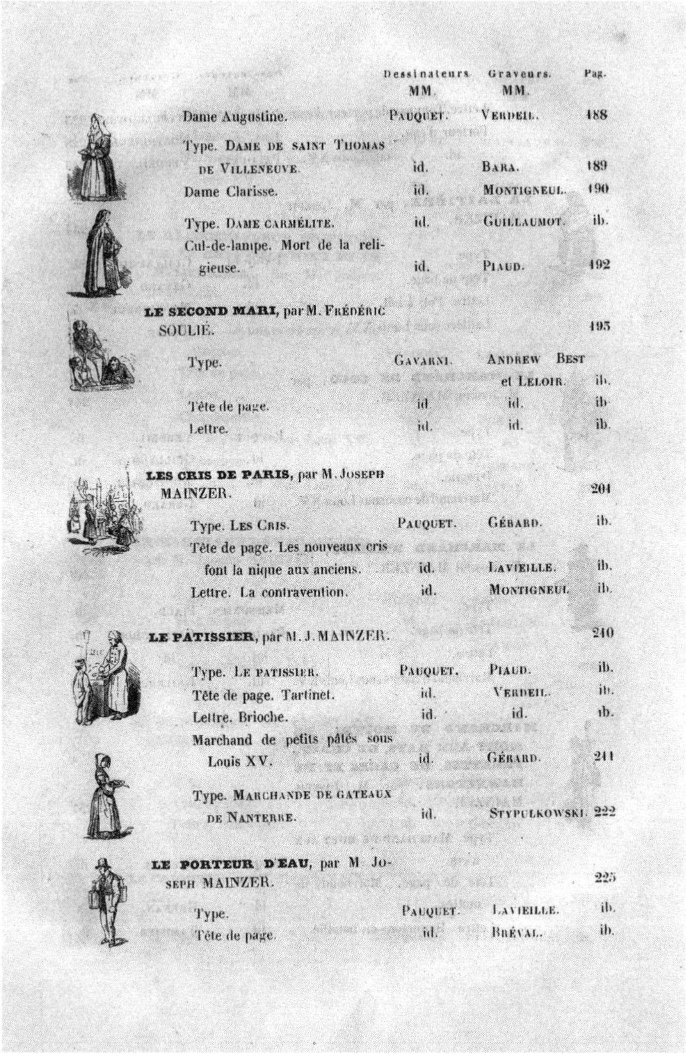

	Dessinateurs MM.	Graveurs. MM.	Pag.
Dame Augustine.	PAUQUET.	VERDEIL.	188
Type. DAME DE SAINT THOMAS DE VILLENEUVE.	id.	BARA.	189
Dame Clarisse.	id.	MONTIGNEUL.	190
Type. DAME CARMÉLITE.	id.	GUILLAUMOT.	ib.
Cul-de-lampe. Mort de la religieuse.	id.	PIAUD.	192
LE SECOND MARI, par M. FRÉDÉRIC SOULIÉ.			195
Type.	GAVARNI.	ANDREW BEST et LELOIR.	ib.
Tête de page.	id.	id.	ib.
Lettre.	id.	id.	ib.
LES CRIS DE PARIS, par M. JOSEPH MAINZER.			204
Type. LES CRIS.	PAUQUET.	GÉRARD.	ib.
Tête de page. Les nouveaux cris font la nique aux anciens.	id.	LAVIEILLE.	ib.
Lettre. La contravention.	id.	MONTIGNEUL.	ib.
LE PATISSIER, par M. J. MAINZER.			210
Type. LE PATISSIER.	PAUQUET.	PIAUD.	ib.
Tête de page. Tartinet.	id.	VERDEIL.	ib.
Lettre. Brioche.	id.	id.	ib.
Marchand de petits pâtés sous Louis XV.	id.	GÉRARD.	211
Type. MARCHANDE DE GATEAUX DE NANTERRE.	id.	STYPULKOWSKI.	222
LE PORTEUR D'EAU, par M. JOSEPH MAINZER.			225
Type.	PAUQUET.	LAVIEILLE.	ib.
Tête de page.	id.	BRÉVAL.	ib.

Figure 11. A page from the table of contents of tome 4, *Les Français peints par eux-mêmes.* Courtesy of the Florida State University Libraries, Special Collections and Archives.

series of three prints titled *Les Petits Métiers* in a larger essay titled "La Musique" provides a humorous take on the randomness of selecting and grouping types: the first category, "Où il faut du physique" (Where physical [not moral] strength is needed) is followed by, but unrelated to, the second, "Où il faut du toupet" (Where a hairpiece / Where nerve is needed). The third category titled "Où il

Figure 12. Bertall, *Les Petits Métiers*, 3e catégorie, "Où il faut de la voix," in *Le Diable à Paris* (Paris: Hetzel, 1846), 2:129. Courtesy of Bibliothèque des livres rares et collections spéciales, Direction des bibliothèques, Université de Montréal.

faut de la voix" (Where voice is needed) concerns the cries and assembles members of the group known as "petits métiers" or "petits industriels" including the pastry seller (who sells *plaisir*, a form of *oublie*), the fruit vendor (who sells *anglais*, a type of pear), the ragpicker, the old-clothes–man, and the flower seller (figure 12). Significantly, Bertall later returns to this topic and catalogs street criers in *La Comédie de notre temps* (1875), in which the figures include musical scores and texts of cries.

Peddlers in *Les Français peints par eux-mêmes*

As Bertall's print illustrates, one significant exception to the loose organization of Curmer's encyclopedic project is the sequence of types representing the social group known as "petits métiers" comprising street criers, peddlers, and itinerant merchants. Whereas other types, such as Balzac's grocer or La Bédollierre's law student, are sequenced willy-nilly, the small-scale tradesmen are grouped together. The task of cataloging this disappearing microcosm in *Les Français peints par eux-mêmes* fell to German composer and journalist Joseph Mainzer. As a foreigner, he explains, he was struck by a thousand sounds that the Parisian no longer hears; as a musician, these sounds arrested his curiosity.[50] Mainzer was a former priest and political exile turned musical journalist and educator.[51] In the spirit of the age's humanitarian and moralist ideas, many progressive thinkers believed choral singing would foster class harmony. Accordingly, in the mid-1830s, Mainzer opened a music school for the working class in Paris and offered singing classes to workers until the authorities, fearing their insurrectional potential, banned the public lessons in 1839. As a choral educator with a sacred mission, explains critic Kerry Murphy, Mainzer chose moralistic texts designed with an ethical focus and conservative scores, because he believed that "vocal music could act as a moral and social agent of change."[52] Given his socialist beliefs, Mainzer was an obvious choice to write no less than seventeen sketches of the *petits métiers* in volumes 4 and 5 of the nine-volume encyclopedia *Les Français peints par eux-mêmes*, including descriptions of the *Cris de Paris,* Les Halles, and a slew of itinerant merchants such as the *pâtissier* or pastry-man, the *vitrier-peintre* or glazier-painter, the *marchand de parapluies* or umbrella vendor, the *marchand de coco* or coco-drink vendor, and the *marchand d'habits* or old-clothes–man.

Curmer's moral encyclopedia more or less replicates social divisions by separating sketches of the elegant world of the upper classes, which dominate the first two volumes, from those of the lower classes, which are available in volumes 4 and 5.[53] Volume 4, for example, opens with an ethnographic and statistical survey of detainees (the incarcerated) and the poor by the economist and jurist Christophe Moreau (he was also inspector general of prisons for the Seine department), while volume 5 is introduced by a statistical overview by Alfred Legoyt, assistant head of the statistics office in the Ministry of the Interior. A number of other republican writers contributed to the later volumes. Together Moreau's and Legoyt's contributions draw attention to a militant undertone in *Les Français* that resonates with contemporary concern with pauperism, prostitution, prison reform, and child labor, concerns that are less easily discernible in the first volume with its introduction by the established critic Jules Janin.[54] Mainzer's advocacy for the *petits métiers* is discreet as compared with the militancy in Moreau, Legoyt, or Arnoult Frémy's "L'Enfant de fabrique" in the first tome of *Les Français: Province*. Though sympathetic to the popular classes, Mainzer never loses sight of his social position or that of his reading audience. Conversely, Mainzer eschews the banter and playfulness that is so prevalent in the first volumes, notably in Balzac's and La Bédollierre's contributions.[55] The sentimental and paternalistic attitude toward the worker that motivated the choral director also fueled the sketch writer.

Mainzer's essay on *Les Cris de Paris* is his first in the series and therefore sets the tone for the sketches that follow. *Petits métiers* and their cries create a sense of place. An intimate familiarity with city noises defines the Parisian just as the distinctiveness of street criers characterizes the capital city for Mainzer. Other commentators writing on the same topic, such as Henry Martin and Jules Janin, make similar claims: "Paris is full of workers that belong only to the big city." To restate the point, Janin adds later: "Only the Parisian understands, loves, and knows how to appreciate the true value of these small-scale tradesmen."[56] "Among the traits characterizing our city of Paris, one of the most salient, if not the most loveable, is surely this storm of cries ranging all the way up and down the scale at once, discordant in all tones, from the most muffled notes to the most acute," writes Martin.[57] Kastner says it well when he coins the term sonorous blazon ("blason sonore") to refer to the signature sounds of a city:

> Big cities have a language; they even have, pardon the expression, their own sort of music that, at all hours of the day, expresses the movement and evolution of life at the heart of the city, whether joyous or somber, laborious or peaceful. Paris, for example, has a strong voice, and whoever heard its pulse during days of riots, whoever, even in the most peaceful times, attuned an ear to the thousand clamors that cross in the streets, that person will never forget what is distinctive in the sonorous chaos that rocks the leisure and strokes the activities of the Parisian giant.[58]

In nineteenth-century Paris, at a time when sound and architectural space were still intimately connected, the reverberations of city sounds represented the uniqueness of place.[59]

Sound Memory

Street clamor defines the city of Paris, and it is this urban music that conveys a sense of being to metropolitan life. Cognizant of the sense of place created by street criers, Mainzer is also conscious that the practice of hawking is declining. For instance in "Le Pâtissier," he describes how the itinerant pastry sellers have changed over time since the reign of Francis I, and he describes the social group as "an almost extinguished race" (2:811). Mapping the decline of a type of pastry known evocatively as "oublie" (a homonym of "oubli" or forgetting) onto the deterioration of the monarchy, he writes wistfully that "the splendor of the *oublie* has been tarnished lately . . . it is fallen royalty" (2:802). The past is consistently depicted as fuller, richer, and more colorful, as compared with the deteriorated and lackluster present. Here Mainzer echoes Janin's statements about the need to capture the everyday before it falls into the abyss of time: "we only wish to find out how to go about leaving behind something of that thing called the private life of a people; for, despite us, we who live today, we will one day be posterity" (1:11). The consciousness of historical change makes the need to remember the disappearing sounds that give Parisians their sense of place all the more pressing.

The sketch of the pastry-man is particularly compelling because, as Mainzer explains, he has long admired the profession of *pâtissier* for which he felt a "devouring passion" as a child. Though occasionally he speaks from experience, most of his essay evokes and consolidates shared cultural memories of either a distant past (the reign of Francis I) or a childhood past familiar to most middle-class Parisians. Temporal distance from this idealized past enhances its appeal for the nostalgic. Throughout the sketch series, Mainzer nostalgically equates the sounds of hawkers with the sounds of childhood: "The Parisian child has grown up amidst used clothing vendors . . . he has been rocked by their tender melodies, he has sucked them with his wet nurse's milk" (2:793). A similar childhood memory is evoked in "Le Marchand de parapluies," in which Mainzer recalls how the nasal sound and green costume of the umbrella vendor made children mistake them for sorcerers (2:883). Mainzer often attributes a fantastic and otherworldly quality to the sounds of street criers, further relegating them to the ghostly realm of memory. He imagines the pastry seller as a "fantastic apparition" "worthy of Hoffmann's pen" with a "satanic" cry of "Hot! Hot!" (2:810). Frequently, the stridency of the cries forces comparisons with cries of distress and sinister thoughts (2:810, 821). They are "vocal monstrosities," with inhuman primordial resonance that sounds like the cry of agony that "strikes our ears in night terrors, in the bosom of uprisings, in the midst of flames and torrents" (2:821). Sounds heard at night while sleeping often resist realist interpretation and persist as dreamscapes.

The cries' association with memory and childhood fantasies is just one way that Mainzer captures their ambiguous relationship to temporality and to the past. On the one hand, in realist terms, the practice of hawking signals the merchant's early morning punctuality and the merchandise's immediate availability for sale. The criers change according to the time of day and year, but return ritually. Yet, on the other hand, the aesthetic reminiscences about criers and their disappearance relegate them to a premodern era. The timelessness of the criers' clothes connects them to the immemorial past, as when Mainzer writes "always, it is by their cry and costume that they have been recognized by the people who need their ministries" (2:879). In other words, a realist impulse to provide a transparent representation of street vendors' labor practices and demeanor competes with a desire to idealize them in keeping with a nostalgic view of the past as fuller and more authentic. As vestiges of a premodern era out of place in their contemporary world, the sounds of the *marchand d'habits* and of the *marchand de peaux de lapins*, Mainzer suggests, are worthy to be placed "under glass and conserved in a cabinet of acoustic rarities" (2:887). In fact in March 1839 (hence much before Gérard de Nerval published on old French ballads in "Les Vieilles Ballades françaises" in 1842, before Comte Narcisse-Achille de Salvandy initiated the Commission on French religious and popular song in 1845, and Hippolyte Fortoul directed the Napoleon project to collect popular song in 1852), Mainzer wrote of the need to research and collect popular music culture before it disappeared, in *Le National*, a newspaper voicing the opposition during the July Monarchy.[60] Similar to folkloric songs, street cries survive as a "sound memory," that is to say, an unadulterated national relic and spontaneous expression of popular voice. To better preserve the memory of street cries, Mainzer included musical scores in his sketch; scores were rarely a feature of textual or graphic works of *Cris*, with the notable exceptions of Jean-Baptiste Gouriet's *Personnages célèbres dans les rues de Paris* (1811) and of Edouard Wattier's *Les Cris de Paris de Vathier* [sic] *avec accompagnement de musique et lithographie par Engelmann* (1822).[61] Other than texts such as these, street criers' voices left few traces.

The Tonality of Street Cries

Mainzer, like many of his contemporaries, also believes that street cries manifest the people's instinctive sense of harmony and closeness to a state of nature. We find a similar Rousseauist overvaluation of the popular classes' proximity to nature in Mainzer's musical reviews, where he writes for instance: "The more a man is close to the state of nature, the more he is subjected to sensory impressions."[62] Music critic Joseph d'Ortigue shares Mainzer's view that working-class hawkers function as agents of conservation and unknowing repositories of the past. For instance, Mainzer claimed (2:855), as did d'Ortigue, that the *Cris de Paris* were related to plainchant or Gregorian chant. D'Ortigue claims that because the ritual practice is "transmitted without variation" down through the ages, the street crier is a better guardian of the ancient tonalities of plainchant than the church is.[63] It is the tonality, reproducing the timbre of Gregorian chant, rather than the words of the street cry that render it distinctive and recognizable:

> And notice that it is the mode, the melodic gush, the prolonged or jerky note with a throaty accent, and not the words that penetrate the depths of the home and strike the ears of the housekeeper. Her ears are so tuned to this scale, to this *tonality*, that she immediately discerns who the vendor is, and which food awaits the consumer at the door.[64]

D'Ortigue's remarks must be read in the context of debates on the revival of Gregorian chant in the mid–nineteenth century. His *Dictionnaire liturgique, historique et théorique de plain-chant* (1853) is one of approximately eighty manuals on the subject published between 1854 and 1860. The subject of plainchant reform elicited the interest of over fifty people at a congress held at Érard's in 1860, and performance methods were also discussed at the abbeys around Paris, notably by the Benedictine monks at Solesmes.[65] As Katherine Bergeron has noted, those partisans of the Restoration of plainchant argued that post-Revolutionary performance practices had destroyed traditional Gregorian melody, resulting in a lost aural sensibility. They followed *Méthode raisonnée de plain-chant* by Gonthier who advocated for a "natural style of singing, a style he believed he could still hear in a handful of chants that managed to weather the centuries of change and neglect—popular chants such as "Gloria," the "Credo," the "Te Deum,"[66] and according to d'Ortigue, in street cries. Thus street cries are perceived as traces of disappearing aural practices that have added value precisely because, in their belatedness, they make the present sound like the past. But just how the past sounded is more fodder for the imagination.

While the writers who discuss them pay much attention to the content of the street cries, they also take special care to describe the tonality of the cries, as we have seen in d'Ortigue's remarks. Fournel, for instance, quotes Mme de Genlis's memoirs in which she reflects on the ways in which the tonality of the street cries changed during her emigration, during the French Revolution. She claims that the cries were gay and sung in the major tone during the ancien regime, but that, after the Revolution, upon her return to France in 1799, most of them were in the minor tone: "they were barely intelligible, exceedingly sad and lugubrious, and almost all in the minor key."[67] Fournel observes that the cries' "tone" has also been modified, losing their "long tail" ("cris *à longue queue*"), "volubility," and "interminable enumerations." Now, the street cry is made "regular, short, and somber."[68] He may well be referencing the atonal or modal sound of plainchant as heard in the street cries; his subjective description, however, also emphasizes that the sound has lost something, in fact, it stands in for melancholy.

The types of music with which street cries are identified provide some insight into what they sounded like to an educated nineteenth-century ear. They are associated with older sound cultures, such as Gregorian chant as well as the music of Jean-Philippe Rameau and the countertenor voice. In "A Note on Rameau," Camille Saint-Saëns refers in passing to street cries and compares their colorless timbre with the sharp, out-of-tune recitative of countertenors (*haute-contres*) attacking the high notes in Rameau. He adds that this toneless singing is "one which our modern ears would not tolerate for a moment."[69] In *La Prisonnière*, Marcel Proust also draws on the analogies to Gregorian chant and to the baroque music of Rameau (Proust attributes lines from Jean-Baptiste Lully's *Armide* to Rameau), to fuel the narrator and Albertine's reflections on the old-fashioned custom of peddling.[70] Listening to "an initial tonality [that] is barely altered by the inflexion of one note leaning upon another" (148), street cries evoke what the narrator calls "Gregorian division," "abrupt changes of tone in the middle of a prayer" in which the chant drags then suddenly accelerates: "after drawling the other words, [the old-clothes–man] uttered the final syllable with a brusqueness befitting the accentuation laid down by the great seventh-century Pope" (162). In the Proust passage, street cries are also compared to the "barely musical declamation" (148), "slightly tinged by even the most imperceptible modulation" (147) in Modest Mussorgsky's *Boris Godunov*, and to Claude Debussy's natural declamation in the recitative in *Pelléas et Mélisande*.[71] The comparison serves to emphasize the melancholy expression in the street cries as well as their mysterious connection to death: "I have always found it difficult to understand why these perfectly simple words were sighed in a tone so far from appropriate, as mysterious as the secret which makes everyone look sad in the old palace" (148). The reflections of Proust, in conjunction with those of Genlis, Mainzer, Kastner, and Fournel, help us hear the specific tonality and interval pattern of street cries in the mid- to late nineteenth century. As traces of disappearing aural practices, street cries were equated with other vestiges of a premodern era, such as the modal scales of plainchant and with the baroque countertenor voice. They resonate foremost as intonations rather than melodies, and the words seem to impress less than the melancholy they convey or inspire.

The *Cris de Paris* combined a visual tradition of graphic and textual sketches circulating in guidebooks or prints, with a musical tradition. These visual and aural genres convey the role of street cries in creating a sense of place. As part of the sonorous blazon of the city, street cries are discussed in terms of a historically significant, if waning social practice. Yet, in addition to their realist, ethnographic treatment, for these writers of the late romantic era, they also evoke the ghosts of the past. Their melancholic tone associates street cries with mourning and loss, whether it be nostalgia for childhood soundscapes or ancient music, or more sinister, even primeval, memories and fears. "Vocal monstrosities," street cries heard in the waking hours can have something of the fantastic, the satanic even. Because street cries as ghostly traces are out of sync with modern times, they sound strident, dissonant, like the sharp attack of the countertenor voice. It behooved Baron Haussmann to shed the itinerant tradesmen who circulated these disturbing cries of their potential for disorder, in his move to clean up and clean out the city.

CHAPTER 3

Sonic Classifications in Haussmann's Paris

The Paris we know today is the result of profound urban renovations directed by Baron Georges-Eugène Haussmann, prefect of the Seine under the Second Empire. Commissioned by Napoléon III, Haussmann extended the work of his predecessors and redrew the city following a rationally designed plan. To him, we owe the wide boulevards, expansive crossroads, and vistas for which modern Paris is renowned. Indeed, Haussmann planned for "la grande croisée" to gut Île de la Cité and reconfigure the urban center along the lines of a cross artificially drawn on the preexisting urban fabric (boulevards Strasbourg-Sébastopol and Champs Élysées-Rivoli).[1] In addition to improving circulation and opening up the streets, Haussmann modernized the city's sanitation systems; implemented a new building code standardizing Parisian architecture; built new public parks, monuments, and railroad stations; and expanded the city limits by annexing the suburbs. The comprehensive process of urban renewal we know as "Haussmannization," however, neither began (nor ended) with the Second Empire; rather it extended policies and projects of previous administrations, notably of police prefects Gisquet, Delessert, and Carlier. Successive renovations, demolitions, expropriations, and gentrification, beginning in the 1830s and coming to a head during the Second Empire (1852–70) caused much social disruption; accordingly, Haussmannization was alternately celebrated for turning the city into a dazzling spectacle or disparaged for imposing the straight line and visual monotony on the old picturesque neighborhoods in the city center. Typically, emphasis is placed on Haussmann's transformation of Paris into a

Figure 13. Cham [pseud. of Amédée Charles Henri de Noé (1819–79)], *Paris entourée de figures symbolisants des boulevards.* Pen and brown ink drawing, 15 × 18.4 cm, Inv: RF23625. Photo: Thierry Le Mage. Musée du Louvre, Paris, France. © RMN-Grand Palais/Art Resource, New York. The bottom reads: "La ville de Paris ne sachant plus à quel boulevard entendre!" (The City of Paris no longer knowing which boulevards to hear).

"City of Light" that delights the eye of the flâneur; however, the evidence from literary guidebooks suggests a broader effect on the senses beyond the visual. Haussmannization, broadly defined, produced a sensory overhaul and changed the soundscape of the city.

The process of Haussmannization involved reordering the sonic environment by cleansing the New Paris of many of the street sounds that had long been a fixture of the old city. Conversely, new, modern soundscapes developed on the boulevards. Many of these changes can be reconstructed thanks to descriptions provided in the numerous nineteenth-century literary guidebooks to Paris by journalists who shared Victor Fournel's nostalgia for Old Paris. Fournel's "artistic and archeological consciousness" put him at odds with Baron Haussmann's transformations of organically grown neighborhoods familiar to the senses into abstractly conceived rational schemes. He felt that the "swarming streets" had been "hacked with scissor cuts; . . . pruned and cleared [like a] forest. [Unity and the straight line tended] to make Paris, since the Revolution, since the last twenty-five years especially, the most splendidly and majestically monotonous city that ever was." Fournel even identified with the street cries he was so fond of: "I am the plaintive and helpless cry of Paris on its way out against Paris on its way in."[2] Peddlers thus become marked as signs of resistance to the new social order, and the sounds of street criers come to symbolize, for those who seek to oppose that order, the disappearing soundscape of the medieval core of the city.

Time eroded the traditional functions of peddlers' street cries, but the transformation of the spatial organization of small-scale tradesmen affected the sound culture of the streets in significant ways as well. Drawing on architectural theory, sound studies, and French cultural history, we can make better sense of how the soundscape of peddling changed during the Second Empire as people became less tolerant of street noise in spaces deemed private, and as the realities of demolition and reconstruction displaced street vendors. Literary guidebooks bear witness to factors that contribute to the decline of street sounds, such as urban renewal, the rise of print advertising, the development of a sedentary bourgeoisie, the implementation of a regulatory culture, and the growth of a capitalist economy. The guidebooks, however, also create a cultural memory by narrating similar idealizing stories of disappearing types for over half a century. The impulse to document the lost acoustic intimacy of Old Paris transforms peddlers in the process into silent and aesthetic artifacts. Preservationists such as Fournel document the fading of older sound cultures, yet by doing so, they also ensure the disappearance they regret and fuel the memory of "the plaintive cry of Old Paris."

The Materiality of Sound Changes, or How to Reconstruct Haussmannian Soundscapes

Literary guidebooks on Paris help us reconstruct the effects of architectural change and of the reorganization of urban space on the practice and sound culture of peddling. A lot could be said about how architectural change affects how the city sounds and how the morphology of the city influences hearing practices. Because sounds are contingent on their environment, they exist or last because they are carried by materials that reinforce, modulate, or weaken their range.[3] When Haussmann gutted the medieval core of the city, his "scissor cuts" transformed how sounds of the city were heard. In addition to the physical changes to the sonic environment, legislation indirectly targeting peddlers' vocalizations regulated where and when they could operate. Taking into account the physical and the social environment successively leads us to consider what position, if any, was adopted on noise abatement.

How did small-scale tradesmen traditionally use city space to make themselves heard over and above the daily clamor? Where did they practice their trade and how did urban renewal displace peddlers, or concentrate them in new areas? Mainzer's essays in *Les Français peints par eux-mêmes* provide a sense of how street criers made themselves audible in the first half of the nineteenth century. Peddlers could be found at markets, but they typically did business in the streets. According to Mainzer's descriptions, criers circulated in the streets crying out their wares so as to be heard far and wide, including on the sixth floor, where poorer people lived (the ground and first floors being reserved for shops and wealthy families). Cries had to be loud enough to soar above the city din and traffic noise. "The deeper and higher the buildings, the more piercing the cry becomes, employing all the strength of lungs dilated by continual exercise in the open air," explains Mainzer. Apropos the reach of the water-carriers' vocalizations, Mainzer further adds that "the cry is emitted, everyone hears it, the inhabitant of the entresol as well as of the attic."[4] High-pitched voices soared in the corridor-like medieval street, lined with multistory dwellings of uneven height. Imagine, for instance, the reverberation in a confined space such as the cul-de-sac on the rue Saint-Martin in the Saint-Merri neighborhood photographed by Eugène Atget in 1911 (figure 14). Haussmann had unsuccessfully planned to triple the narrow width of rue Saint-Martin in this plebeian and labyrinthine neighborhood, which had been the site of uprisings and epidemics. Since the alignment, width, and length of streets affect how voices carry, one can sense how Haussmann's new boulevards, which were as wide as their buildings were tall (eighteen meters),[5] would not return echoes or provide the same clues for spatial location, as would old narrower streets in which the width of the street was easily one half of the height of the buildings.

Resonant spaces such as courtyards and stairwells, or covered streets such as *passages* and arcades, similarly helped amplify and carry peddlers' voices. These spaces particularized sounds so that they were perceived as distinctive of place. The *laitière* or milk-woman could be heard near the Palais-Royal and the Passage Véro-Dodat. Since these covered streets protected pedestrians from being run over by traffic, hit by whip lashes, or spattered with mud, they could safely look and listen to their surroundings; in effect, these same safeguards made it easier for peddlers to be heard and to secure the attention of buyers.[6] Criers such as the *raccommodeur de faïence* or porcelain repairman, and the *porteur d'eau* or water-carrier would approach stairwells and courtyards. The *chaudronnier* or boilermaker, as Mainzer explains, would explore each street and frequently hold up in the courtyard or stairwell to psalmody his cry and communicate more directly with the servant who may not have heard him. Peddlers and street musicians penetrated into these enclosed liminal spaces

Figure 14. Eugène Atget. *Cul de sac, Fiacre, 81 Rue Saint-Martin, 4th Arrondissement, Paris,* 1911. Reprinted with permission of the Bibliothèque nationale de France.

or common areas in residential buildings to better reach paying audiences.[7] In *Paris et les Parisiens au XIXe siècle*, Paul de Musset recalls with emotion how he would regularly run into the *porteur d'eau* in his home's stairwell; in those days, the loyal water-carrier was practically a member of the family.[8] Stairwells as well as other close quarters provided Musset with daily intimate encounters that became less frequent once street criers were forbidden in insular spaces such as parks, squares, and courtyards. Similarly, Henry Martin—with somewhat less exasperation than Delphine de Girardin—relates how the Cries followed one everywhere, "not content to harass you during your strolls, the Cries pursue you right to your courtyard, right to your stairs; they station themselves right at your door."[9] The constant physical proximity of criers fostered what architect Juhani Pallasmaa calls "acoustic intimacy," though Martin might have stressed that such closeness and intrusion was a mixed blessing.[10]

When the detractors of Haussmann deplore the gutting of the Old Paris, they regret the warmth and tactility of these picturesque encounters, which created a sense of place and gave the city character. Yriarte explains the new detachment as a spatial effect when he states that "the straight line has killed the picturesque and the unexpected. The rue de Rivoli is a symbol, a new street, long, wide, cold, on which stroll well-dressed, wooden people who are as cold as the street."[11] George Sand took the opposite position in *Paris-Guide* when she mused that the New Paris relieved the pedestrian of incursions into his reveries: "Now that wide inroads, too straight for the artistic eye but eminently safer, permit us to walk at length, hands in our pockets, without straying or being forced to consult at every instant the policeman on the corner or the affable costermonger, it's a benediction to stroll along a large sidewalk, without listening to anything or looking at anything, in the dreamer's highly agreeable state of mind that nevertheless does not impede seeing or hearing."[12] Sand's musings attest to the growing appeal of wide urban spaces amenable to reverie and private reflection. As the bourgeoisie's expectations for segregated and quieter lifestyles grew, interior spaces such as courtyards and stairwells were made more private by closing them off to street traffic, in a move parallel to the insularization of the home interior.[13] New investments in sheltered private spaces, and in wide open, but regulated, public spaces that impeded reverberation made the peddlers' voices less audible to poor residents on the upper floors, and thus the traditional practices of trades such as the water-carrier were rendered less functional.

Small commercial stalls or *échoppes* were yet another casualty of the regulation of space in the New Paris. The *échoppe* was approximately a one-meter-wide makeshift stall, made of wood and nestled against a public building, a church, or a private house, where foods were sold or services rendered. The *rémouleur* or knife-grinder, the *savetier* or cobbler, the *ravaudeuse* or mender worked in *échoppes* or stalls. As Charles Vincent explains in *Paris Guide*, an anthology written for the Universal Exposition of 1867, rising rents, increased sanitization, and closely regulated circulation led to the decline of these stalls: "It is because wide streets make for high rents, and because high rents beckon luxury boutiques that drive further out poor neighborhoods. Stalls look like warts on renovated churches; municipal surgery therefore removes them with the utmost care. . . . In this New Paris that one wants to see clean and glowing, everything conspires against the stall; stall-keepers therefore disappear little by little from public thoroughfares, which they used to fill with life and gaiety."

The "surgical" removal of *échoppes* from the cityscape, Vincent makes clear, not only restricted the spaces of small-scale tradesmen, but also the sound of the city: gone were the volubility and verve that characterized the sound of informal street commerce. By smoothing the city's lines, planners flattened its soundscape. Vincent concludes that today the formerly garrulous *savetier* has become the "taciturn" *cordonnier* in the grip of a merciless landlord, who waits for customers to come to him, quietly.[14] Material and spatial reconfiguration of the city under Haussmann that exiled the *petits métiers* from the new neighborhoods consequently reordered the soundscape of Paris.

In *Les Industriels du macadam,* Élie Frébault records more specifically how urban renewal projects in the late 1850s, combined with the Universal Exposition of 1867, affected small-scale tradesmen. If experienced street singers could make as much as ten francs a day in working-class neighborhoods, he writes, "the new neighborhoods [are] a bad deal. A virtuoso with experience never wanders there." The song sheet vendor cursed the litany of transformations of the capital, "the demolitions, the restorations, the widening, rectifications, and opening of new streets, *places,* and squares, and in general all the public works currently underway": the construction of new boulevards impeded his trade and forced him to move to the outer city.[15] Urban renewal and beautification also irritated the *carreleur de souliers* or cobbler who foresaw, according to Frébault, that his humble trade would be unwelcome on the widened streets of the elegant New Paris. The *marchande de saucisses* or sausage and grilled meats vendor complained that the demolitions forced her to continually relocate her stand, and as a result, her regular customers could not find her. The old-clothes–man who confided in Frébault bemoaned his lost business during the Universal Exposition of 1867 because his usual clients gave their old things to poor relations in town visiting the fair.[16] Displacements such as these forced some small-scale tradesmen off the streets and in the process transformed the sound culture of new neighborhoods. Once road construction was complete, however, the boulevards drew some peddlers back.

Whereas urban renewal projects from the 1830s through the Second Empire displaced some peddlers from their traditional occupational spaces such as *échoppes,* stairwells, courtyards, and squares, they opened new venues to others on overcrowded boulevards, where idle and unwitting customers could be solicited at street level. Here peddlers' voices did not need to carry far to find customers, but rather to goad passersby at hand into buying what they sold. Some criers expanded their trade into the more affluent sections of the city, on the boulevards, at outdoor festivals, at the balls, and in the theater district, where more people would congregate. Indeed, we followed the flâneur in chapter 1 as he encountered peddlers and street musicians on his strolls on the

Champs Élysées. According to Mainzer, the *marchand de coco* or vendor of coco-drink (a lemon and licorice flavored water) and the *pâtissier* or pastry-man went everywhere including the Champs Élysées, the Champs de Mars, the entrance to the Tuileries gardens, as well as the Faubourg du Temple. Frances Trollope describes the "numberless ambulant cisterns" serving lemonade at a public fête on the Champs Élysées.[17] And, with a mix of tacit horror and fascination, Balzac attests to the intense level of activity of popular commerce on the boulevards and theater district in the 1830s in "Histoire et physiologie des boulevards de Paris de la Madeleine à la Bastille":

> Beginning at the Porte Saint-Martin Theater until the Turkish Cafe (on the Boulevard du Temple) . . . at night it's frighteningly animated. Eight theaters incessantly beckon spectators. Fifty outdoor vendors sell comestibles and feed the people, who give two cents to their stomachs and twenty to their eyes. It is the only point in Paris where one hears the Cries of Paris, where one sees the teeming multitudes and those rags so stunning to the painter.[18]

Among the locations in which commentators describe a heavy presence of street vendors, special attention goes to the Boulevard du Temple. This area also known as the Boulevard du Crime because of the melodramas performed there, was demolished by Haussmann's renovations in 1862 to make way for the Place de la République. Yet, even before its demolition, the Boulevard du Temple, like the Pont Neuf (another traditional area of popular entertainment), was subject to police surveillance. In "Le Boulevard du Temple" (1844), Gérard de Nerval for instance, like Fournel later on, waxes nostalgically about the *saltimbanques* and *forains*, entertainers (such as Bobèche) who filled the streets of the Boulevard du Temple with farcical jokes and popular laughter during the first quarter of the century. Street noise for Nerval calls to mind a popular sociability that loosely bound social classes together, as the poor drawn to the performances resisted spending their last penny at the cabaret and the rich paid the most talented performers with their well-chosen applause. As Augustin Challamel put it: "the land of Bobèche, the boulevard du Temple, was the rendez-vous of all social classes seeking pleasure equally!" Nerval reflects on how much "embellishments" and urban renewal under the July Monarchy have changed Paris's popular theater district—usually not for the better: "In truth, popular laughter is waning: police regulations have killed it."[19] Louis Énault in the 1850s reports a similar threat to the volubility of the Pont Neuf where street vendors gathered:

> [The Pont Neuf] has been abandoned to street vendors that exploit small purses: chestnut sellers and coco-vendors, safety chain makers, and outdoor Aragos who discover spots on the sun, and help one see, when the night is clear, the man on

the moon; . . . male and female ragpickers, tinkers, chimney sweeps, organ grinders, violin players, guitarists singing *romances*, print sellers who despite you sneak their bulletins in your pocket, the eau-de-Cologne vendor—today, that is the Pont Neuf's usual population; it lives there at war, under the strict surveillance of the sergeants and police agents.[20]

Where peddlers congregated, these accounts suggest, so did police, with the hope of controlling the volubility of street noise. However, if we are to believe Edmond Texier, hawkers' skill at firing up the crowds and using noise to their advantage defeated the police at every turn: "Oh Parisians, no matter what governments do, you will be eternally subject to the golden language of orators!"[21] The forces of order wage war, with limited success one imagines, against the peddling noise of informal commerce.

As we move toward the end of the century, the commotion on the boulevards reached new intensities. During the Universal Exposition of 1867, which drew newcomers to Paris, Frébault reports that many foreign buskers swelled the ranks of locally grown talent on the boulevards. Frébault also comments on how aggressively the *musico* pursued passersby, until he received his "petit sou" or little coin.[22] "There is not one moment's repose either for the ear, for the eye, or the brain," wrote Edmondo de Amicis in 1879. The Italian journalist goes on to describe how vendors assail the stroller: "In every corner there are a thousand mouths which call you, a thousand hands which beckon."[23] Edward King, the Paris correspondent for the *Springfield Republican* and *Boston Transcript*, who was sent to Paris for the Universal Exposition of 1867, also reacted to the intrusive way peddlers assailed passersby with their whispered taunts, catcalls, and gestures: "The orange woman too, is an institution in each street, and she understands how to make it very uncomfortable for you to pass her, unless you buy. A little satiric underbreath [*sic*] of criticism, pungent as orange juice, may remind you to help the poor."[24] In spite of police surveillance, boulevards were full of commotion, smells, jostling, and noise as hawkers shouted out the news, sang new popular tunes, thrust foodstuffs at unwitting customers, or advertised fashionable consumer goods in loud aggressive voices.[25]

The material changes to the soundscape we associate with Haussmannization broadly defined—the destruction of medieval streets filled with familiar sounds that fostered acoustic intimacy or the widening of boulevards that drew noisy but anonymous crowds—were accompanied by changes to social policy that developed prior to the Second Empire. Although the hubbub of street noise remains a persistent motif in literary guidebooks and journalists' accounts throughout the century, policy makers attempted to curb the clamor. Disturbances of the peace ("bruit et tapages injurieux ou nocturnes") were already actionable offenses in the penal code of 1810, but efforts were renewed during the July Monarchy to clamp down on noisemakers.[26] During his term as prefect of police from 1831 to 1836, Prefect Henri Gisquet campaigned against noxious street merchants and musicians and endeavored to enforce a new standard of public tranquility. Hot on the heels of the ordinance of December 1831, targeting street performers, *saltimbanques*, and organ-grinders discussed in chapter 1, Gisquet moved forward in January 1832 with an ordinance that sought to drastically reduce the numbers of "marchands ambulants" or itinerant vendors across the board. In 1837, he issued a ban on the public use of drums, horns, and other loud instruments used by peddlers. In his memoirs published in 1840, the prefect explained his intent to contain the invasion of Parisian streets by vendors who competed with shopkeepers and to limit their numbers to only the most indigent peddlers who had no other way to make a living. In Gisquet's widely held opinion—we have heard it before in Anspach's diatribe against vagabonds and beggars who used street music as a cover for mendicancy—peddlers made no contribution to the city's economy and their nomadism was threatening. If he conceded that peddling can work as a palliative for mendicancy, he also justified his move to limit the number of peddlers in Paris on account of their repulsive ("grossièreté," "repoussant") presence and seditious influence. Even more controversial was his campaign against town criers ("crieurs publics") who called out news headlines and political news. According to Gisquet, such an "overabundant" and "anachronistic" trade—he stated as self-evident that newspapers and print advertising had replaced oral publication for all classes— had "become dangerous and useless."[27] Whereas Gisquet denied peddlers any productive economic role and stressed their parasitic existence, his successor was more circumspect. Prefect Gabriel Delessert, less intent on controlling street vendors, acknowledged that they had few other means of survival and recommended that they neither be apprehended nor their merchandise seized on a regular basis.[28] Indeed, some commentators such as Henry Martin recognized that peddlers played a significant role in the supply and distribution of foods in working-class neighborhoods.[29] As Jules Janin cavalierly put it, informal commerce satisfied the poor man's desires for luxury items at knock-off prices[30]—the *chiffonnier* will rent you a used dinner jacket and the *regrattier* will sell you the leftovers of a banquet.

In a city such as Paris with a population explosion, itinerant merchants supplemented inadequate municipal functions, such as access to water and food, as well as waste management and recycling (scavengers and ragpickers). (The ordinances of 1851 and 1859 in fact explicitly recognized the significance of street commerce to food distribution.) They also catered to the underserved needs of the working class. As Maxime Du Camp assessed in 1870, approximately six thousand itinerant merchants ("marchands des quatre saisons" or costermongers) appealed to poorer workers whose schedule did not permit them to travel to the centralized market at Les Halles. Ordinances, however, served the interests of the bourgeoisie and their fear of competition. Several police ordinances restricted street vendors from entering local Parisian markets and crying out wares was expressly banned.[31] Although today we might also look positively upon peddlers' impact on competition in the marketplace, the belief that street vendors unfairly competed with shopkeepers led to their strict surveillance in nineteenth-century Paris.

The Second Empire continued the policies of the prefects under the July Monarchy, of issuing ordinances that controlled commotion in the streets, regulated circulation, and rendered the practice of using street commerce as a livelihood for recent and seasonal migrants more and more difficult. Haussmannization's sensory overhaul thus represents less of a radical break with the preceding decades than a continuation and expansion of earlier social policy and changing attitudes toward street noise. Prefect of Police Pierre Carlier's ordinance banning loud instruments on thoroughfares (June 1851) and regulating "marchands ambulants" (October 1851)—both revisions of Gisquet's 1837 and 1832 regulations—preceded Napoléon Bonaparte's coup d'état of December 1851, and Haussmann's nomination as prefect of the Seine in 1853. The ordinances of October 1851 and December 1859 renewed efforts to curb street vending by imposing a permitting system (peddlers had to wear a medallion). In 1851, the stipulation was added to Gisquet's legislation that all peddlers must have resided in the capital for one year before they could obtain a nontransferable permit. In 1860, after the annexation of Paris's suburbs, the ordinance on "marchands ambulants" was extended to the new area, but peddlers could hawk in either the new or the old arrondissements, not both. In 1860, the same office was charged with permitting street musicians and itinerant tradesmen, and the consolidation of the two previously distinct occupations in law suggests intensified control of the sonic landscape of the city.[32] Yet, as we have read, policing these repeatedly issued laws was not always effective. Throughout the nineteenth century, legislation was enacted with limited success to curb vagrancy and vagabondage, including informal commerce (perceived as a cover for mendicancy and otherwise uncontrollable and disorderly activity), and to encourage sedentary, formal commerce that could be subject to quality control, price monitoring, and fiscal control. The ordinance on public markets of 1865, for example, made it illegal to "announce by cries the nature and price of merchandise" and to "call out to passers-by with comments on behavior or appearance."[33] In other words, hawkers were to be excluded based on a concept of a society characterized by order, sedentariness, and social, demographic, and fiscal stability.[34] It should be noted, however, that most of these ordinances do not explicitly attempt to curb the sound of street criers, but rather to restrict their presence in the city. Limitations on where peddlers can go are de facto regulations on how much noise from street commerce is tolerable in a given area. Yet, when faced with a resident complaining of street cries on Rue Rambuteau, a police officer (commissaire) could only respond that that was not an actionable offense.[35]

Despite the accumulation of police ordinances implicitly intent on curbing noxious behaviors, there was no clear policy against noise in comparison with intolerance for bad smells, smoke, mud, and overcrowding, factors more closely associated with sanitation and health in the nineteenth century. Clearly for Haussmann, cleaning up the city involved tackling congestion on the streets, traffic vibrations, stenches, and noise, conceived of broadly as an entangled onslaught on the senses,[36] but abating noise pollution per se was not one of the primary concerns of the regime, which followed the era's general stance on the innocuousness of noise.

Nineteenth-century city dwellers had a high tolerance for noise, not because they failed to experience it (we have read repeated evidence to the contrary), but because they did not feel entitled to lodge official complaints about sounds they rarely heard as "noise"; only nocturnal rowdiness was considered a legitimate (actionable) public nuisance, and most city clamor did not reach the threshold of intolerance, at least until mid-century. Alain Corbin suggests that noise did not become subject to legislation and regulation because noise was understood as a justifiable part of the "traditional rowdiness of artisans and the din of the 'cries of Paris.'"[37] Catalogues of police ordinances can give some idea of which noises proved annoying or caused enough discomfort (the preferred French word is *incommode*) to be targeted by regulation; these include coachmen's cries, the clank of carriages overloaded with metal scraps, loud instruments used on thoroughfares, and street singers.[38] There are few, if any, mentions of loud sounds that would startle twenty-first-century urbanites, such as the whinnies or hoof beats of horses, or the bellows of animals going to the slaughterhouse: as opposed to the noise of street singers, considered valueless and unnecessary, these everyday animal sounds were easily tolerable because they had economic value.

Regardless of any legal standard for thresholds of intolerance, many writers complained forcefully about bells and traffic noise. For example, the photographer Nadar lashed out in an 1883 pamphlet against bell ringing titled "Le Cas des cloches," addressed to the *ministre des Cultes* and to "mayors, city counselors, deputies and even senators." The fact that he appealed to municipal officials in Aix-les-Bains as well as a wider range of officials and to French public opinion suggests that "pointless" peals of bells and the "right to silence" were topics that had fairly broad support among the leisured ("gens de loisir"), even in the absence of legislation on levels of urban ambient noise. Invoking adamantly an infringement of his right to silence and to sleep, he asks: "How then can one violate the free enjoyment of my sense of hearing by tearing my eardrum with the permanent and relentless screeching of these intolerable bells?"[39]

Whereas city ordinances targeted the loud coachmen rather than noise produced by conveyances, writers complained about traffic noise. Foreigners were especially sensitive to its din: as an Englishwoman accustomed to macadamized or paved roads in London, Trollope complained about Paris's noisy pavements, wherein she heard the distant threat of popular unrest:

> The exceeding noise of Paris, proceeding either from the uneven structure of the pavement, or from the defective construction of wheels and springs, is so violent and incessant as to appear like the effect of one great continuous cause—a sort of demon torment, which it must require great length of use to enable one to endure without suffering. Were a cure for this sought in the Macadamising of the streets, an additional advantage, by the bye, would be obtained, from the difficulties it would throw in the way of the future heroes of a barricade.[40]

When the Moroccan scholar Muhammad as-Saffār accompanied his ambassador to France in 1845–46, he was also overwhelmed by traffic noise on the streets of Paris: "The uproar of the carriages and the wagons does not cease day or night. The glass in the windows is perpetually rattling and shaking from the terrible din. For days sleep eluded us because of the frightful roar that never stopped. It felt as though we were standing at the seashore or next to a turning grindstone."[41] And, indeed, the newspaper *L'Illustration* reported on November 15, 1845, that Paris had 28,520 vehicles just for carrying people.[42]

The problem persisted with Haussmannization. David Jordan cites a minister who asked Haussmann to macadamize the rue de Grenelle to muffle the omnibus traffic noise that kept his employees from working.[43] While indeed paving the streets with asphalt, cement, or even wood planks, in addition to widening them, would reduce traffic sounds, street paving presented a number of engineering challenges, some of which are discussed by medical doctors and hygienists such as J.-B. Fonssagrives, who take seriously what had been humorously alluded to by Balzac in "Monographie du rentier."[44] When one considers that "along the Madeleine-Bastille line omnibuses passed more than 10,000 times in a twenty-four hour period in 1880," it is worth questioning in fact, along with Hazel Hahn, whether the sensory overload on the boulevards at the fin de siècle ran counter to Haussmann's intended regulation of the circulation of goods, people, and vehicles throughout the city.[45] The assault on the senses is certainly what the caricaturist Cham conveys in his drawing representing allegorized boulevards of Paris each trying to scream louder than the next. The drawing shows one older thoroughfare (Boulevard de l'Hôpital) competing with several of the new axes inaugurated by Haussmann, including the Boulevard Sebastopol (1858), the Boulevard Malesherbes (1861), and the Boulevard du Prince-Eugène (1862, but renamed Boulevard Voltaire in 1870). In the middle of the image, the allegorized City of Paris stands ear-stricken, her mouth open, and her hands on her ears. Cham clearly suggests that the New Paris is so noisy as to provoke disorientation, migraines, even madness (figure 13). As a hygienist during the Third Republic, Fonssagrives promoted the concern that no residences were fully sheltered from the "incommodious" noise of peddlers such as cobblers and coopers; he felt that the noise from omnibuses and carts, which infallibly "cause[d] windows and nerves to vibrate," led to nervous disorders in provincial tourists, women, children, and the infirm.[46] His concerns about neurosis were echoed by Nadar's invective on the insalubriousness of bell ringing, as well as by formalized sentiments expressed in a more light-hearted vein, in the 1830s, by Delphine de Girardin and Bertall. Under the influence of late-nineteenth-century hygienists such as Fonssagrives, thresholds of intolerance would change in the late nineteenth and early twentieth centuries when noise control and abatement became more of a priority for citizens and city governments, even if France remained behind other European nations.[47]

The Plaintive Cry of Old Paris, or How to Preserve Acoustic Artifacts

As a scholar of nineteenth-century French literature, my own interest lies in the writers who were among the first to express their antipathy for noise, rather than in the relatively slow-growing (at least until World War I) campaign for noise abatement on the part of urban planners, municipal officials, and hygienists in France.[48] Although literary works draw attention to issues of noise control—for instance rants about excessive numbers of street musicians on the boulevards discussed earlier—literature often invites closer study of the quality rather than quantity of sound. Writers tell us about the creative role of sound and its potential to generate ideas about the self, the city, and art. This is why the writings of Victor Fournel and the poetry of Charles Baudelaire can tell us so much about which sounds stroked their ears amid the clamor of the city, in which forms they captured the imagination, and how they were mythologized as sites of cultural memory through idealization, aestheticization, co-optation, or resistance. Street cries rose above the din with special stridency in the city's concert.

When Fournel identifies with "the plaintive cry of Paris on its way out," he tones down the stridency of militant *petits métiers* voices, intensifies their pathetic sound, and gives free reign to his aural reminiscences. For the nostalgic Fournel, street cries become symbols of the charms of urban existence, especially of the city life that he remembers, or perhaps imagines, as it once was. Nostalgia heightens his awareness of the sounds that he thinks make Paris both an intimately familiar place and a picturesque old city. As I discussed earlier, the *flâneur* on a stroll through the city listens to "the homily of a soap merchant" and the "dithyramb of a watch merchant" using musical terms that suggest the sounds are decorative, artistic perhaps, but not utilitarian.[49] These sounds, now merely ornamental, are divested of their economic purpose; likewise, their controversial history, especially the functions of criers in specific historical moments such as the French Revolution or the July Monarchy when tradesmen were politically active, is erased in favor of a sound image frozen in an idealized past. The nostalgic construction of peddlers as a shared cultural memory depends as much on remembering their picturesque attributes, as on forgetting their "shady" past.[50] By the eighteenth century, the peddler was widely associated with sedition, and he was regularly perceived as trafficking in defective merchandise or spreading malicious and subversive information.[51] Some street criers, notably the *oublayeur* (who sold a pastry called *oublie*), reputedly scoped out residences to which they gained access in view of robbing them. Both Fournel and Mainzer recount the story of Louis Dominique Cartouche, a notorious brigand who posed as an *oublayeur*. Fétis also refers to street musicians' bad reputation as thieves and spies.[52] Hawkers are frightening because of these protean abilities to defy bourgeois attempts at categorization.

To get a better sense of the discourse on class inherent in the representations of peddlers, it is useful to look back to Louis-Sébastien Mercier's *Tableau de Paris* (1781–89) and *Le Nouveau Paris* (1799). These two works illustrate well the complexity and evolution of the street crier's connotations in the eighteenth century. New in Mercier's *Tableau de Paris* is the perception that street cries are changing as they are no longer tolerated—they are becoming an unintelligible and ear-wrenching noise, as those wanting silence seek to separate themselves from the noisy. Mercier's commentary reveals a judgmental and moralistic attitude toward the noisy peddler:

> No, nowhere in the world is there such a city where male and female hawkers have more piercing and shrill voices. One has to hear them burst out beyond the rooftops; their throats overcome the noise and clamor of the intersections. It is impossible for the stranger to understand anything; the Parisian himself only

distinguishes things out of routine. The water-carrier, the old hat crier, the scrap metal vendor, the rabbit skin seller, the fishmonger, it is for whomever to sing the merchandise in the highest and most heartrending mode. All these discordant cries form an ensemble, of which one has no idea when one has not heard it. The idiom of these ambulant criers is such that one has to study it to distinguish what it means. Servants have a much better trained ear than the academician; they go downstairs for the academician's dinnertime, because they know how to distinguish from the fourth floor, from one end of the street to the other, if mackerels or fresh herring, or lettuces or beets are being called out for sale. As the endings share more or less the same tonality, only usage teaches these learned servants not to err, and it's inexplicable cacophony for all others.[53]

In this description of Paris street cries, Mercier explains that the ability to understand the sound culture of the streets distinguishes Parisians from foreigners, and elites from servants. In contrast to the narrator's own perception of criers' voices as "shrill," "piercing," "heartrending," and "discordant," female servants will easily make sense of each different cry. The (male) academician is thus separated from the (feminized) working classes through their relationship to street noise.[54] To regain the upper hand, the academician must study this "inexplicable cacophony," this strange "idiom." It is no wonder that when Mercier imagines the perfect city in *L'An 2440: Rêve s'il en fut jamais* (1770), he hears "none of those confusing and bizarre cries that used to hurt [his] ears."[55]

Returning to the subject of street cries in *Le Nouveau Paris* written after the Revolution, Mercier emphasizes this time the politicization of criers, especially newspaper hawkers, their ability to circumvent censorship, and their ensuing power to control and to proliferate the word (sound). As compared with his description of the criers in the earlier *Tableau de Paris*, Mercier is less ready to dismiss the cacophony of street cries, recognizing now that the *peuple* loudly communicate their revolutionary spirit.[56] "It has been in vain that silence has been imposed on these commentators. They contend that they are privileged heralds: one would sooner capture sound than their bodies."[57] Mercier is referring to the royalist *chansonnier*, Ange Pitou, who captivated his large audience to the extent that guards dared not arrest him, and he defied attempts to silence him until his final deportation. Fournel remembers Pitou and Mercier when he claims that popular song was "the natural and often formidable complement to the liberty of the press."[58]

In fact, during the Revolution, traditional iconographic series of *Cris de Paris* disappeared in favor of a proliferation of new discursive uses of the word "cry" in political pamphlets, suggesting the degree to which the sounds of cries emanating from the lower classes held political resonance.[59] Historians who have studied the sound culture of eighteenth-century France insist on the significance of songs and public outcry as vehicles of popular political power and revolutionary protest.[60] The loud voices of town criers, pamphleteers, broadsheet sellers, social agitators, and spreaders of rumor defy upper-class rules of civility, and express the people's right to sovereignty in 1789, as well as in 1830, and again in 1848. The association between street cries and public unrest continued in the nineteenth century, when titles of periodicals such as *Le Charivari* and *Le Tintamarre* relied on the metaphor of the cry and other street clamor to signal their oppositional agenda.

Georges Kastner, citing the *History of the French Revolution* by Edmond and Jules de Goncourt, describes the proliferation of cries during the period with an excess that conveys dizzying alarm: "Listen to these voices: rustling, murmurs, fanfare, cries, song, anger, laughter, speeches, sermons, thoughts, advice, screams; these thousand, these millions of voices suddenly unleashed, unchained, growing, tempestuous, rising from Paris at all hours, these millions of enemy and clashing voices, each perhaps hoarse but whose stream of racket dizzies France with its discord."[61] Kastner adds that in the post-Revolutionary era, during 1830 and 1848, the echo of the "collective cries" and "terrible dissonances" continues to resound. Although (surprisingly perhaps) the term "charivari" is not listed, the Goncourt Brothers and Kastner implicitly evoke this age-old noise-making ritual, which was once a plebeian right to self-regulate offenses to the community. Now, however, as elites, they fear the incursion of lower-class noise into their sought-after tranquility. What Kastner unwittingly refers to as the "deluge of the people's vocal manifestations" poses an implicit threat to the bourgeois status quo.

When folklorists and scholars focus on street cries in the second half of the nineteenth century—after 1848—they practice selective amnesia, evacuate criers' shady past, and promote an idealized image of hawkers. Peddlers are no longer represented as a political threat, but rather as dehistoricized and depoliticized stereotypes or aesthetic artifacts. Accordingly, they satisfy the nostalgic commentator's longing for social harmony, in which everyone knows their place. From Fournel to Franklin, we find many clichéd remarks that carry over from one text to the other or repeat statements made by Jean-Baptiste Gouriet and Mainzer. Indeed, through selective recall of the past, they construct cultural memory as an ordered and harmonious narrative of shared memories of street vendors and repeatedly circulate these memories among their contemporaries in a variety of media including guidebooks, archives, prints, photographs, collectibles, and later recordings. Thus cultural memory of street criers acquires permanence without context, a canonical status that effectively masks class prejudices by fixating on reassuring images of a declining population of *petits métiers*.[62] The ability to muffle unpleasant sounds makes these cultural memories worth preserving in the present. The "plaintive cry" of the peddler eventually becomes a metonym for the working class as a whole, whose raucousness turned to whimper favors bourgeois aspirations to tranquility.

When Mercier wrote "the idiom of these ambulant criers is such that one has to study it to distinguish what it means," he posited that one of the objectives of academic scholarship is the mastery of lower classes' troubling difference in a way that will prove influential to later commentators. Mainzer and Fournel refer to the need to "put some order into a complicated subject, into this immense clamor ["tintamarre"] of cries,"[63] as each amateur folklorist sets out to collect, sort, and contextualize the perceived disappearance of street cries. Sound recording was being imagined and invented in this period: in 1856, the photographer Nadar imagined something he coined "an acoustic daguerreotype," adding "Have you not dreamed, as I have, of this instrument whose need we all feel?"[64] Édouard-Léon Scott de Martinville first attempted to transcribe sounds in 1857 using the phonautograph, followed by Charles Cros's and Thomas Edison's inventions of sound recording with the paleophone in 1877 and the phonograph in 1878.[65] The possibility of fixating acoustic traces, however, obviously preoccupied many prior to the devices' inventions. In a passage cited earlier, Mainzer refers specifically to the practice of conservation and modes of display in the museum when he writes that the sounds of the *marchand d'habits* should be "placed under glass and conserved in a cabinet of acoustic rarities."[66] As Classen remarks in *The Deepest Sense*, attitudes toward touching museum objects changed in the nineteenth century; whereas in previous eras, visitors could manipulate artifacts, now "rarities," displayed in glass cases as Mainzer describes, were "positioned outside time and space, and thus removed from ordinary human interaction."[67] Bertall's vignette representing a devil[68] looking at glass-encased miniature street criers and other noisy objects (we can see a coco-vendor and a mender, as well as a carriage wheel), placed at the end of Balzac's essay "Ce qui disparaît de Paris" in *Le Diable à Paris* (1846) and later recycled as a frontispiece in *Le Diable à Paris: Paris et les Parisiens à la plume et au crayon* (1868), humorously illustrates the attempt to preserve lost sounds. Bertall references the eighteenth-century practice of collecting ceramic porcelain figurines representing peddlers. Criers are not only desonorized but miniaturized; sonic relations figure class and economic relations as miniature street vendors face their monumental observer and potential buyer. At the top of the case, a sign difficult to decipher reads "Conserves gamme," which may refer to preserving the musical scale of street noises (figure 15).

The impulse to document and conserve street cries is akin to rendering practices that once had a function in the community into artifacts valued as art for art's (or curiosity's) sake. It is also part of a tacit project of social control and

Figure 15. Bertall, vignette, *Le Diable à Paris: Paris et les Parisiens à la plume et au crayon* (1868), frontispiece. Courtesy of McGill University Library, Rare Books and Special Collections, Montreal.

sonic classification. Such preservation took place once technology permitted. In the first decade of the twentieth century, linguist Ferdinand Brunot of the Sorbonne University collected phonographic artifacts for his "Archives de la parole." Brunot explained that sound clips of popular idioms, the working class, or provincial accents, as well as standard vocal specimens would be included in his comprehensive "Musée de la parole," because, when the voices of the present day had been extinguished, his generation owed it to their successors to enable them to revive everything that might hold scientific merit.[69] Other sound recordings, such as a series of imitations of common street cries by the singer Jean Péheu, now preserved in the Bibliothèque nationale de France's sound archives, offer a trace of the past of a different kind.[70] Although Fournel condemned the desire for order and the straight line that characterized Hauss-mannization, he was unaware that this same spirit of centralization guided the work of the archivist, who imposes order on the chaos of popular sounds, and whose project constructs the distance between the silent observer and the noisy peddler that will eventually consign them permanently to a timeless past.

Toward the end of the nineteenth century, street cries were symbols of the charms of urban existence, local color, and the picturesque. For some, the charm had been worn thin. The city was no longer in concert, but rather an uncontrol-lable proliferation of cries and criers. Henri Beraldi thought one should sweep up all those discordant notes: "Every day there is something new: nobody can make sense of it anymore. Yesterday, it was the 'cricri' of an iron castanet, today it is the 'psitt' of a rubber pear. Cries and noises that, once again, resist musical notation, and it matters little. To lead as one should these performers, what is needed is not an orchestral conductor's baton—but a broom."[71] For others, such as Abbé Valentin Dufour, editor of the seventeenth-century *Lettres d'un Sicilien* by Marana: "their antiquity, their perpetuity endear them to us all the more; we have endeavored to share them with our readers to remind them of our fathers' customs, to make them love them." He adds that

> In fact, we can observe that the Cries of Paris disappear daily to the detriment of the picturesque, but to the advantage of the tranquility of the good burgher, whose ears are no longer tired by the more or less harmonious concert of the street cries of modern Paris: the thousand voices of the press and the billboards of advertisers have been substituted for the street cries of the Middle Ages. Who dares declare that this is not the sign of progress claimed by our century full of discoveries, the century of science and enlightenment?[72]

Ever conscious of a historical break with the past, Abbé Dufour can refer to the charms of street cries because they have lost their purpose, and no longer disturb those demanding a quieter lifestyle. Dufour clearly relies on sound to demarcate social classes. He also aligns ancien regime sociability with dis-order and constructs the modern "enlightened" urban lifestyle as quieter and more visual.

Street cries have been transformed, Dufour suggests, from a primarily aural to a visual phenomenon in the form of mass-market advertising. Nineteenth-century posters in effect often appropriated the iconography of the street crier to advertise merchandise.[73] Deafening street sounds therefore continue to shape print media metaphorically. Fournel, in fact, compared how the "typographi-cal eloquence" of posted ads and city signs, and the "symphony" of street cries competed for the flâneur's attention in a passage I cited earlier from *Ce qu'on voit dans les rues de Paris*.[74] Yet late-nineteenth-century laws in France toned down the volume on aural in favor of print advertising. Regulations on peddlers' and buskers' cries were extended to hawkers who were forbidden to shout out the news in 1889; in contrast, the 1881 law on the freedom of the press lifted earlier restrictions on postering (*affichage*).[75] We should keep in mind, however, that Dufour neglects other modern transfigurations of street cries: other than billboards and sandwich men, the cries find new life in twentieth-century commercial jingles, infomercials, and other oral/aural forms of publicity. Commercial posters and more broadly print culture did not wipe out oral-based advertising. Inasmuch as they coexisted, they mutually informed literary texts. The works of Charles Baudelaire or Stéphane Mallarmé provocatively refer both to print and aural, high- and lowbrow, commercial and aesthetic culture, as I discuss in the next chapter. As Philippe Hamon insightfully comments, nineteenth-century literature anticipates 1960s pop art by productively drawing on "talking images" (*images parlantes*) or media that mix verbal and visual such as street cries and advertising slogans.[76]

In the sources examined here, the street crier is commodified—if street cries were once a means used by the lowest class of merchants of selling their wares, they now have become currency, a means of producing wealth for the middle classes. Preserved under glass, as it were, peddlers are no longer heard but seen, their evanescent sound afforded the permanence of an image (a print, a poster, a postcard, a score, or a museum record) that can be bought and sold. Though opposing Haussmannization's reorganization of the sonic environment, Fournel's work ultimately idealizes the street crier and echoes Haussmann's silencing of working-class noise. In Fournel, we hear the flâneur's attempt to compose the city as a concert, and the amateur historian's rendering tradesmen mutedly picturesque; however, the frequency with which he treated the topic suggests that street cries resist complete co-optation and retain an element of the inassimilable: the shrillness of the cry that Charles Baudelaire captured so well in "Le Mauvais Vitrier."

CHAPTER 4

Listening to the Glazier's Cry

As attentive listeners to street noise, as well as observers of spectacles on the boulevards, nineteenth-century French poets were keenly attuned to the transformations of the sonic ambiance of Paris by the prefects of the Seine, especially Baron Haussmann. They listened to the ways in which old and new soundscapes collided and coexisted; they took note as high-pitched transient sounds such as street cries emerged against the continuous but lower-frequency rattle of traffic. Amid the ubiquitous street nuisances that overwhelmed nineteenth-century ears, the cries of peddlers hawking merchandise or services were invested with particular emotional force and artistic potential. Traditionally, those cries were associated with the multimodal genre of the *Cris de Paris* and with the flâneur-writing that flourished in nineteenth-century literary guidebooks to Paris. These two interrelated discourses come together in writings on the *Cris* by the likes of Joseph Mainzer, which were an integral part of panoramic literature with their portrayals of the flâneur's daily encounters with peddlers. They are also the background for my readings of Arsène Houssaye's and Charles Baudelaire's prose poems inspired by the glazier's cry. These poets accentuate the cry's euphonious or strident qualities to connote sentimental or ironic reactions to social inequities. Glaziers were both makers and breakers of windows; the way poets perceived their activity influenced whether their cries sounded like songs that brought people together or shrieks that tore them apart. Houssaye exploits the capacity of prosaic rhythms and refrain to record and memorialize the disappearing street cries of Paris. Part of what makes Baudelaire's poetry modern is precisely the way he uses noise to disrupt Houssaye's sentimental rhetoric.

Listening to the city streets is not in itself new in the nineteenth century. City noise in general was a motif with roots in antiquity. The noise of Paris was a traditional literary motif used to evoke the capital's overwhelming vastness and excessive disorder. Guillaume de la Villeneuve's thirteenth-century "Les Crieries de Paris" enumerates the ear-deafening cornucopia on offer, but the better known example is Boileau's satire. Following the Roman poet Juvenal, Nicolas Boileau lists all the insufferable cries in the city that hinder his sleep in "Les Embarras de Paris" (1666). In the eighteenth century, the noise-averse Jean-Jacques Rousseau indelibly marks Paris as a "city of noise, smoke, and mud" at the end of book 4 of *Émile ou De l'éducation*. Responding to Rousseau's dysphoric motif of urban noise, the French Romantics naturalize the murmur of the street by comparing the city to the beehive or the ocean. Victor Hugo amplifies the analogy in the chapter "Paris à vol d'oiseau" from *Notre Dame de Paris*; in a sonic panorama that rivals poetic prose, the city sings like an orchestra. These examples suggest that the trope of the noisy city carries over from century to century, but until the 1830s, the motif rarely, if ever, suggests the kind of disorientation, social conflict, and existential malaise we find later in Baudelaire's poetry.[1]

The Baudelairean speaker hears noise at the street level: the street around him deafeningly screeches. Such a disorienting, loud experience defies conventional motifs. The rapid pace of mid-century urban renewal renders traditional topoi obsolete. Instead, new poetic forms are needed to account for new volumes of noise and newly changed sonic relations. Although both Houssaye and Baudelaire single out the glazier's cry as prototypical of these new sonic relations, they differ in their dramatizations of the flâneur-poet's encounter with the window-mender. Is what they hear a "song" or a "cry"? What distinguishes these two types of sound? How should they be transposed into poetic language? I draw on a network of discourses including the picturesque and flâneur-writing, panoramic literature on the *Cris*, and reflections on populist song, in order to show how different writers harmonized the glazier's cry into poetic prose. If Houssaye senses tears in the glazier's song when Baudelaire hears a piercing and discordant cry, it is because the two poets' perceptions of sonic relations are at odds, as are their understandings of the disruptive potential of noise in art.

Aural Flânerie in Houssaye and Baudelaire

Charles Baudelaire's identification with peddlers such as ragpickers and glaziers is well known. Walter Benjamin, in his widely influential reading of Baudelaire, gave currency to the affinity between poet and ragpicker by finding a modern heroism in the poet's attraction to society's marginal classes (whether the apache or the itinerant tradesmen such as the ragpicker).[2] This affinity also stems from the discourse on flânerie. In the section "Tableaux parisiens" of *Les Fleurs du mal*, a series of poems influenced by "panoramic literature" and added to *Les Fleurs* after its initial publication,[3] the poet-flâneur encounters and identifies with peddlers and other members of the *lumpenproletariat* as he strolls through the old "faubourgs" and marginal neighborhoods of Paris to which Baron Haussmann's renovations confined the poor. The *petits métiers* or small-scale tradesmen are also omnipresent in "panoramic literature,"[4] so it comes as little surprise that Baudelaire would pepper his poetic works with urban encounters with itinerant lower-class workers and the poor. Baudelaire was a consumer and critic of picturesque sketches of *petits métiers*. In his essay "On Some French Caricaturists," he commented appreciatively about representations of the working class in the work of the caricaturist Joseph Traviès: "Traviès has a deep feeling for the joys and griefs of the people; he knows the rabble through and through, and may be said to have loved it with a tender sympathy. . . . those tramps of his are generally very lifelike, and all their rags and tatters have that almost indefinable fullness and nobility of a style readymade, such as nature often provides in her odd moments."[5] Baudelaire's own poetry, whether in verse or in prose, evinces a similar investigation into the joys and the troubles of the *petits métiers* and the poor.

Baudelaire's early poetry draws extensively on panoramic types, be they beggars, street musicians, or tradesmen. He drew freely from picturesque literature in his early years, in juvenilia inspired by buskers and their "plaintive," "humble" street music, such as "Tout à l'heure je viens d'entendre," "Le Raccommodeur de fontaines," and "À une jeune saltimbanque."[6] "À une jeune saltimbanque," an 1845 sonnet possibly written in collaboration with Alexandre Privat d'Anglemont (a writer known for his anecdotal sketches about Paris), describes a poor female street harpist singing *romances* and accompanied by a street child performer on tambourine. Formerly a paragon of beauty, she has now been brought down to the street where, as the poet's fallen muse, she begs. Like "La Muse vénale" (The Venal Muse), the poem draws on the picturesque to critique the collapse of patronage, which has left the poet, like the street performer or prostitute, to beg miserably for a living. Contact with the modern urban beggar forced a new relationship between rich and poor, one no longer defined by traditional relations between almsgivers and beggars based on doctrines and customs of Christian charity. Both this poem and "À une mendiante rousse" (To a Red-Haired Beggar-Girl) are dedicated to a street singer and guitarist with red hair.[7] The poet-flâneur identifies with the poor beggar-musician and, in a parody of courtly homage, lauds the beauty he finds in such destitution. As noted in discussions of Delphine de Girardin, Maria d'Anspach, and Victor Fournel in chapter 1, beggar-musicians, often specifically identified and linked to the picturesque urban scene, elicit from flâneurs and flâneuses strong reactions to their poverty, vagrancy, and mendicancy. Baudelaire, however, avoids the anecdotal by not identifying the musician (the address after all is to "a" not "the" celebrated redheaded beggar) and turns the poem into a voyeuristic fantasy. "À une mendiante rousse" becomes a parody of giving (or not) homage, and a reflection on poetic language and courtly love poetry.[8] "Le Vin des chiffonniers" (The Ragman's Wine) also from *Les Fleurs du mal*, again avoids specific identification of its subject[9] while evoking a drunken but voluble ragpicker who stumbles against walls like a poet. The comparison underscores the analogy between the stumbling ragpicker and the jerky language of modern poetry. By avoiding the strategies of literary guidebooks that treat the celebrities of the streets as known and knowable, Baudelaire represents urban encounters as "shocks" (as Benjamin states) that disconnect the social and poetic fabric, forcing readers to attempt a meaningful if elusive interpretation of the fragments of metropolitan experience.

Le Spleen de Paris (*The Parisian Prowler*) moves even further away from the picturesque and the anecdotal. Although there are also a large number of paupers, street people, and beggars in the prose poems, depictions of individual street types are mere pretexts for broader reflections on sonic relations. For example in "Les Veuves" (Widows) and "Le Vieux Saltimbanque" (The Old Acrobat), the narrator identifies with the misery of the working class by contrasting the isolation of a widow or of an old acrobat with the sense of the social evoked by the noise of military music, public concerts, buskers, vendors, and the general hustle and bustle in the streets. An ambiance of noise hovers over the city in *Le Spleen de Paris*, as in the multiplicities of confused voices Baudelaire refers to as "un immense bruissement de vie . . . la vie des infiniment petits" ("a vast buzzing of life filled the air—the life of the infinitely small"), or as "une foule de cris discordants" ("a multitude of discordant shouts"), hanging in the air as the tangible evidence of an alienated humanity's presence.[10] In *Le Peintre de la vie moderne*, urban noise and harmonious beauty coexist in an unexpected equilibrium as when Baudelaire writes of M.G.'s admiration (one he undoubtedly shares) for "l'étonnante harmonie de la vie dans les capitales, harmonie si providentiellement maintenue dans le tumulte de la liberté humaine" ("the amazing harmony of life in the capital cities, a harmony so providentially maintained amid the turmoil of human freedom").[11] The drone of traffic is frequently evoked in Baudelaire's poetry, but noises such as knocks, whistles, shouts, and cries that signal sudden changes to the sonic environment are especially salient in *Le Spleen de Paris*. Indeed, what makes Baudelaire's poetry about peddlers distinctive are the number of unsettling encounters with the noisy working poor that disrupt not only urban experience, but also the coherence of meaning and the possibility of transparent communication in the prose poem.[12]

In the dedicatory letter to Arsène Houssaye that serves as preface to *Le Spleen de Paris*, Baudelaire again refers to the formative role of urban encounters and especially of peddlers in his poetry. The inspirational function of the strident cry of the *vitrier* or glazier—a sound that carries through the street and up to the top floors of the surrounding buildings—is evident in this passage addressed to Houssaye: "Vous-même, mon cher ami, n'avez-vous pas tenté de traduire en une *chanson* le cri strident du *Vitrier*, et d'exprimer dans une prose lyrique toutes les désolantes suggestions que ce cri envoie jusqu'aux mansardes, à travers les plus hautes brumes de la rue?" ("You yourself, my dear friend, did you not try to translate the *Glazier*'s strident cry into a *song*, and to express in lyrical prose all the woeful associations that cry sends all the way up to attics, through the street's thickest fogs?").[13] Baudelaire refers to Houssaye's "La Chanson du vitrier," first published in 1850, as an antecedent to his own work. This homage, however, is not so straightforward an honor.[14] Irony can complicate Baudelaire's epistolary admiration, as we saw in "À une mendiante rousse," where the address had already thwarted easy interpretations. As a well-known critic and editor of *La Presse* and *L'Artiste*, and a writer with political aspirations, Houssaye represented the establishment. As such, Baudelaire flattered him in the dedication to *Le Spleen de Paris* because he needed his support. He published "Le Mauvais Vitrier," for example, in 1862 in *La Presse*, when Houssaye was still its editor. Nevertheless, he did not respect the bourgeois artist class that Houssaye embodied. The dedicatory letter thus contains the tension already articulated in the *Salon of 1846*, in which Baudelaire mocks the bourgeoisie, but also recognizes that he needs their patronage and (financial) support. That *chanson* or song is typeset in italics raises several questions that invite further examination, namely the issue of whether or not the glazier's cry can be ascribed the melodious qualities we associate with songs, and what relationship exists, if any, between the "song" of the glazier and "lyrical prose." This chapter sounds the depths of this relationship between the perception of the cry and its transposition into poetic writing.

The dedication to Houssaye mitigates the need for flattery while imposing a distinction between Baudelaire's complex ironic prose poetry and his precursor's sentimental narrative poem about an individual destitute glazier.[15] Indeed it is tempting to preserve the dichotomy that raises the stakes of Baudelaire's modernist prose poetry above that of the more conservative Houssaye. Many scholars follow Baudelaire's lead in dismissing Houssaye's poem and use it as a mere foil to "Le Mauvais Vitrier," but it is worth listening carefully to the treatment of the glazier's cry in "La Chanson du vitrier." Houssaye transposes the cry in his prose poem, not with conscious irony, but in a manner that refers in innovative ways to the discourse on aural flânerie, as well as to the aestheticization of popular street sounds in literary guidebooks that were examined in earlier chapters. The formal experimentation with song and the prose poem form in Houssaye's text evince an attempt—in some ways quite successful—to harmonize the glazier's strident cry, and as such, throw into sharp relief Baudelaire's rejection of the trope of the city as concert.

Houssaye's poem begins with a statement about flânerie and the idle stroller's receptivity to street cries:

> Oh! vitrier!
>
> Je descendais la rue du Bac ; j'écoutai,—moi seul au milieu de tous ces passants qui à pied ou en carrosse allaient au but,—à l'or, à l'amour, à la vanité,—j'écoutai cette chanson pleine de larmes.[16]

> Ho! glazier!
>
> I was walking down Rue du Bac; I listened—alone among all the passers-by, on foot or in carriages, darting to their destination,—toward gold, love, vanity,—I listened to this song full of tears. (my translation)

For readers of literary guidebooks, it is a familiar scene depicting the flâneur amid, rather than above the streets, with his ear attuned to a city soundscape that most Parisians do not listen to anymore. Moreover, Houssaye implicitly draws on the discourse of literary guidebooks when he refers to specific locations (*Rue du Bac*, a street with illustrious past occupants in today's Seventh arrondissement; *Rue des Anglais* in the present-day's Fifth arrondissement near the Sorbonne; *Place Maubert*, historically a marketplace also in the Fifth). He evokes both the disinterestedness of the idle flâneur in search of distractions—rather than profit, love, or other selfish pursuits—and describes the sordid lifestyle of the *vitrier*, his family, and his peer group.[17] The fact that Houssaye dedicates his poem to E. T. A. Hoffmann, the author of an iconic text in flâneur literature, "My Cousin's Corner Window," suggests his interest in being read in this vein. In Hoffmann's tale, the flâneur-figure confined to his room remains truly detached from the scene he observes from his window. The same cannot be said of Houssaye's narrator who has more in common with another idler, Hugo's speaker in "Le Mendiant" from *Les Contemplations*. Houssaye's, like Hugo's, poem dramatizes the speaker's self-satisfaction; neither first-person speaker, however, understands the beggar's real needs.[18] In Hugo's "Le Mendiant," the pensive speaker does not even listen to his interlocutor, even though the poor man is portrayed as an individual (rather than a type) with a life story to tell. In Houssaye, the glazier does tell his story, but the narrator remains silent upon hearing it, vainly satisfied with his fraternal gesture, or overcome with emotion.[19] By providing anecdotal details of the tradesman's life story, Houssaye presents the glazier as known and knowable, even though the narrator cannot actually decipher the signs of the man's destitution. Houssaye's approach contrasts with Baudelaire's avoidance of the anecdotal in poems such as "À une mendiante rousse," and in "Le Mauvais Vitrier" where the glazier's story remains untold, irrelevant even. The failure of Houssaye's narrator to understand or remedy the glazier's dire situation—his failure to actually hear what the glazier tells him repeatedly, that he is hungry and needs money to provide food for himself and his family—is fairly typical of flâneur literature. We have seen how Fournel and others experience urban distractions with all their senses, but as bourgeois idlers they do not dwell on the socioeconomic significance of what they perceive. Were they to do so, they could not maintain the moral detachment and economic disinterestedness that enables their idleness.[20]

Houssaye's poem references panoramic literature on the type of the glazier. These texts frequently describe encounters among passersby and peddlers, as in this humorous sketch by Delphine de Girardin of a pedestrian's travails as he gets on and off the sidewalk to avoid mishaps or dangers, such as the glazier's hooks:

> A little farther, you get back on the sidewalk. You see a glazier coming toward you. "He carries on his back wings of light," meaning that the rays of light play on the large windowpanes he carries on his hooks. As these wings have a frightful wingspan, you move a little to the right to let him go by without knocking them.[21]

In contrast to Girardin's detached passerby, who decidedly avoids an encounter with a faceless but frightening tradesman that would be too close for comfort, Houssaye's and Baudelaire's narrators welcome the glazier, albeit for different reasons. Their use of panoramic types is indeed dissimilar. The findings of scholars such as Richard Burton and Steve Murphy apropos the historical context of Baudelaire's glazier are significant for understanding the two poets' divergent use of popular ethnographic discourse. Aside from Girardin's reference, which is not widely known, the main panoramic discourse on the *vitrier ambulant* appears in Joseph Mainzer's typology of the glazier in *Les Français peints par eux-mêmes* and in Émile de la Bédollierre's essay "Le Vitrier ambulant. Le Vitrier-peintre" in *Les Industriels. Métiers et professions en France*. Both these *physiologies* classify and rank the types of glaziers, separating "the vulgar scribbler of letters" from the "true artist," the unskilled "vitrier ambulant" from the diverse types of skilled laborers, the "ouvrier-peintres."[22] Sometimes the categories overlap in a narrative about coming down in the world. As talented shop owners,[23] *vitriers-peintres* had aspirations of being artists, but fell to the rank of artisans, then to the lowly status of *vitriers-ambulants*. In Houssaye, the glazier is equally unskilled and set on an irrevocable course of downward social mobility. In Houssaye's poem, but also in Baudelaire's, the *vitrier* has lost his specialist artistic skills (he has no palette and no colored panes of glass) and is therefore, to quote Burton, "rendered as economically and socially superfluous."[24] Both Mainzer and La Bédollierre refer to the probity and "the instinct for plotting and profitability" of the "vitrier ambulant" in contrast to the "faineance" of the "ouvrier-peintre," but they also comment on glaziers' participation in riots, adding that, as window-breakers as well as window-menders, the tradesmen "often speculate on others' misfortunes."[25] Indeed, multiple sources attest to the colloquial, political connotations of the "glazier" as "chasseurs de Vincennes," the infantry corps of Vincennes involved in the insurrections of June 1848 and December 1851, therefore adding to the subversive dimension of the glazier already alluded to in the *physiologies*.[26] Given Mainzer's and La Bédollierre's bourgeois bias, it is hard to assess the objectivity of their colorful remarks, which fuel the era's anxieties and satisfy expectations about the dangerous classes in a manner comparable to the unease felt by Prefect Gisquet. Attempts to define and classify the subaltern status of peddlers merely result in reaffirming bourgeois habits of thinking about marginality. The protean instability of the glazier, at once skilled and unskilled, or honest and criminal, prevents him from being comfortably assimilated into the urban picturesque.

Houssaye's glazier is apolitical and powerless, completely lacking the calculating instinct Mainzer attributes to the type. In contrast to Mainzer, who largely avoids the topic of pauperism in his series on street criers, Houssaye develops a sentimental discourse on economic marginalization through the portrayal of the glazier, while staying clear of any direct political commentary given his position within the establishment. When the narrator notes that the glazier has given "une année de misère à la République" founded in 1848, we understand that the poem first published in 1850 is set in 1849.[27] That choice of date avoids any direct commitment to the progressive values of the June Days Uprising and any possibility of implied criticism of the new Bonapartist regime (the election of Louis-Napoleon Bonaparte to the presidency in December 1848 was followed by the proclamation of the Second Empire on December 2, 1851, by coup d'état).[28] Houssaye does, however, share Mainzer's ethnographic commitment to documenting the everyday life of his contemporaries and to preserving an archive of aural folklore for future generations. Nostalgic like Mainzer and Fournel, Houssaye aims to capture the sound of the cry that he too invests with strong emotion. Houssaye's narrator, then, oscillates between the flâneur's detachment and the sentimentalist's concern about pauperism.[29]

It is worth considering whether the lack of clear direction in the poem stems from its appropriation of a cry, a type of sound that often defies control and that is subject to semantic drift (by its intensity the cry can mean distress as well as elation). Houssaye's poem is all about the response to a cry. In his poem, the cry, supposed to be attention-getting and an effective advertising tool, goes unanswered, unheard even by those in the marketplace. He evokes the "voix d'en haut" he would expect, in vain this time, to reply—"pas une servante, pas une bourgeoise, pas une fillette, n'avaient répondu, comme un écho plaintif" (not one maid, not one bourgeoise, not one young girl had responded like a plaintive echo).[30] Houssaye does not mention the sixth floor or garrets that are explicitly referenced in Baudelaire. Even the narrator fails to properly respond to the cry as an economic signal; he does not purchase windowpanes, rather he inadvertently breaks them. The cry has lost its efficacy as a sales strategy. The poem has aestheticized the cry. Although it is no longer functional, it is still beautiful and symbolic of the picturesque quality of Parisian streets.

Transposing the Cry into Song

Although no characters respond to the glazier's cry, the poem repeats it as a refrain, a device that adds a sense of musicality to poetry. The use of refrain in a poem whose title is "Song" and the exact phrasing and linguistic register of the refrain are significant because they determine to some extent whether the cry is heard as an address or a lamentation and whether it is directed toward action (conative) or emotional response (expressive). Houssaye transposes the "cry" into a "song" by transforming the prepositional phrase "Au vitrier" from the locative to the vocative, "Oh! vitrier!" Although some have suggested that this change is typical of "Houssaye's sentimentality and/or ignorance,"[31] it is also possible to interpret the transposition as a thoughtful process of harmonization, germane to musical ethnographers' attempts to record sound artifacts. The exact phrasing of the glazier's cry, both linguistic and musical, was the subject of great scrutiny among composers and musicologists such as the conservatory-trained Kastner, and the music educator and critic Mainzer. Although Mainzer uses the prepositional phrase "au vitrier," the locative is not the only or the main form of the glazier's cry. Variations on the interjectional phrase "oh vitrier" were common. For example, Kastner cites "oh! vitri!" in his musical treatise Les Voix de Paris as does vaudevillist Eugène Grangé in Les Vitriers. Other variants include "Ohé le vitrier" and "ô vitrier."[32] When the caricaturist Bertall depicts a glazier in a series of representations of peddlers in La Comédie *de notre temps*, he adds a caption that reads "Oy! vitrier" (figure 16). Bertall is closest to capturing the traditional official call of the peddler that marked oral publication with the abbreviated form of "Oyez . . ." or "hear ye," but the other variants suggest that many people did not hear the cry as such.

Composers and musicologists were attuned to the sound of the glazier's cry and documented its timbre in their works by textually and musically describing precisely how it sounded. Notating the cries is part of an ethnographic preservation project that has some, such as Kastner, Mainzer, and later Bertall including musical scores along with the traditional lyrics. Kastner, moreover, devotes considerable space to the contractions used by street criers, linguistic forms common in the "old rustic idiom" spoken by peasants who have recently immigrated to the city:

> [These contracted forms] consist principally in the tightening of two syllables into one, or in the retrenchment of several syllables, what one calls in grammatical terms, *syncope* and *apocope*. They frequently determine the suppression of the silent 'e' which is no less a cause of embarrassment for itinerant tradesmen seeking to formulate their cries, than for composers trying to set to music the text of a song.[33]

Putting street criers on a par with composers, Kastner identifies the importance of syncopation in the cries: indeed, elsewhere Kastner explains that composers such as Grétry follow the example of "gens du peuple" or working-class people and banish the silent 'e' from some of their music, because it "opposes the free emission of voice."[34] Although there is no "e caduc" or /ə/ in "vitrier" /vitʁije/ as there is in "vitre" /vitʁə/ [window], altering the terminal /je/ to an /i/ vowel shortens the overall sound of the word, /vitʁii/. La Bédollierre also comments on phonetic contractions in the cries resulting from erasure of the /ə/, when he states that the southern regions from which glaziers originate, notably the Limousin and Piedmont, accentuate the closed-vowel /i/: "V'là l'Vitri . . . i!"[35]

Finally, it is Mainzer who has the most compelling description of the musical phrasing of the glazier's cry:

> It would be difficult to indicate the melody of *Au vitrier!* with the notation style in use. These two words undergo variants, and sometimes become incomprehensible for whoever hears, but does not see, the vendors, as for example when the words are transformed into these: *Au i-tri-i!* They are also half-sung, half-spoken. The first syllable *au* is sung very high and cried out loudly, whereas the word *vitrier* is spoken softly, and is almost muffled by the first sound. This sound often reminded me of the convulsive hiccups of seasick passengers, at the tragicomic moment when struggle begins between the desire to keep down and the need to throw up overboard what ails their stomach.
>
> I met a glazier who sang a descending chord in F minor.[36]

Figure 16. Bertall, *Le Vitrier, La Comédie de notre temps* (1875). Courtesy of Bibliothèques des livres rares et collections spéciales, Direction des bibliothèques, Université de Montréal.

Like Kastner, Mainzer documents the elisions and syncopations in the cry, which is dominated by the sharper phoneme /i/. Mainzer, however, is intent on conveying, on transposing the cry's musical qualities. As he shows in the musical score, the cry is a descending F minor arpeggio that accentuates the loud, high-pitched vocative "o." The rhythm is significant too as it attacks the

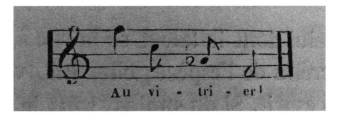

Figure 17. Score of the glazier's cry from *Le Vitrier-peintre* by Joseph Mainzer, in *Les Français peints par eux-mêmes*, 4:301. Courtesy of Florida State University Libraries Special Collections.

vocative on a quarter note and ends by propagating the cry with a resonant vowel on a half note. Like Mainzer, Bertall attests to the same general shape of the rhythm and melody; both men document the cry as one long high note followed by two descending shorter notes, and ending with a long note, which is one octave lower that the initial note, as we can see when their scores are set side by side:

Though both scores show similar rhythm and melody, the differences in how they register the vocative and the ending invite further scrutiny. Bertall's score uses a grace note and quarter note to lean in to the "oy" in an upward glissando, as compared with Mainzer's unadorned quarter note vocative. This ornamentation could be an attempt to imitate the jerkiness of the countertenor voice that Joseph-Louis d'Ortigue mentioned in his music criticism, discussed in chapter 2. Whereas Mainzer ends on a half note that fades away, Bertall emphasizes a sixteenth note for the final /e/ followed by a rest, such that the cry has lost the "long tail" that Victor Fournel remembered in *Les Cris de Paris*.[37] Bertall renders the cry more monotonic by pairing it down to a two-note scale, and one can wonder whether the loss of detail is merely incidental to our comparison. Because of these divergences between Mainzer and Bertall, the scores can only give us today an approximate idea of what the cry sounded like; yet, there is enough agreement between the two scores composed thirty-five years apart to extrapolate the descending melody of the cry and to attest to its continuity over the mid-century decades of urban renewal that impacted peddling.

Moreover, Bertall specifies for which type of voice the part is intended: the tenor, the highest male voice, whose popularity peaked in the romantic era. Tenors were classified in the period and the "grand tenor" may refer to the clarion sound of the dramatic or heroic tenor. The designation "grand tenor" on Bertall's image could mean that the notes are to be sung higher than written depending on the performer's skill, since the score does not exploit a tenor's range (from C3 one octave below middle C to C5 one octave above it or A4); moreover, according to Hector Berlioz, tenors liked to sing the phoneme /i/, which showed off their skill.[38] It is with an ironic mixing of high and low then that Bertall applies this "grand" designation to such a piddling subject. Mainzer may also attempt to deflate his own serious discussion of the cry when he compares it with the hiccups of a seasick passenger; yet, the analogy between the cry and bodily convulsions corresponds to the uncanny and monstrous quality of the cries.

When Houssaye uses "Oh! vitrier!" as a refrain, he does not reproduce the elisions and syncopation that Kastner and Mainzer discuss. "La Chanson du vitrier" is not aiming for sonic realism; accordingly, the poem rephrases the glazier's cry in line with poetic conventions, namely the apostrophe and the standard linguistic register. He elides traces of the "old rustic idiom," the linguistic marker that identifies the glazier as foreign (the very difference the narrator has a hard time acknowledging). Used as the opening phrase, a conventional site of invocation, "Oh! vitrier!" approximates an apostrophe: "Ho! Glazier!" sounds like "O glazier!" Apostrophe characterizes the lyric because it usually animates an absent, inanimate addressee through the artful use of language.[39] What do we make of the use of apostrophe in this passage that describes a glazier who is actually alive and present? Is his a ghostly presence? "Oh vitrier" could imply that the speaker is not expecting an answer because he invokes an absent body with longing. If literary apostrophe produces a speaking subject and (an imaginary) object of address, in this case someone who calls out to a glazier whose presence is rhetorically abolished, and an actual *vitrier*, we must conclude that Houssaye's poem puts this very circuit into question. Instead, he harmonizes the cry, and by making it sound melodious, the glazier's voice loses its Occitan, lower-class accent, and achieves a ghostly presence in the poem.

In addition to aestheticizing the cry by transforming it into a refrain, the poem further moves away from the cry's function in the marketplace by blurring the source of the glazier's cry. When the interjection is attributed to different speakers, the "oh!" expresses the full range of connotations from "surprise, frustration, [to] discomfort, longing, [and] disappointment."[40] Whereas the first and second occurrences clearly emanate from the glazier himself, the sources of the subsequent cries could either be the narrator, the boy-bartender, the potential clients, or the glazier.[41] The ambiguity suggests the narrator's identification with the glazier. The cry becomes a sound memory, as the narrator starts singing the song of the glazier himself: "Au vitrier" becomes "Oh!

vitrier!" If the poem itself is as moving as it is intended to be, then the reader might also repeat the "dolorous music" of the glazier from memory. One might even say that the cry's repetition suggests its resonance at the level of collective cultural memory. In fact in his *Confessions*, Houssaye relates an anecdote that evinces the emotional impact of "La Chanson du vitrier" on those who heard it declaimed by Léon Beauvallet of the Comédie Française at an 1852 performance in which the monologue "broke his voice in a sob that wrung out the tears from everyone."[42]

Houssaye's theatrical adaptation of his poem further suggests the *pathos* this work is meant to generate. "La Chanson du vitrier" was adapted into a play starring Beauvallet and Delphine Marquet, whose text was published in *Le Violon de Franjolé*. A note in the 1859 edition states that the well-to-do at this princely theater made a substantial donation to the Montagne Sainte-Geneviève neighborhood. This suggests that the play successfully toyed with the audience's senses of guilt and self-satisfaction.[43] The dramatic adaptation does away with the male narrator and introduces a woman (with a daughter named Berthe) as a main character. (A female listener referred to as "madame" is addressed in the fifth paragraph of the prose poem "La Chanson du vitrier," but she is not involved in the story as told to her/us by the narrator.) In the play, she is on her way to a romantic rendezvous when she runs into the glazier, who startles her. The exhausted glazier breaks his window panes when he falls of his own weakness. The woman offers to give him her purse and to drive him home; when he refuses, she rights the wrong she was about to commit with her lover. The poem is designed to elicit tears and thus conforms to a commonplace sentimentalist trope.[44] The sound of the glazier's cry becomes invested with (metonymic) meanings, laden as it is with the individual glazier's story, that of his entire peer group of poor tradesmen; it becomes the voice of *la misère*. Both because of its association with cultural memory at a time of the decline of the *petits métiers* and because of its timbre, it elicits sadness in those who hear it. Moreover, the formal structure of the poem with its refrain reinforces the melancholic effect.[45] Refrains are typical of songs and act as mnemonic devices. They provide closure and, in this case, the refrain ensures we do not forget the glazier's cry, even if we do not remember the socioeconomic reasons that cause the desperation we hear. The pathos of the cry neutralizes its potential radicalism.

Song Rhythms as Sound Memory

It should be clearer now why Houssaye titles his prose poem *chanson* or song, but what could the title have meant for Baudelaire? When Baudelaire italicizes the term *chanson* in his dedicatory letter, the italics signal the presence of an ironic layer that supplements the literal reference to the title of Houssaye's poem. While seeming to refer positively to his antecedent's work, the quotation of the title word contains an implicit jab at "a genre charged with populist intentions" to borrow Sonya Stephens's phrase, as an unsuitable model in Baudelaire's search for a new hybrid genre of prose.[46] Baudelaire, however, was sensitive to the power of song, but perhaps not in the same way as Houssaye. Putting aside Baudelaire's prejudicial remark, let us further consider what Houssaye may have intended by a title emphasizing the interrelationship between high and low culture, between song, the picturesque, and poetry, or more aptly prose poetry. Houssaye experimented with "primitive poetry," the title given to the fourth section of his works, Œuvres poétiques (1857), in which we find the poem on the glazier and several other poems titled "Song of. . . ." In a postface included in the 1850 edition of his complete poems, Houssaye in fact addresses his own strategy of eschewing "la vétusté des rimes" (antiquated rime): "il a osé être poëte dans le rhythme [sic] primitif sans rime, sans vers et sans prose poétique, comme dans les Syrènes et la Chanson du vitrier" (he dared to be a poet in primitive rhythms, without rhyme, without verse and without poetic prose, as in The Sirens and The Song of the Glazier).[47] What attracted Houssaye and some of his contemporaries to "primitive" or folkloric material was precisely its perceived naiveté and authenticity and the ease with which it lodged in memory, as Théophile Gautier explained: "ces chants naïfs, que jamais musiciens ni poètes n'ont pu imiter . . . [n'ont] souvent ni rime ni raison; pourtant l'impression est profonde, et le motif, une fois entendu, s'empare invinciblement de vous" (these naïve songs, that neither musicians nor poets could ever imitate, have neither rhyme nor reason; but the impression left is deep, and the motif, once heard, takes hold of you invincibly).[48] Gérard de Nerval had evoked a similar idea about the value of popular airs residing in their appeal to memory in "Il est un air pour qui je donnerais / Tout Rossini, tout Mozart, tout Wèbre" (There is an air for which I would give / All Rossini, all Mozart, all Weber) in Odelettes (1834). Much later, Arthur Rimbaud would famously evoke the appeal of "refrains niais, rhythmes naïfs" ("ridiculous refrains, naive rhythms") in "Alchimie du verbe" (Alchemy of the Word).[49]

In light of the popularity of song during this era, Houssaye's transposition of street cries—urban folklore rather than rural folklore—into prose poetry makes sense. Early-nineteenth-century poets had mined this popular resource in song-poems such as "Tableau de Paris à cinq heures du matin" by chansonnier and vaudevillist Marc-Antoine Désaugiers (1802).[50] Others, such as the songwriter Pierre-Jean de Béranger and Marceline Desbordes-Valmore had also cited familiar street cries in their verse, respectively, the cry of the old-clothes–man "vieux habits, vieux galons!" in "Vieux habits, vieux galons ou Réflexions morales et politiques d'un marchand d'habits de la capitale (Novembre 1814)" and that of the night crier "Réveillez-vous gens qui dormez" from "Le Crieur de nuit"; both song-like poems use the cry as a refrain, as does Houssaye. Yet, they are less concerned with "translating" street cries than with evoking a culturally significant figure or context.[51] Aloysius Bertrand also evokes street noises in his prose-poetry. "Le Clair de lune," for instance, quotes the same cry as the Desbordes-Valmore poem, and in "Octobre," we can hear peddlers' voices: "Les petits Savoyards sont de retour, & déjà leur cri interroge l'écho sonore du quartier" (The little Savoyards are returning, and already their cry questions the neighborhood's sonorous echo).[52] The sadness and social consciousness that permeate Houssaye's poem are not evident in the romantic poems discussed, but they are present in Louisa Siefert's sonnet "Marchand d'habit!" from *Rayons perdus* (1868). The sonnet describes the decline of the tradesman's voice and concludes that a whole "poem of misery" can be heard just in his cry "Marchand d'habit!":

Ce petit homme grisonnant
S'en venait encore à l'automne,
Le regard vif, l'air avenant,
En poussant son cri monotone.

Mais qu'il est changé maintenant !
Le regard est noir, l'air atone;
Et, sur les syllabes traînant,
Sa voix chevrotante détonne.

A peine un hiver a passé
Et le revoilà si cassé,
Qu'à l'entendre mon cœur se serre . . .

Poursuivant un maigre débit,
Oh! quel poëme de misère
Dans ce seul cri: Marchand d'habit![53]

That little graying man used to pass through in fall, bright-eyed, engaging, crying out his monotonous call.
How he's changed now! Dim-eyed, dull sounding, and his quivering voice jars as it drags on the syllables.
Barely one winter has gone by and there he is again so broken that to hear him my heart sinks.
A meagerly flowing song, oh! What a whole poem of misery in only this one cry: Old-Clothes–man! (my translation)

"La Chanson du vitrier" is one of Houssaye's many poems that explicitly appropriate popular sounds. In his study of the cultural transfer between high and low art forms in *Nerval et la chanson folklorique*, Paul Bénichou briefly discusses Houssaye's limited success with the transposition "Fresque byzantine" on the air of the hymn "Jésus Christ s'habille en pauvre" (Let all mortal flesh keep silence), another poem about Christian charity.[54] "La Chanson du vitrier" stands out as a lone example of a transposition of an urban street cry, rather than a traditional hymn of the kind Bénichou examines. Unlike his romantic antecedents, Houssaye attempted to transpose popular sonic material into high art, but he did so by experimenting with prose poetry rather than the octosyllabic sonnet form Siefert used. Houssaye's experimentation with appropriations of popular sounds in his poetry should be considered as part of his contribution to the development of the prose poem. By introducing the formal features of popular song, such as refrain, repetition, assonance, and doing away with classical rhymed verse (especially rich rhyme), he attempted to restore a more "primitive" accent and natural elocution to French verse.[55] "La Chanson du vitrier" uses refrain to heighten periodicity, to transform the functional into the lyrical, and to convert strident distress into pathos. The song-form strives for a kind of closure that naturalizes the suspect ideological message about fraternity the poem is at pains to convey. But cries are hard to contain or control.

Despite his undercutting of Houssaye's "song," Baudelaire too had admitted the mnemonic effect of song in his essay on Pierre Dupont in *Réflexions sur quelques-uns de mes contemporains* (1861), as little as a year before the publication of the dedicatory letter in *La Presse*, and just six months before the private letter of December 25, 1861, that Baudelaire addressed to Houssaye testing ideas about his prose poems. In *Réflexions*, he writes that the cry is destined to imprint itself eternally in all minds:

> Pierre Dupont belongs to this natural aristocracy of minds that owes infinitely more to nature than to art, and that, like two other great poets, Auguste Barbier and Marceline Desbordes-Valmore, find only by way of their souls' spontaneity the expression, the song, the cry destined to imprint itself forever in everyone's memory.[56]

Both Dupont and Desbordes-Valmore, according to the 1861 Dupont essay, share a "spontaneity" and a "natural" talent (meaning an artistic instinct rather than a cultivated or learned art) that convey to their poetry "un accent rajeuni, renouvelé par la sincérité du sentiment" (2:173–75; a rejuvenated accent, renewed by sincere sentiment). The link between song and cries is clear in both Baudelaire's 1851 and 1861 essays on Dupont. He refers to *Le Chant des ouvriers* as a "cri de douleur" (cry of pain) in the 1851 Dupont essay (2:31) and as a "cri de ralliement" (rallying cry) in the 1861 Dupont essay (2:172). The few comparisons Baudelaire makes between Dupont's songs and cries correspond to the language he uses in his essay on Desbordes-Valmore in *Réflexions sur quelques-uns de mes contemporains*. For Baudelaire, Desbordes-Valmore's poetic cries resemble "troués profondes" (profound holes), and "explosions magiques de la passion" (magical explosions of passion) that impose themselves on memory.[57] Baudelaire therefore appreciated the explosiveness, sincerity, and staying power of the song-like poetry of some of his contemporaries, though not of Houssaye's.

Populist song had an impact on Baudelaire's formative years.[58] Baudelaire was a member of bohemian circles where songs were prized, including bourgeois *romances*, drinking songs, music sung at public balls, popular *rondes*, and satiric songs. He even admits the value of Désaugiers's songs over philosophical poetry (2:11). Baudelaire's juvenilia clearly suggest the influence of attentive listening to street music, auditory skills that carry over into his major lyrical work. It is common knowledge that several poems of *Les Fleurs du mal* are song-like; "L'Invitation au voyage" (Invitation to the Voyage) is certainly the best known. "À une mendiante rousse," whose parody of courtly homage I briefly discussed earlier, also borrows many formal features of song, notably the use of the *impair* or imparisyllable (here the heptasyllable), *vers mêlés* or variations in metrical patterns (7/7/7/4), and couplet rhymes that ignore the rules of alternation (all this poem's rhymes are masculine, thus avoiding the silent 'e').[59] The Baudelaire we commonly associate with serious poetry was also a lyricist. Consider the light verse of "Le Jet d'eau," which started out as a song with a musical score by Victor Robillard and was possibly inspired by "La Promenade sur l'eau" by Pierre Dupont.[60] The song-like qualities of Baudelaire's verses such as "La Mort des amants" inspired many transpositions.[61] Similarly to his contemporaries Théodore de Banville, Champfleury, Dupont, and others, Baudelaire strove to relax classical verse by integrating some of the features of popular song, notably its verve and contrasts, as well as the liberties it took with meter and rhyme. Baudelaire half acknowledges Houssaye's attempts to create a poetic prose "musicale sans rythme et sans rime," by quoting the leading critic's own words "without rhyme or verse" in the dedicatory letter, but *Le Spleen de Paris* seeks to transpose a different kind of musicality. The implicit contrasts between "musicale sans rythme et sans rime" and words that follow, such as "heurtée" ("choppy") and "soubresauts" ("jolts") suggest that Baudelaire wanted to do "quelque chose de nouveau" (something new) as he states in his letter to Houssaye of December 25, 1861.[62] That would mean moving forward—rather than looking back either to what Houssaye calls "rythmes primitifs" or to his own juvenilia. In *Les Fleurs du mal*, the poet wished for "les sons nombreux des syllabes antiques, / Où règnent tour à tour le père des chansons" (1:15; sounds of ancient syllables, / Where reign in turn the father of all song [25]). By contrast, in *Le Spleen de Paris*, the statement "Les chansonniers disent que le plaisir rend l'âme bonne et amollit le coeur" (1: 318; "Popular singers say that pleasure makes the soul kind and softens the heart" [61]) from "Les Yeux des pauvres" (The Eyes of the Poor) is full of irony, as the narration exposes the narrator's smugness.

In "Le Mauvais Vitrier," Baudelaire does not attempt to "translate" (the term he used in the dedicatory letter), nor to transpose the glazier's cry as Houssaye had. Indeed the poem does not cite the glazier's cry in any of its variants ("Oh! vitrier!," "Au vitrier," etc.). Rather the poem describes the perverse *effect* that hearing the "cri perçant, discordant" (1:286; "piercing, discordant cry" [14]) has on the poet-speaker, allegedly prompting him to drop a flowerpot on the glazier, shattering his panes of glass in an explosive noise. It is worth remarking that different adjectives are used to describe the sound of the cry in the dedicatory letter than in the poem. Whereas the poem refers to a *piercing* cry, the letter uses the rare word *strident*. As Charles Nodier writes in his *Dictionnaire des onomatopées*, "this is how we qualify a hard noise, a little shrill, a little quivering, produced by a very refractory body, attacked by a file or a saw. This expressive and true word, happily based on *stridere* in Latin, has not yet been admitted into our linguistic usage, that it could only enrich."[63] Indeed, the latter adjective, found only once in Baudelaire's corpus, was rarely used at all before the nineteenth century, and its literary frequency is greatest in the period we are discussing, between 1850 and 1899.[64] A comparison of the relative frequency of the words *harmonieux* and *strident* using an online graphic tool such as Google Ngram Viewer (that charts the evolution of the percentage at which the search term appears in a given time frame in the corpus of books digitized by Google in a given language) shows that, whereas use of *harmonieux* varies little over the course of the nineteenth century, that of *strident* rises steadily from about 1830. The word's emergence could suggest a newfound need, beginning in the industrial age, to characterize the increasing number of loud and harsh sounds in the environment. We can conclude without a doubt that Baudelaire's word choice, which aptly captures a new kind of discordance, is especially modern. He heard a new shrillness in the cries that was neither part of the tradition set by Boileau's "embarras de Paris," nor that of the urban picturesque exploited by Houssaye.

Although Baudelaire emphasizes the stridency of the cry, "Le Mauvais Vitrier" represents a functional circuit of communication; in contrast, recall that "La Chanson du vitrier" harmonized the cry but short-circuited communication. In "Le Mauvais Vitrier" the glazier's cry is not explicitly transcribed, but the narrator's response subtly propagates the final note of the cry: /e/. The Baudelairean narrator responds by crying out "Hé! Hé!" and then something like "Come-on up!" reported in indirect speech ("et je lui criai de monter"), after hearing the glazier. Murphy explains that the Baudelairean poem suggests an imaginary echo, as the cries "au vitrier!," "hé!," "et," "criai," and "monter!" rhyme, significantly disseminating a high-pitched, resonant /e/ that would contrast with the low-pitched ending syllable posited by Mainzer and Bertall in their musical transcriptions of the glazier's cry. I might add that the poem ends with the speaker's cry, "La vie en beau," which inverts the vowel sounds /i/ and /o/ in the glazier's syncopated cry, "Au i-tri-i." Ellen S. Burt, however, argues that Baudelaire's narrator does not so much as reply to the glazier as a subject, but rather as a "placeholder," as if "aiming over the glass-seller's shoulder at someone else." "Hé hé'" she suggests is less a reply than a "summons" or a "challenge."[65] One thing is certain; the cry calls on us to question how, not whether, to respond.

The Demonic Effects of Stridency

The differences between the two poems' transpositions of the cry and circuits of communication tell us a great deal about how sound is conceived. Houssaye's poem is grounded in the assumption that the sounds stand in for real things or people as properties of those sources, and accordingly the poem describes the subject's interactions with his surroundings. Instead of adopting a realist standpoint on sounds, Baudelaire's poem explores the sensation of sound as a mental construct and the behaviors sounds elicit. It is interesting that the speaker invites speculation about the cry's relationship to the crier by evoking, in the poem and in the dedicatory letter, the city's thick fog and dirty atmosphere that would make the crier hard to see but easy to hear. The sound the poet actually hears is less relevant than the *effect* the sound has on the listener. The opening of the poem sets the focus not on the material or substantive world, but on the mysteries of the mind, the "impulsion mystérieuse et inconnue" (1:285; "mysterious and unknown impulse" [13]), the energy, the forces that motivate people to act. In fact, the digressive structure of the narrative, in which the story of the encounter with the glazier is delayed by a series of anecdotes about impulsive behaviors, should be read as a means of frustrating the process of interpretation.[66]

One of the forces in the poem that leads the speaker to act is the devil, who also appears in verse in *Les Fleurs du mal*, and who reflects Baudelaire's strong interest in Edgar Allan Poe's work. Demonic figures also make appearances in other prose poems such as "Les Tentations ou Éros, Plutus et la Gloire" (The Temptations, or Eros, Plutus and Fame) and "Le Joueur généreux" (The Generous Gambler). Baudelaire's poem parodies the ambiguous content in Houssaye's text. "La Chanson du vitrier" falls far from its apparent target—to write a poem about Christian charity and fraternity—and instead conveys an implicit violence and cruelty, even Satanism, toward the working class.[67] Like Mephistopheles, the narrator befriends his victim to secure his downfall. The satanic surfaces again as repressed content in Houssaye's poem in the comparison of the glazier to Jesus Christ and Niccolò Paganini. On the one hand, Houssaye turns the glazier into a kind of Christic figure deprived of manna by the public, who is crucified at the hands of the bourgeois narrator; the more enigmatic comparison to Niccolò Paganini on the other hand could refer to the violinist's extreme virtuosity that some thought resulted from a pact made with the devil.[68]

Moreover, in panoramic texts about the glazier and other street criers, allusions are made to the violent, fantastic, and sinister overtones of the cries. Indeed, street cries surface in childhood memories, which can easily be infused with superstitions dating back to times immemorial or with the fantastic and the magical. These associations are all the more powerful because criers are often heard in the early morning hours, while the listeners are still half asleep, and their reverie is interrupted by street noise, as evinced in Kastner's symphony *Les Voix de Paris*, Alfred Lebeau's prelude to *Les Cloches du monastère*, and in Proust's *La Prisonnière*.[69] In Ensemble Clément Janequin's recording of Kastner's symphony, one can hear the sharp attack of the countertenor voice interrupt the lullaby melody and cry out "V'là le vitrier." Apparently following this pervasive model, Baudelaire sets up his glazier poem so that the speaker, whom we can count among "les plus rêveurs des êtres" (1:285; "dreamiest of creatures" [14]) has recently woken. He hears the strident cry of the glazier, which could sound like what Mainzer describes in this passage, following the one I quoted earlier that ended with the musical score:

> I will cite another [glazier] that can be regarded as a rarity of the species, and whose cry is worthy of being consigned to the page, to be transmitted to our descendants. This one ordinarily haunts the elegant neighborhoods of the Chaussée d'Antin. At the end of *Au vitrier!* he ascends the scale by quarter-tones, like on a violin string or piano, and once he is thus very high on the scale, his cry transforms into a whistle so shrill, so piercing, that it cuts the air like a diamond cuts a window pane. Perhaps he has imagined this bizarre whistling as a symbol of his trade; or, perhaps it gives him the magic power to shake and shatter the panes he mended the previous day, just as the organ's strong vibrations can sometimes break cathedrals' stained glass windows.[70]

Here again Mainzer evokes preservationism and musical notation, traits that should be familiar to the reader. It is particularly significant that the passage attributes a disturbing shrillness and a subversive violence to the glazier, both maker and breaker of windows.[71]

The Baudelairean narrator's violence in "Le Mauvais Vitrier" is not then as random as it first appears. The poem literalizes satanic undercurrents already present in Houssaye's text and in the discourse on the glazier's cry. The stridency of the cry and the flights of fancy and fear that it elicits are themselves topoi of the literature. Even though Baudelaire borrows common topoi, he rejects the clichéd sentimentalism of Houssaye and exposes social hypocrisies in "Le Mauvais Vitrier," as he does in other poems such as "Les Yeux des pauvres" ("The Eyes of the Poor") and "La Fausse Monnaie" ("The Counterfeit Coin"). Quoting the glazier in a supposedly realistic mode as Houssaye did, would indeed not nearly be as effective as evoking the connotations of the cry in the collective imagination and unleashing them in the poem.

The interpretation I am proposing relies on the cry's uncontainable effects. The pure vocality of the cry cuts through rhetoric and would appear to reach outside the text (though as I indicated the cry signals to other discourses on the glazier, as a historical figure, literary type, and collective fantasy). In Baudelaire's poem, however, no other characters hear the cry, which becomes subsumed in the actions of the narrator ("Une action d'éclat" [a brilliant action]) and the glazier ("un bruit éclatant" [a brilliant sound]).

A reading of "Le Mauvais Vitrier" as a self-contained narrative accounts well for the playful self-reflexivity of the poem. The speaker's actions are determined by the very words he uses to describe his motivation. Even before the glazier arrives on the scene, an irresistible force pushes him to commit a "brilliant action."[72] The poem artfully turns words and puns into actions.[73] In a parodic gesture, Baudelaire substitutes Houssaye's "verre" with a "pot" ("prendre un pot," "prendre un verre" are informal expressions meaning "to have a drink"), which he uses quite differently, but both encounters end with an aggravation of the glazier's destitution. The flowerpot that the narrator throws down on the glazier, as Culler observes, also recalls Poe's and Baudelaire's own "flowers of evil." The pun on the homonyms "verre"/"vers" (glass/verses) draws an analogy between the glazier and the poet "who refuses to give his readers a rose-tinted view of reality" and who rebuffs their expectations of "pretty glosses" rather than "evocations of reality."[74] Although "Le Mauvais Vitrier" does exhibit the self-reflexivity that has been ascribed to it, while referring punningly to its literary intertexts (Poe, Houssaye), this interpretation seems to silence unduly the poem's coming to terms with urban noise, a reality that breaks through throughout *Le Spleen de Paris* (as it already had in *Les Fleurs du mal*[75]) and resounds beyond it, in much of the "street poetry" that was inspired by Baudelaire.

The differences between Houssaye's euphonious glazier's song and Baudelaire's embrace of strident dissonance are evidence of his modernist attention to noise. Baudelaire introduces discordant breaks into the harmonious weave of the lyric.[76] Many prose poems pursue the modernist attention to noise as disruption of the ideal. In "La Chambre double" (The Double Room), the disruption to reverie sounds striking and visceral, like a heavy blow of a pickax in the stomach. In "Une mort héroïque" (A Heroic Death), a whistle interrupts the artist's enthralling performance. The prose poem "Le Crépuscule du soir" (Twilight) inextricably entangles harmony and discordance, or "ululation," both human and inhuman, familiar and monstrous, originating above and below; as a result, oxymoronically, harmony sounds dismal and infernal. In this way, Baudelaire's ironic prose poetry avoids falling victim to its own rhetoric of social hypocrisy as Houssaye's does.

What does dissonance mean in this context? In Baudelaire's poetry, dissonance and harmony are indissolubly bound.[77] Noise erupts in the prose poetry to disrupt the pathos and sentimentalism (sometimes even the optimism) that promote the resolution of conflicts and the fulfillment of expectations. Rather than harmonize noise by translating it into "song" or refrain as Houssaye did, Baudelaire breaks the melodic line by forestalling idealization with strident interruptions. There is no attempt in Baudelaire's poem to assimilate the cry into the knowable and the repeatable; in fact, Baudelaire ends "Le Mauvais Vitrier" with a tension between the spontaneous fury of the speaker's cry and the appeal to an aesthetic ideal, "la vie en beau," in such a way as to draw attention to the incompatibility of the dissonance of the cry and the harmonizing impulse of the urban picturesque. In Baudelaire's prose poetry, chance urban encounters, unexplained demonic impulses, lexical uncertainty, and especially irony create the "noise" that makes the poetry disturbing, hence discordant.[78] The poet seeks to jar the reader by transitioning between emotional states and mixing things up as it were: "Le mélange du grotesque et du tragique est agréable à l'esprit comme les discordances aux oreilles blasées" (The mix of grotesque and tragic appeals to the mind as do discordances to blasé ears).[79] Indeed, escape to a contemplative state is always already a dead end in Baudelaire's poetic universe, because of the recognized imperative to stay grounded and come to grips with street noise.[80] This willingness to hear the dissonance of the outside world would have a lasting impact on the way Baudelaire's followers, from Charles Cros and Jean Richepin to Jules Laforgue, Joris Karl Huysmans, and Stéphane Mallarmé, represented the clamor of the streets and noisy tradespeople in their poetry.

CHAPTER 5

"Cry Louder, Street Crier"
Peddling Poetry and the Avant-Garde

Criez plus fort, crieurs des rues;
Fouettez vos fouets; geignez, cochers!
À travers l'espace lâchez
Toutes vos phrases incongrues!

· ·

Que ton baume tourbillonnant
Enivre et souffle, en bourdonnant,
Ma pauvre Pensée, et ne laisse
Jamais le temps de m'envahir
Aux spleens qui viennent m'assaillir.

Cry louder, street crier;
Whip your whips; groan, coachmen!
Unleash across space
All your incongruous phrases!

· ·

Let your whirling balm
Blow and intoxicate, buzzing,
My poor Thoughts, and never
Give time to invade me
To the spleens that assail me.

—"Le Bruit," Georges Lorin

"Le Bruit" by the avant-garde poet Georges Lorin records the intensity of city noise in Paris where loud coachmen, carts, animals, and street musicians assail the flâneur-poet, but instead of toning down this clamor to render the city as harmonious concert, Lorin, following Charles Baudelaire, begs street criers to shout louder so that they may deafen him, make his head spin, and assuage his spleen. Street noise is reclaimed by these poets as an antidote to bourgeois complacency and as a critique of the sonic relations that condemn noxious behavior. Throughout this book, we have heard how street noise strained the relationship between the lower classes, including seasonal workers and peddlers, and those in the central bourgeois neighborhoods expecting a quieter lifestyle. Myths about the sonic relations among social classes had been crystallized in the tradition of the *Cris de Paris* that classified street types such as glaziers; poets and artists could recycle this familiar material to reaffirm or to challenge different ways of listening. Noise in the poems discussed in this chapter signals the alarming social question of the era, what to do about the poor and specifically the intrusiveness of their noise, which threatens the sensitive bourgeois ear. Noisy peddlers practice a declining trade that endears them to nostalgists, but their resilience under modern capitalism and their resistance to the market forces armed against them explains why they fascinate poets. For these reasons, poets often identified with peddlers, who like them exercised a marginalized trade and used street noise artfully to try to capture the attention of bourgeois consumers. Because the pressures of the market economy on poets and itinerant tradesmen are commensurate, poetry about peddling addresses relationships of scale and the commercialization of the word through the development of the mass market press.

This chapter follows representations of peddlers from Baudelaire to François Coppée, Charles Cros, and Jean Richepin, and finally to symbolists such as Stéphane Mallarmé and Joris Karl Huysmans. It considers whether they perceived the city-as-concert as harmonious or dissonant by analyzing the extent to which their poems reflect or inflect the discourse on the picturesque. Poetry about peddlers incorporates the vitality of street noise, the formal experimentation of popular song, and the aural acuity of flâneur-writing into the art of the establishment or the avant-garde. Such mixing of high and low registers, already the purview of panoramic literature, is especially salient when Mallarmé's *Chansons bas* are read alongside Jean-François Raffaëlli's illustrations of types in the tradition of the *Cris de Paris*. The parodic poetry of Cros and Richepin, written in reaction to Coppée's moralizing sentimental *dizain*, in a way sets the stage for Mallarmé's "lowly songs."

Morality and Parody in Poems on Peddlers by Coppée, Cros, and Richepin

François Coppée, who like Arsène Houssaye garnered success early and joined the Académie Française in 1884, dedicated a number of poems to the small-scale tradesmen, workers, and petits-bourgeois living modestly on the margins of Parisian society. A famous—or infamous—poem from *Les Humbles* (1872) titled "Le Petit Épicier de Montrouge," for instance, tells the petty life of a shop-keeper, in the grand style of alexandrine rhymed couplets. Like many naturalists, Coppée depicted the lower classes. He favored the outlying area around Paris, the zone beyond the fortifications not subject to urban renewal, where the popular classes had moved when Haussmannization forced them out of the city center (for example in the southeast of Paris). Coppée's poetry, however, idealizes the *banlieue* as an escape from Paris rather than as the ghetto it was.[1] The poet-flâneur takes the reader on an imaginary stroll through the streets in *Promenades et Intérieurs*, a series of trite scenes written in pared-down, virtually prosaic alexandrine verse. Coppée shared with the Parnassian poets, such as Banville and Houssaye, an appreciation of the constraints of finely tuned verse, but unlike them he innovated by depoeticizing his verse, so that he can be said to emulate in poetry the naturalist novelist Émile Zola. Like snapshots and sound bites, the street scenes that embody the aesthetic of the fragment are written in *dizain*, the ten-line form revived by Coppée.[2] Consider for example this *dizain* (no. 23) that describes a clichéd vignette of a *grisette* singing at her window,[3] a young poor, but generous woman who gives a coin to the barrel organ player when she hears him in the street below:

> De la rue on entend sa plaintive chanson.
> Pâle et rousse, le teint plein de taches de son,
> Elle coud, de profil, assise à sa fenêtre.
> Très-sage et sachant bien qu'elle est laide peut-être,
> Elle a son dé d'argent pour unique bijou.
> Sa chambre est nue, avec des meubles d'acajou.
> Elle gagne deux francs, fait de la lingerie
> Et jette un sou quand vient l'orgue de Barbarie.
> Tous les voisins lui font leur bonjour le plus gai
> Qui leur vaut son petit sourire fatigué.

> From the street, one hears her plaintive song.
> A pale red-haired girl, a face full of freckles,
> she sits sideways at the window sowing.
> Well-mannered, she knows she may be unattractive.
> A silver thimble is her only jewel.
> Her room is bare with a few mahogany pieces.
> She earns two francs, sowing,
> and throws a penny when the organ-grinder comes by.
> All her neighbors happily bid her good day,
> thus earning her little weary smile.[4]

Coppée's poem shares Houssaye's sentimentalist approach to working-class types. Both stress the pathetic qualities of the "plaintive song," and neither attempts to jar the readers/listeners out of their complacency. The woman's generosity toward the organ-grinder masks any social animosity toward the type and the intrusiveness of street music. By referring to her charitable gesture, the poem represents the peddler as a beggar in need of assistance, while at the same time promoting a harmonious view of society in which everyone knows their place. The rhyme "gai/fatigué" aptly captures the resignation of the well-mannered, but weary *grisette*. Whereas Baudelaire's flâneur was fascinated by the city's discordances, Coppée's stroller seeks to make unfamiliar neighborhood sounds familiar.[5]

Coppée was parodied by a group of younger nonconformist poets who mocked his clichéd scenes and his appeal to bourgeois sentimentalism or self-satisfaction and who despised his success. This resentment was later exacerbated when Coppée, a member of the jury, rejected their submissions to the third *Parnasse contemporain*. Coppée had been one of the favorite targets of a group centered on Verlaine called the "Vilains Bonshommes" or Naughty Fellows in the early 1870s. One of these naughty fellows, Arthur Rimbaud, included a parodic sonnet titled "Paris" in the group's *Album zutique*, formed of a polyphonic sequence of proper names, slogans, street signs, and what we might call "sound bites," though none are properly street cries.[6] Seeking to mock the third *Parnasse contemporain*, these bohemians regrouped later in 1876. Gathered around Nina de Villard, they included, among others, Charles Cros and Jean Richepin, and excelled at parody. Cros makes extensive use of syncopated language, popular references (including to peddlers), repetition, and song, in the second edition of *Le Coffret de santal* (1879), which incorporated his contributions to the collective *Dixains réalistes par divers auteurs* written in Nina de Villard's salon.[7] Cros had an excellent ear for parody and word play; accordingly, a fellow avant-gardist and member of the Hydropathes, Georges Lorin, dedicated a poem entitled "Le Bruit" to Cros.[8] It is not surprising that such an audiophile would also be the inventor of sound recording. Incidentally, at roughly the same time as the publication of *Dixains réalistes*, he submitted a scientific essay on the "Procedure to Record and Reproduce Phenomena Perceived by the Ear" to the Academy of Sciences.[9] Cros-the-inventor and Cros-the-poet share an interest in recording sound. These preoccupations suggest that we read his poems on street cries as attempts to record street noise and, more broadly, as part of the cultural obsession with the preservation and capture of lost sounds evident in the work of Fournel, Mainzer, and Bertall, as well as of Nadar and Martinville.

In one of the realist *dizains* in *Coffret de santal* titled "Jours d'épreuve," ironically referring to the poet's tribulations, Cros mocks Coppée's sentimentally trite musings and street scenes:

> Jadis je logeais haut, tout contre la gouttière:
> Tapi souvent à ma fenêtre en tabatière,
> Rêvant à ma misère, à tant d'affronts subis,
> J'écoutais les marchands de légumes, d'habits:
> Et les tuyaux des toits, chefs-d'œuvre des fumistes,
> Rayaient de noir le fond de mes grands yeux si tristes.
> J'entendais quelquefois un doux bruit de grelots,
> Et me penchant, j'aimais ce gros homme en sabots
> Qui se hâtait pour vendre aux phthysiques jeunesses
> La consolation du tiède lait d'ânesses.

> Long ago I lived up high, right up against the gutters:
> Often nestled in my bay window,
> Dreaming of my miserable state, of so many insults suffered,
> I listened to the vegetable sellers, the old-clothes–men:
> And the pipes in the roofs, those masterpieces of chimney sweeps,
> Streaked the depths of my big sad eyes with black.
> I would sometimes hear the soft noise of a bell,
> And leaning over, I loved that big fat man in clogs
> That hastened to sell to phthisic youths
> The consolation of warm donkey's milk.[10]

Cros's speaker listens to a commonplace street scene heard from an open garret window: he evokes the trope of street cries soaring above the streets to be heard by working-class or bohemian inhabitants of the top floors. The poem records the lasting power of sound memory as he remembers the cries of the old-clothes–man, the costermonger, and the milkman. He hears the sound of provincial vigor in the milkman's wooden *sabots* or clogs and the ringing of his *grelots* or bells (though peddlers' instruments were repeatedly targeted by city ordinance[11]). Enjambment heightens the fast-paced beat of the clogs of the heavy-set vendor hastening to sell donkey's milk as the syntax and lack of punctuation in the last three lines of verse straddle the line-limits. Donkey's as opposed to cow's milk was prescribed to consumptives (phthisics) or youth weakened by debauchery as Louis-Sébastien Mercier records in *Tableau de Paris*.[12] Mainzer also poked fun at the practice of circulating the jenny-ass to sick people throughout Paris in fashionable carriages marked with false advertising: "Lait assaini d'ânesses nourries aux carottes" (Sanitized Milk of Carrot-Fed Donkeys).[13] At first, it seems as if Cros's poem is a record of the soundscapes of peddling in the manner of the urban picturesque; yet, close attention to the poem's language reveals it to be a parody of literary guidebooks and Coppée's flâneur-writing.

Cros tweaks the imagery to avoid the nostalgia that such sound memories frequently nourish, by drawing attention to the excessive sentimentality of the speaker whose plight is exaggerated in the title "Jours d'épreuve." The speaker, who even dreams of his own misery, has big sad eyes that are streaked with black from the chimney soot, just like those of the abused nineteenth-century child par excellence, the *ramoneur* or chimney sweep. He debunks this last cliché with the humorous rhyme *fumistes/tristes*, where "fumiste" refers literally to a chimney engineer (a step up from *ramoneur*), and figuratively to a clown, prankster, or bohemian writer who enjoys mystification and seeks to disconcert readers. Those sad eyes are mercilessly mocked when we think of them as the masterful work of a *fumiste*. Fumisme is a type of parodic humor and iconoclasm developed by nineteenth-century avant-garde poets working in collaboration, including the groups that produced the *Album zutique* (1871) and the *Dixains réalistes* (1876), as well as groups such as the Hydropathes and the Chat Noir cabaret.[14] These bohemian groups were on the margins of the literary establishment and discounted by writers seeking recognition among the naturalists, the symbolists, or the academy. The *fumistes* sought to deride and transgress bourgeois values and aesthetic movements (hence the *Dixains*'s subversion of Coppée and the Parnassian school) through word play, pastiche, and parody, both in print (poetry and journals) and in cabaret performances. *Fumisme* prefigures the black humor of dada and surrealism, but it also harks back to the ribaldry and irreverent laughter of the Middle Ages; many *fumistes*, for instance, celebrated Rabelais, Villon, and what they coined "l'esprit gaulois" or Gallic spirit in cabaret performances, journals, and poems.[15] To further undermine the over-romanticizing sounds, "Jours d'épreuve" introduces pedestrian language (*gouttière, tabatière, sabots*) that brings down to earth the speaker perched up high.[16] The poverty-stricken poet who listens to vendors cry out merchandise he cannot perhaps afford to buy recalls the posture of the thirteenth-century author of "Les Crieries de Paris." In his poem that set the model of the genre, Guillaume de la Villeneuve transposes the cacophony of cries advertising things he cannot afford, but he does so with an ear for the lowbrow irreverent humor that characterizes "l'esprit gaulois."[17] Cros's *dizain*, then, functions on several different levels as a rejoinder to the tradition of word play and badinage dating back to Villeneuve, as well as a *fumisterie* and rich parody of Coppée's sentimental representation of the *banlieue*.

In "Morale," a loose parody of Coppée's "Noces et Festins," the speaker captures the "ter lin tin tin" of the *marchand de coco* through onomatopoeia:

Sur des chevaux de bois enfiler des anneaux,
Regarder un caniche expert aux dominos,
Essayer de gagner une oie avec des boules,
Respirer la poussière et la sueur des foules,
Boire du coco tiède au gobelet d'étain
De ce marchand miteux qui fait ter lin tin tin,
Rentrer se coucher seul, à la fin de la foire,
Dormir tranquillement en attendant la gloire
Dans un lit frais l'été, mais, l'hiver, bien chauffé,
Tout cela vaut bien mieux que d'aller au café.

To thread rings astride wooden horses,
To watch a dog play dominos,
To try to win a goose at a game of *boules*,
To breathe the dust and the sweat of the crowds,
To drink warm *coco* from the tin cup
Of a shabby merchant who says *ter lin tin tin*,
To return home to sleep alone, at the end of the fair,
To sleep peacefully awaiting fame,
In a fresh bed in summer and in winter a nice warm one,
All this is worth much more than going to the coffee-shop.[18]

Like "Jours d'épreuve," "Morale" captures the sound of the coco-vendor who rang a bell and dispensed a lemon-licorice flavored beverage into a tin cup from a silver tap on a canister he carried on his back. The type is immortalized in countless literary guidebooks, such as *Paris et les Parisiens au XIXe siècle*. There, Paul de Musset remarks upon the vendor's inability to compete with new beverages and imported tastes: "with his white apron, his fountain on his back, this modest cupbearer from the people enlivened summer fairs, promenades, and avenues with the sound of his bell. But already, on the Quay of the Tuileries, in the summer, one can see mobile icehouses with cold beverages. Soon we will have as they do in Florence lemonade shaken for one sou a glass, sorbets, and ice creams for two sous. Licorice in luke-warm water, despite it being a healthy and cough-suppressing drink, will not sustain the competition."[19] Or to quote Élie Frébault's memories apropos the coco-vendor from *Les Industriels du macadam*: "You were for me a last relic of the good old days . . . and I feel the gentle sympathy for your memory that good souls feel for races that disappear."[20] Although "Morale" documents the same piddling subject as literary guidebooks do, their goals in evoking street cries differ.

Far from indulging wholeheartedly in the nostalgia that feeds Frébault's and Musset's memories, Cros's poem evokes a dreamscape[21] of the fair to better debunk the cliché. A closer look at the poem's language helps us understand how parody introduces dissonance into the familiar tune, not by stressing the stridency of the cry as did Baudelaire, but by poking fun at the sentimentalism that seeks to assimilate the peddler into the familiar city-as-concert. The sound of the coco-vendor, accentuated by enjambment and onomatopoeia, figures prominently as a mnemonic trigger, but the suspension of disbelief is curtailed suddenly by the last lines. The rhyme "gloire/foire" reveals the speaker's disingenuousness: what kind of lasting fame can be gained without work? And if fame is the goal, what contrast exists between flitting away the hours at the fair or at the coffee shop? Setting this issue aside, I might add that the poem makes interesting use of nonlexical onomatopoeia (to borrow Derek Attridge's term[22]) to record or transpose the sound of the coco-vendor's cry. Onomatopoeia is more common in song-forms, but relatively rare in standard nineteenth-century French poetry; some of the more salient examples appear later in Jules Laforgue's *Les Complaintes* (1885) or in Stéphane Mallarmé's translation of E. A. Poe's "The Bells" (1888)—as well as in the early modern examples of Guillaume de la Villeneuve's and Clément Janequin's *Cris de Paris*. We hear in "ter lin tin tin" an echo of the shrill, nasal cry of the street vendor, the very type of high-pitched sound Joseph Mainzer described on numerous occasions in his essays in *Les Français peints par eux-mêmes*. We might also hear the clank of glasses, the tinkling of bells, or the refrain of a drinking song. The poem may imitate the "ter lin tin tin" as heard by (real) nineteenth-century Parisians, but at the same time, aided by the rhyme "étain/tin," the reader's attention is returned to the sounds on the page. Onomatopoeia as a figure ironically throws out of tune what would be a familiar melodic line to readers of literary guidebooks: did the cry really sound like the nonsensical "ter lin tin tin"?

Another participant in the *Dixains réalistes* with Cros and fellow member of the avant-garde literary club of the Hydropathes, Jean Richepin sought inspiration in the language of the popular classes, notably that of peddlers. Mixing high and low struck a dissonant note that would discomfort the smug bourgeoisie, in a way that recalled Baudelaire's aphorism in *Fusées*: "The mix of grotesque and tragic appeals to the mind as do discordances to blasé ears."[23] Richepin shares with Cros a desire to shock the bourgeoisie. A classically trained but colorful rebellious bohemian writer, Richepin fashioned himself after the wayward medieval poet François Villon. Richepin's work draws on the verve of popular language and culture to lambast the bourgeoisie's complacency toward poverty.[24] One of the most original features of *La Chanson des gueux* is that, unlike Houssaye's "La Chanson du vitrier" or Hugo's "Le Mendiant," Richepin writes in the voice of peddlers using *argot* or slang, cries, and songs. The wretchedness and destitution of those who live on the underside of the City of Light described in *La Chanson des gueux* (1876) so scandalized the establishment of the Third Republic that Richepin, like Baudelaire before him, was put on trial for indecency.[25] After spending one month in jail and paying a hefty fine, the modern Villon and his beggars or *gueux* were famous. The section "Les Quatre Saisons" of the collection includes several poems about the seasonal migration of street criers to the big cities, including the violet seller in "Achetez mes belles violettes," the chickweed vendor in "Du mouron pour les p'tits oiseaux," and the organ-grinder in "Variations du printemps sur l'orgue de Barbarie" and its complement "Variations d'automne sur l'orgue de Barbarie." This section recreates, for the reader-turned-flâneur, the experience of being barraged with street cries while on a stroll through the markets or streets. We can wonder, then, how will the reader-flâneur respond: with fascination or revulsion, or with ironic distance or pathetic identification? By way of an answer, consider that among Richepin's choice of types, we find mostly the poorest among street vendors, those for whom the trades were a cover for mendicancy or sometimes prostitution; the women who picked pimpernel or violets in the early morning hours on the rural outskirts of Paris, beyond Montmartre to the north, or in the south Hauts-de-Seine near Sceaux and Clamart, and sold them on the streets for one *sou* could hardly make a fortune.[26] Richepin however depicts the *marchande de mourons* as a tired but diligent and honest worker, who is an old woman (not a prostitute) responsible for two grandchildren. This poem, like "Achetez mes belles violettes," cites the peddler's cry, in this case, "Du mouron pour les p'tits oiseaux," as a refrain, thus revisiting some of the techniques in Houssaye's "La Chanson du vitrier." The poem narrates the day's work of the *marchande de mourons* from her own point of view, resorting to free indirect discourse to render her motivational mantra, "Un sou par-là, deux sous par-ci!" While Richepin's attempt to give the subaltern peddler a voice distinguishes his poetry among texts exclusively narrated from a bourgeois standpoint, the poet's emphasis on feelings of sympathy and sadness betray his paternalism. His pathos mars his undertaking.

As such, Richepin's songs are much more sentimental and far less parodic than Cros's *dizains*. Yet, by loosening the parodic knot, tugging at heartstrings, and flaunting his disregard for the establishment, Richepin achieved wide popular appeal, whereas Cros's finely tuned literary prank, conceived at least initially in spite against the Parnassian school, circulated in a small circle of initiates. Richepin's "Le Marchand de coco" uses onomatopoeia ("drelin din din") as does Cros's *dizain* "Morale," but the jarring effect achieved by Cros is missed by Richepin. Whereas Cros self-consciously treats the cry as a cliché so as to short-circuit any affect, Richepin repeatedly quotes variations on the familiar coco-vendor's cry "À la fraîche! À la glace! Qui veut boire?" Nobody cares to partake of the vendor's drink, and even the speaker concedes that it is not that tempting. Richepin's poem, narrated in the scratchy voice of the weary coco-vendor, elicits our pity at the signs of the trade's waning vitality. Despite its purported decline, there was a real craze for this street type at this time.[27] Maupassant for instance published "Coco, coco, coco frais!" in 1878,[28] and in 1881 Deransart, whose "Qui qu'a vu Coco dans l'Trocadéro" was sung by Coco Chanel, wrote "Les Cris de la rue" that featured the *marchand d'habits* and the *ramoneur*.[29] Richepin and the members of his lively bohemian circle sought to counter the placidity of the Parnassians and reconnect with the vitality of popular culture. The interest in the common people that these poets shared with naturalist writers explains why they turned to the picturesque imagery and folkloric rhythms of street types for inspiration. Yet, contrary to writers of literary guidebooks, Cros and Richepin heard what was jarring about peddlers' vocalizations. In the wake of Baudelaire, they used these sounds in their poems to discomfort bourgeois blaséd ears and to draw attention to the dissonance of the sonic relations that the urban picturesque implicitly harmonizes.

Mallarmé Sings Low, with Raffaëlli on Bass

Combining the tradition of the Baudelairean analogy with the parodic playfulness of Richepin and Cros, the symbolist Stéphane Mallarmé also wrote poems known as "Chansons bas" that explicitly draw on the tradition of the *Cris de Paris*. Mallarmé had evoked street music and street performers in two early prose poems dedicated to Baudelaire. Both develop the analogy between poet and street performer, or between the lofty transcendence of poetic language and the pedestrianism of the everyday, common in Baudelaire and in Théodore de Banville. In "Plainte d'automne" (Autumn Lament), a sorrowful narrator listens to an organ of Barbary through the open window, but, unlike Coppée's grisette in Dizain no. 23, he does not give him a coin. Rather, the outdated air he hears crystallizes past memories and melancholic thoughts. A child street singer in "Pauvre Enfant pâle" (Poor Pale Child) shouts his head off, literally. "Pourquoi crier à tue-tête dans la rue ta chanson aiguë et insolente?" ("Why do you bawl out your sharp, cheeky songs in the street at the top of your lungs?"), asks the narrator; crying out at the top of his lungs does not win the street-child handouts from almsgivers putatively located on the upper floors, but rather "they" turn him into a criminal who will be decapitated (hence, the pun "crier à tue-tête," literally meaning "to cry your head off").[30] The unexplained adversarial relationship between the narrator and the singer recalls that in "Le Mauvais Vitrier." While "Plainte d'automne" toys with the sentimental, "Pauvre Enfant pâle" more cynically links street singers and criminality, raising—or ironically exposing—the specter of (self-serving) bourgeois fears of vagrancy and immigration.[31]

Mallarmé wrote two sonnets and six quatrains at the behest of Jean-François Raffaëlli to accompany the artist's illustrations of peddlers for the seventh installment of *Les Types de Paris*, an illustrated album of tradesmen published in ten installments in the newspaper *Le Figaro* in 1889. The centennial of the French Revolution and the World's Fair of 1900 renewed interest in the street culture of Old Paris[32] and ushered in a wave of books on the subject of street criers, including Victor Fournel's *Les Cris de Paris, types et physiognomies d'autrefois*, Abbé Dufour's *Lettres d'un Sicilien,* and Albert Arnal's *Paris qui crie*. Known for his portraits, drawings, and book illustrations, Raffaëlli conceived the project for which he drafted the types in color engravings and then solicited the participation of naturalist writers such as Alphonse Daudet, Émile Zola, Guy de Maupassant, Octave Mirbeau, and others. Raffaëlli's art combines observation with moral reflection on a "neglected class of individuals,"[33] and accordingly, his aesthetic is best understood as an extension of the urban picturesque. Raffaëlli pursues the art of flânerie as developed by Balzac and Fournel—sensual observation followed by analysis and introspection—but, like Coppée, he strolled in the impoverished suburbs, not the elegant boulevards. As Arsène Alexandre suggests, the term "picturesque moralist" that Baudelaire applies to Constantin Guys, could just as well apply to Raffaëlli.[34] The artist's work raises questions about just how far he departed from the iconography of mid-century realism and the picturesque.[35]

Despite Raffaëlli's relationship to the urban picturesque, he is often linked to impressionism. In his review of the fifth impressionist exhibition, "L'exposition des indépendants en 1880," Huysmans praised the newcomer Raffaëlli's "correct painting style, terribly savant despite its frank allure."[36] Contemporary reviewers commented on his precision; "among the impressionists, Raffaëlli is what we call a great finisher [*finisseur*]. He treats every detail with care, touches up, and retouches constantly."[37] Raffaëlli was well received at the exhibition, as Huysmans's positive assessment suggests, despite unanimous claims that his work was not really impressionist. Raffaëlli was simply at the right place at the right time.[38] Certainly Mallarmé, who had a close relationship with Édouard Manet and several impressionist artists, seems to have considered Raffaëlli among the leading members of this circle.[39] Like other impressionists, Raffaëlli demonstrated an interest in collaboration between artists and writers, as can be seen in his illustrated editions of *Croquis parisiens*, *The Raven*, *L'Après-midi d'un faune,* and *Le Tiroir de laque*.

To briefly assess how Raffaëlli diverged from the impressionist aesthetic, it is helpful to compare his treatment of the chestnut vendor (figure 18), with a

Figure 18. Jean-François Raffaëlli, *Le Marchand de marrons parisien* in *Croquis parisiens*, 1880, etching facing, p. 49. Reprinted by permission of the Bibliothèque nationale de France, Paris.

sketch of the same topic by Henri de Toulouse-Lautrec, who is better known for his treatment of cabaret stars and dancers rather than street types (figure 19). Raffaëlli's *Le Marchand de marrons* accompanies a poem on the same subject by Huysmans that appeared in *Croquis parisiens* (1880). Raffaëlli represents the vendor's wrinkled face, eyes, and clothing up close and in detail. Nestled in a doorframe, the merchant, on the alert for customers, appears worried that he may not make a day's wage. His hand is also prominent, suggesting the heat

Figure 19. Henri de Toulouse-Lautrec, *Le Marchand de marrons,* ca. 1897, crayon lithograph in black with scraper on white gray wove paper, sheet: 14 7/16 × 10 7/8 in.; 36.6713 × 27.6225 cm; image: 10 5/8 × 7 9/16 in. Courtesy of Smith College Museum of Art, Northampton, Massachusetts. Gift of Oriole Ferb Feshbach and Peter Farb.

of the chestnut warmer that prevents frostbite. Indeed, Huysmans's poem describes scurrying passersby who seek shelter from cold weather. In contrast, Toulouse-Lautrec sketches the chestnut vendor from the back so that his face, his identity even, remains unknown. The customers around him are equally ghostly. Behind the vendor, on the right of the image, a working-class man and a girl stand idle. Coming toward us, at left of the image, a well-dressed woman with a bulldog strides past the vendor, without stopping to buy chestnuts. Her lanky figure and feather-topped hat recall Toulouse-Lautrec's images of the famous *cancan* dancer Jane Avril, as seen for instance in the poster *Divan Japonais* (1892–93). Her angular jacket clashes with the vendor's rounded back. The figures' shadows extend the lines of the indistinct buildings, drawing attention to the formal arrangement of the work. In the foreground, a bulldog rather comically anchors the street scene.[40] Whereas Toulouse-Lautrec drafts the fleeting encounter with detachment, Raffaëlli emphasizes the *marchand de marrons*'s miserable situation in a poignant portrait. Similarly, some of the other works exhibited at the fifth impressionist exhibition, with titles such as "Chiffonnier éreinté" or "Balayeur souffrant du froid" overtly elicit pathos. In his review, Armand Silvestre went so far as to compare Raffaëlli's "touching" street scenes to Coppée's naturalist poetry: "*Balayeur souffrant du froid* or *Street Sweeper Suffering from the Cold* is as touching as one of François Coppée's Parisian elegies. There's a poet in Mr. Raffaëlli, beside a painter extraordinarily able to convey detail."[41]

The Raffaëlli/Mallarmé collaboration manifests the alliance of visual and textual that is traditional in the iconography of the *Cris de Paris*. In 1888, when Raffaëlli undertook to illustrate *Les Types de Paris*, he asked Mallarmé to send him some short poems to complement his drawings. Mallarmé's eight light-hearted and humorous poems are assembled under the heading "Chansons bas." The titles of these five quatrains are "Le Marchand d'ail et d'oignons," "Le Cantonnier," "Le Crieur d'imprimés," "La Femme de l'ouvrier," and "La Marchande d'habits." A sixth quatrain, "Le Vitrier," was composed but left out of Raffaëlli's book. Two sonnets complete the series: "Le Savetier" and "La Marchande d'herbes aromatiques."[42] I quote from Raffaëlli's August 23, 1888, letter:

> L'article s'appell*erait* "Petites gens de la Rue" ou quelque chose d'approchant.—Si vous pouviez choisir pour ces quelques vers la délicieuse petite tournure que vous avez employée dans tant d'invitations, adresses, etc., cela ferait un petit bijou. . . .

> The article would be called "Small-Scale Street Vendors" or something like it.—If you could choose for these few verses the delicious turn that you employed with many of your invitations, addresses, etc. . . . that would be a gem. . . .[43]

Mallarmé had only "tiny rough sketches" of the drawings in hand when he wrote most of the poems, and two served as inspiration for the sketches rather than the reverse.[44] Most of the verses do not correspond to the scenes in the drawing. In Raffaëlli's 1888 letter, he explains the terms of the collaboration:

> Je ne vous demande pas de faire des vers SUR mes dessins, mais à côté, et ce sont vos vers que mes dessins ENCADRERONT.

I am not asking that you write verses ABOUT my drawings, but on the side, and your verses will be FRAMED by my drawings. [45]

Raffaëlli did not intend that Mallarmé's verses interpret the drawings, but rather supplement them—in fact, his main concern appears to have been layout, as he wanted to make one full page of each type and its accompanying text. The resulting collaboration updates the traditional illustrations of the *Cris de Paris*, containing type and caption. In this case, however, the relationship between text and image is discordant as Raffaëlli's pathos strikes a different chord than Mallarmé's bathos. [46]

Raffaëlli and Mallarmé's collaboration invites verbal and visual interplay within the image/text pairing in the *Cris de Paris* genre, but also within the discourse of the picturesque. The format in this installment as compared with the other units is quite distinctive. Each of the sketches contains a title in red ink. The two works in color—the lavender seller and the old-clothes–woman—attest to Raffaëlli's innovations in color engraving. [47] Let us consider for instance Raffaëlli's illustration of the *marchande d'habits*, a female peddler who sold old clothes (figure 21). Among the quatrains, only this one was not based on a drawing supplied by Raffaëlli; rather the artist made the image after the poem's composition. [48] The image refers to narratives about the popular type prevalent in panoramic literature. In fact, Raffaëlli's image is strikingly similar to the *marchand d'habits* by Jean Louis Ernest Meissonier accompanying Mainzer's essay in *Les Français peints par eux-mêmes*. [49] Both show a figure in a three-quarter pose holding out a hat and looking up and out of the image frame, presumably at an unseen buyer located in a garret. Raffaëlli scrupulously follows the conventions of the *Cris de Paris* genre that we saw deployed in the medieval woodcut and in prints by eighteenth-century engravers (figure 3 and figure 5). Raffaëlli's peddler in this image is isolated from the context of her labor; no customers are represented. She is identified only by the accessories of her trade—in this case, a man's umbrella, hat, and coat. [50] These accessories are not chosen randomly; on the contrary, they signify required traits of the bourgeois man, namely respectability, foresight, and caution, which the *marchande* will gladly sell you if you lack them. The strength of the *marchande* is visible in her posture (she stands legs apart) and in the way she forcefully holds out the hat and umbrella. Her precisely drawn face is youthful and thoughtful, unlike the dour expression in Bertall's caricature (figure 20). The visible strokes, which give the image of the *marchande d'habits* a dynamic quality, attest to Raffaëlli's impressionism, but the colors, blue, white, and red may be less realistic than symbolic of the nationalist force Raffaëlli ascribes to these Parisian types. The precision of the detail, the woman's pensive, serious expression make it clear

Figure 20. Bertall, *Une marchande à la toilette, Le Diable à Paris: Paris et les Parisiens à la plume et au crayon*, 1868, 3:114. Courtesy of McGill University Library, Rare Books and Special Collection, Montreal.

that the type is not a caricature and hence cannot be interpreted as an illustration of Mallarmé's comic scene. The image might even recall the whole "song of misery" Louisa Siefert evoked in her sonnet "Marchand d'habit!" There is an intimacy in Raffaëlli's image of the old-clothes–woman, as well as a narrativity (by way of its realist iconography) that are at odds with Mallarmé's ironic verses:

Figure 21. Jean-François Raffaëlli, Stéphane Mallarmé, *La Marchande d'habits, Les Types de Paris*, 1889. Courtesy of Special Collections, University of Miami Libraries, Coral Gables, Florida.

Le vif œil dont tu regardes
Jusques à leur contenu
Me sépare de mes hardes
Et comme un dieu je vais nu.

The piercing eye with which you see
What they contain essentially
Separates my rags from me
And naked I go as a diety.[51]

Mallarmé, rather, picks up on other aspects present in panoramic treatments of the *marchand(e) d'habits* and the *revendeuse à la toilette*. The latter bought and sold clothes among society's elite (often elite women) and acted as a money-lender, whereas the former (either male or female), operating primarily in the Latin Quarter, was students' or poor people's last resort prior to the pawnshop. While these two types are not identical, they share a similar shrewdness. Mallarmé parodies clichés about the speed with which the old-clothes–woman figuratively undresses the client, as she eyes how much she can make on each item of clothing during the transaction. The outmoded word "hardes" (which Weinfield translates as "rags") aptly conveys the poor or worn quality of the wardrobe of a speaker at the old-clothes–woman's mercy. The vendor's lucrative skill at obtaining the best price while leaving the client near destitute—virtually naked—is a stock scene in narratives about the *marchande d'habits* and even more so the *revendeuse à la toilette*. Narratives such as Mainzer's "Le Marchand d'habits," Arnould Frémy's "La Revendeuse à la toilette," Balzac's "Une marchande à la toilette ou Madame la Ressource en 1844," never fail to emphasize how much power the vendor has over the client.[52] Bertall's caricature of the *marchande à la toilette* captures the wiliness of the gaze, which has nothing to do with the pensive look of Raffaëlli's type (figures 20 and 21). The feminization of the trades turns this power, real or imagined, into the potential threat of female independence in the marketplace.[53] Mallarmé's poem narrates the act of dispossession by the tradeswoman from a first-person male point of view (the adjective "nu" is masculine). "La Marchande d'habits" therefore implicitly reflects late-nineteenth-century buyers' fear of being victims of fraud when dealing with peddlers who favor differential pricing and reject the fixed price system of shopkeepers.[54] Raffaëlli's drawing, in contrast, elides the anxieties surrounding informal commerce. Some of these anxieties about destitution are deflated however in the last line of Mallarmé's verses, when the speaker regains his transcendence and ironically compares his nakedness to a God's nudity. The pared-down style of the quatrain playfully mimics the nudity of the poet.

The lighthearted analogy between poets, beggars, nudity, and gods points to the poem's bawdiness, the *esprit gaulois* associated with the Cries. The oral dimension of the *Cris de Paris* tradition is brought to the fore in Mallarmé's title "Chansons bas," literally "lowly songs," which attributes the poetic qualities of song to the "bas peuple" in keeping with the traditional association of peddler and poet. (In view of the gradual reinsertion of sound into the graphic representations of the *Cris de Paris*, it is worth remarking that Mallarmé's *chansons bas* were later adapted into art songs by Darius Milhaud.[55]) The Mallarmé/Raffaëlli collaboration stays within the tradition by pairing text and image, but goes beyond it by allegorically referring to the process of poetic creation thus further abstracting the peddler from his original historical purpose.

The humor of "Chansons bas" seems uncharacteristic for a poet reputedly serious, arcane, and difficult. The series are odd little poems that do not correspond to the image that many readers have of Mallarmean poetry. The mix of high and low in these poems, in fact, debunks the myth of Mallarmé as the ivory-tower poet who disdains popular culture, a revisionist interpretation of Mallarmé's works that has achieved consensus in the last decade.[56] Mary Shaw proposes that it is worth considering Mallarmé as a "man of his own time" who shares a sense of the "reversibility of extremes of humor and seriousness" with contemporary *fumistes* and other "proto-dada groups."[57] While Shaw argues that Mallarmé extensively combines popular entertainment with highbrow culture, she does not discuss "Chansons bas." It is clear that "Chansons bas" have not garnered the level of attention by Mallarmé scholars that "Le Mauvais Vitrier" has of Baudelaire specialists. They have therefore not been considered in their connections to the visual/verbal tradition of the *Cris de Paris*, or criers' treatment in panoramic literature, nor have they been read in the broader context of other poems appropriating street cries by Mallarmé's avant-garde contemporaries such as Cros and Richepin.

Although they share the same subject matter as many symbolist poems on street life in the tradition of Baudelaire's ragpicker and glazier, Mallarmé's poems are much more light-hearted and ironic. Consider "Le Marchand d'ail et d'oignons" (The Seller of Garlic and Onions):

> L'ennui d'aller en visite
> Avec l'ail nous l'éloignons.
> L'élégie au pleur hésite
> Peu si je fends des oignons.

> The boredom of paying a call
> With garlic we forestall;
> The tearful dirge won't wait
> If onions I should grate.

The poem evokes the smells emanating from the onion vendor's produce and humorously draws attention to its virtues for bourgeois callers and poets alike. Those who dread making social calls can reduce their duration or their need by eating garlic; similarly, the abilities of the elegist can be enhanced by cutting up onions, which will make tears fall easily. Mallarmé establishes an analogy between the artist and the stonebreaker in "Le Cantonnier" (The Roadmender):

Ces cailloux, tu les nivelles,
Et c'est comme troubadour,
Un cube aussi de cervelles
Qu'il me faut ouvrir par jour.

You break pebbles for your sins,
And as a troubadour
I too must open a cube of brains
Each day and year by year.[58]

"Le Cantonnier" equates the task of the quarryman with the strenuous mental effort of the troubadour who seeks the formal perfection of the cube. The poet, moreover, exercises daily the hard labor of making poetry resound. Another *chanson bas*, "Le Savetier" extols the creativity of the cobbler. He is at once the poet's peer in creativity and the adversary who would pin down the poet's restless wanderlust. These poems establish an abstract analogy between poet and peddler that masks any economic relationship that would force an interaction. In contrast, "La Marchande d'herbes aromatiques" stages a confrontation with the tradespeople, when the speaker remarks on the seller's effrontery as seen in the detail of the raised eyebrow ("ce cil/Osé"):

Ta paille azur de lavandes,
Ne crois pas avec ce cil
Osé que tu me la vendes

Don't think I'm willing to pay cash
For the lavender straw of azure hue
You sell by flaunting a daring lash[59]

There is, however, no real fraternity between poet and peddler as we overheard in Houssaye's "La Chanson du vitrier." Keeping the tradespeople out of earshot, the sight of peddlers is an invitation to reflect on the poet's own posturing. Is he who peddles words so superior to the cagey *marchande* who falsely, but effectively, advertises lavender? If one is searching for a unifying theme in "Chansons bas," one could in fact find it in the unstable alliance between poet and street crier that runs through most of the series. "Flaunting a daring lash" as it were, the Mallarmean speaker relies on ironic dissonance to avoid the sentimentalism manifest in Siefert's or Houssaye's treatment of street types—as well as in Raffaëlli's drawings.

Jules Laforgue and Joris Karl Huysmans share with Mallarmé an interest in combining the bathetic and the ludic to subvert the seriousness of pauperism. In the prose poem series "Types de Paris," Huysmans evoked peddlers and *petits industriels* working in the *banlieue parisienne*, especially the impoverished area near the Bièvre river in southeast Paris, the antithesis of elegant Paris along the Banks of the Seine.[60] For instance, in "Le Marchand de marrons" (The Chestnut Seller), whose illustration by Raffaëlli I discussed earlier, the chestnut-seller's cry reoccurs as a refrain in the narrative: "hue! philosophe, hue! entonne à tue-tête, jusqu'à la pleine nuit, au clair du gaz, sous le froid, ton refrain de misère: eh! chauds, chauds, les marrons!" (shout! philosopher, shout! intone at the top of your voice late into the night, under the cold light of the gaslamps, your miserable refrain: "Ah-hot, hot chestnuts-ah!"[61]). Despite the use of "a miserable refrain," the prose poem however resists harmonizing the chestnut vendor. The poem resounds with the gossip, chatter, grieving, dramas, and drunkenness that swirl around him, but the vendor in his *échoppe* or stall remains "impassible" to these street noises. No one buys his chestnuts. By comparing the vendor's nasal twang ("nasillard") to an obstinate complaint ("complainte obstinée"), the narrator insists on the crier's stubborn resistance to modernity. Likewise, Jules Laforgue's "Grande Complainte de la ville de Paris, prose blanche" (Grand Complaint of the City of Paris, White Prose) aptly conveys the dizzying excess of street noise without sentimentalizing the crier. The prose poem begins "Bonne gens qui m'écoutes" (Good people who can hear me), imitating the hawker who hassles passersby, and continues with a collage or a quodlibet reminiscent of the polyphonic works of Clément Janequin and Jean Servin; Janequin's "Voulez ouir les Cris de Paris" (1528) and Servin's "Fricassée des Cris de Paris" (1578) use the same techniques of collage, accumulation, and polyphony with parodic intent as Laforgue, except that "Grande Complainte de la ville de Paris" mixes quotations of print advertising, posters, and signs with slogans, public cries, and other "white noise" pervading the modern metropolis. As a fractured catalog of sound bites, the poem accrues references to commercial terms.[62] Although written as a prosaic listing, "Grande Complainte" implies the lyrical form associated with the Renaissance—the complaint—used in most of Laforgue's other rhymed song-like verse, such as the "Complainte variations sur le mot 'falot, falotte'" (Complaint Variations on the Words "Light Beam, Beam Light"), which evokes the ragpicker and the lantern bearer ("un falot" refers to a lantern, whereas the adjective "falot, falotte" means *colorless*). Huysmans and Laforgue appropriate street noise in their prose poetry to catalog the city's vastness, but also to reflect upon the belatedness of the crier within modern networks of commercial exchange. Poets hear the peddler's cries distinctly in the city amid a whirl of sound bites, but they represent them as obstinate and impassible—even "blank" as in the expression "prose blanche"—rising against the sounds of modern capitalism.

Any critical rapprochement between poet and crier invites us to question the commercialization of the word. In a city where everything is on offer, what happens to peddling poets? Can they sell their poetry in the marketplace? This question preoccupied Mallarmé. Although Mallarmé had clear ideas about the book as a total, creative enterprise in the late nineteenth century, he was no less cognizant of the potential for reciprocity between industry and art, and of the importance of the press in his time, as he professes in his journalistic essays on the London Annual International Exhibition (1871–72), in "Étalages" (Displays), and in "Le Livre, instrument spirituel" (The Book, A Spiritual Instrument) from *Divagations*.[63] It is nevertheless ironic to publish poems about street criers in *Le Figaro*, the newspaper being one of the most representative forms of the rise of print culture, the same commercial venture that hastened the decline and obsolescence of street criers—and the publication of poetry.[64] In "Étalages," Mallarmé describes how, to quote Dina Blanc's summary, "first peddling their own scandals within the pages of the newspapers, books are once again out on the streets, beckoning to their clients, to end up idle in the hands of their purchasers, where they do nothing more than keep life's banality at bay."[65] Writers have to hawk their merchandise, as it were, on the street, "Le vulgaire placard crié comme il s'impose, tout ouvert, dans le carrefour" ("the common pronouncement appropriately shouted out openly in the square") as do peddlers and street criers.[66] The newspaper vendors' cries are heard once again in "Étalages" when the narrator describes men of letters hastening their step and averting their gaze at "the sacred volume" illuminated by gaslight. In "Le Crieur d'imprimés," one of the quatrains in *Types de Paris*, Mallarmé had in fact evoked glibly the unfailing regularity, no matter the banality of the headline, with which the newsvendor (plied with alcohol) gaily hawks the first issue of the day. Resisting change, he shouts out the news despite the new legislation forbidding it that passed March 19, 1889.

In "Le Crieur d'imprimés," perhaps more dramatically than in the other quatrains, the poet implicitly stakes out his difference from the newspaper seller: he has had his revelation and lives "hors et à l'insu de l'affichage" (outside of and unbeknownst to advertisement), "selon un pacte avec la Beauté" (according to a pact with Beauty).[67] Although Mallarmé explores the affinities between the poet and street criers in *Chansons bas* and *Types de Paris*, ultimately he maintains his difference from the peddlers. Any contact with the peddlers remains at the level of abstraction. His speakers are not affected by their sounds and smells, even when the sense of olfaction would necessarily be solicited by the intrusive smell of cobbler's pitch, onions, and lavender. Each poem turns away from the peddler back to the speaker. Similarly to Huysmans's flâneurs in *Croquis parisiens*, Mallarmé's aloof speaker is isolated from the crowd where tradespeople hawk their wares.[68] Despite the mild resentment expressed toward the peddlers in the sonnets,[69] the poet is successful in maintaining an emotional detachment from the noisy peddler, something that proved more challenging for some of the authors discussed in the first chapter, such as Old Nick, Girardin, and Anspach, whose neurasthenia betrayed a fear of the lower classes' encroachment on the bourgeois sphere, or Fournel, Houssaye, and Richepin, whose solidarity with the *peuple* irrespective of its sincerity led them to delve into popular culture. In fact, the ironic distance that Mallarmé maintains contrasts with the empathy that characterizes Raffaëlli's drawings of working-class and marginal types.

Although the relationship of criers to the print and market economy (including the use of billboards and sandwich boards to advertise) was changing, Mallarmé could still admire, albeit at a distance, that street vendors embodied a fragile combination of artistic talent and commercial purpose—the crier, like the poet, capitalizes on the tuneful quality of the cry to attract buyers who may or may not be successfully lured away from the mass-produced (journalistic) commodities available in the marketplace. Poets may even reclaim the belatedness of the crier who resists the fall into consumerism.

Extending the Baudelairean analogy between flâneur-poet and street type, poets sound out the streets for inspiration. The return in force in avant-garde art of street types that are the mainstay of both literary guidebooks and *Cris de Paris*, whether they be coco-vendors, old-clothes–men, organ-grinders, or flower sellers, is a testament to their resiliency. Through their tacit references to the graphic tradition of the *Cris de Paris*, the popular discourse on the disappearance of street criers and peddling in the commercial press, the "Chansons bas" thus implicitly comment on the love-hate relationship between avant-garde art and mass market consumerism, between advertising and aesthetics that Mallarmé explored in other writings. Poets' embrace of the sounds of the peddling classes in the late nineteenth century signals the widening rift between the silence-seeking bourgeoisie and the noise-loving avant-garde. By pitting the street crier against bourgeois conservatism, conformism, and capitalism, Mallarmé continues in the iconoclastic and parodic vein explored by bohemians and *fumistes* such as Cros and Richepin. They reveled in the "esprit gaulois" of the *Cris de Paris* and mocked the bourgeois tendency to oversentimentalize the decline of peddling, while remaining indifferent to its social meaning. Coppée and Raffaëlli took a different path, as they sought to depict street types as sympathetic individuals, with conscientious detail that eschewed romantic idealization. Whereas Coppée tended to harmonize peddlers by making their stories seem quaint and their voices sound melodious rather than shrill, Cros, Richepin, and Mallarmé, to varying degrees, use parody and bathos to sound the dissonant note a peddling poetry can ring. Avant-garde poetry celebrates the intrusiveness of street noise by pumping up the volume, as Georges Lorin intoned:

Criez plus fort, crieurs des rues;
. . . .
Car, cher bruit, c'est dans ta clameur
Que le regret se noie et meurt,
Et que fleurit l'indifférence.
Pour qu'il ne puisse revenir
Étourdis l'Affreux Souvenir!

Shout louder, street criers
. . . .
For, dear noise, it's in your clamor
That regret drowns and dies,
And indifference flourishes.
So that he cannot return
Deafen Frightening Memory!

Conclusion

One hundred and twenty-five years after the publication of *Les Types de Paris*, in another time and place, you can still hear the jingle of street vendors peddling their services. As I drafted this conclusion in Montreal's Mile End neighborhood, I was struck by surprise when I heard the amplified voice of the knife-grinder in the back alley. The *rémouleur*—it could have been Gilles or Tony l'Aiguiseur—circulated slowly in the streets alerting potential customers that he was available at this moment to sharpen your knives, your scissors, and your tools. No longer on foot, trailing sharpening equipment in a wagon, and crying out his services as in the olden days, today's *rémouleur* drives an old cantine truck with a bell—or perhaps an amplifier. He takes pride in his trade, which is his life's work, as it was his father's before him, but avoids the trapping of modern businesses (he has no website, telephone number, or set schedule). The *rémouleur* survives today because he continues to meet the needs of his clientele. Yet, his appeal also undeniably rests in the way he evokes a bygone era and contributes to neighborhood folklore. Radio segments, blogs, online photo montages, and museum exhibitions keep the memory of this traditional trade, and many other *petits métiers*, alive.[1]

As a visual and textual phenomenon, the *Cris de Paris* proliferated in nineteenth-century France, even while the numbers of actual peddlers and the volume of their cries declined throughout the century. Many circumstances account for this decline, especially urban renewal both prior to and during Haussmannization, as well as social policy targeting disturbances of the peace and the commotion of street commerce. Also relevant are socioeconomic changes that pitted itinerant vendors against sedentary shopkeepers, or garrulous against taciturn salesmen. Street vendors' dependence on bargaining was superseded by fixed-priced sales, and small-scale traders were supplanted by large centralized markets and department stores. *City of Noise* documented shifts in attitudes toward noise that lowered the threshold for intolerance of street nuisances that intruded into bourgeois interiors. Despite all these changes, however, representations of street vendors flourished in nineteenth-century France.

Efforts to control and limit street vendors by the likes of Prefect Gisquet and Baron Haussmann effectively toned down street noise, but did not result in the prompt disappearance of peddling. In the mid- to late nineteenth century, the peddlers and their clamor still drifted into certain neighborhoods, however sporadically, but they soared resonantly in the collective memory of Parisians. Indeed, writers from Honoré de Balzac in "Ce qui disparaît de Paris" in 1845 to Rowland Strong in *Sensations of Paris* in 1912 evoked the disappearance of peddlers, often trading heavily on nostalgia for earlier, simpler times. The imagined disappearance of peddlers was in fact necessary to sustain the idea of modernity as capitalist development and industrialization. Peddlers, as the narrative goes, could not compete in the sedentary bourgeois economy expanding under the Third Republic, in which consumers shopped in department stores and at regulated central markets. Their role in the economy faded, even as it became easier to buy porcelain figurines of street vendors from merchants selling such bibelots at quiet, fixed addresses. Nevertheless, the value of the peddler, like most commodities, increased in proportion to hawkers' (perceived) scarcity. The charm of street cries then came from their vestigial status as remnants of a fading sound culture, equated with the acoustic intimacy and picturesque character of Old Paris.

When Fournel evoked the "plaintive cry" of Paris on its way out, he captured how Parisian street cries sounded to the nostalgic amateur of Old Paris. Whereas many Parisians, used to their neighborhoods' sounds, lived immersed in street noises they may no longer have consciously heard, visitors to the city, amateur historians, and musicians listened to them attentively. These listeners often detected changes to the music of the street that heightened their awareness of a break with the past. As a critic of Haussmannization, Fournel mourned the acoustic intimacy being destroyed by the reorganization of space, and he heard in the somber vocalizations of criers the hollowing-out of the old city. Along with Balzac before them and Proust after them, these listeners heard in street cries a resistance to modernity.

A new awareness that the past was slipping away, that France had entered the modern age, and that it behooved writers to transmit their memories to the next generation spurred interest in the history of medieval Paris and its popular street culture. Thus archivists, bibliophiles, amateur historians, and music scholars revived the *Cris de Paris* and circulated compilations, reproductions, and adaptations in a variety of media. Chapter 2 surveyed a range of musical and visual examples from Georges Kastner's symphony *Les Voix de Paris* to Gustave Charpentier's *Louise*, and from prints by François Boucher and Paul Gavarni, to caricatures by Bertall and photographs by Eugène Atget. The active circulation of the *Cris de Paris* as cultural memory shows the degree to which the tradition remained relevant in the nineteenth century, not just because it revived the past, but also because it structured the present. They were repeatedly evoked as a sonorous blazon essential to the city's character and sense of place. For that reason, any panorama of Paris worthy of Louis-Sébastien Mercier would not have been complete without a reference to the *Cris de Paris*. The *Cris* embodied the opposition between noisemakers and silence-seekers and thus were useful in drawing a distinction between bourgeois and working-class identities. Throughout, this book argues that the *Cris* expressed sonic relations or distinctions among social identities based on perceptions of how much noise is made by a given group.

In chapter 1, we paid close attention to sonic relations in descriptions by Girardin, Old Nick, and Anspach, where street noise is presented as an intrusion from which the unshielded ear cannot protect itself. Implicitly, the *Cris* recall the ritual of the charivari, but in the nineteenth century, the people's right to make noise was undercut by a new expectation of tranquility among the bourgeoisie. New levels of anxiety about the incursion of street noise, evident in the legislation considered in chapter 3, showed how attitudes toward peddlers channeled social unease surrounding vagrancy, pauperism, criminality, and migration. Traditional customs of almsgiving faltered in the nineteenth century as the numbers of chronically poor grew, so cries begging for charity were often perceived as a burden, even an affront, on the senses. Violations of the invisible but ear-wrenching boundary between bourgeois private sphere and street were treated comically in the satirical sketches discussed in the first chapter, but gained in gravity in examples discussed in the third and fifth chapters, such as Gavarni's "Le Petit Commerce" series, Raffaëlli's chestnut vendor, or Fernand Pelez's violet seller. These set the stage for my reading of Baudelaire's "Le Mauvais Vitrier" as an ironic commentary on the intrusions into the poet's state of reverie, and the neurasthenia caused by noxious peddlers' vocalizations. Similarly, Mallarmé's poem "Pauvre Enfant pâle" sardonically mocks the defenseless ear by turning the peddler's high-pitched cry into a sign of his criminality and certain decapitation. Call-outs from the poor are ignored with difficulty and the vulnerability of the ear strains the bourgeoisie's fragile status quo. Poets, caricaturist, and painters force listeners to confront their response to the crier; they cannot turn the ear like the eye away from catcalls and are forced to confront their complacency.

The *Cris de Paris* also shaped how peddlers were heard by modulating their sounds and attenuating their troubling difference. When heard as harmonious *Cris*, they no longer sounded like a "frightful charivari." For the cries of peddlers to be remembered much indeed had to be forgotten and harmonized—especially their connections to civil unrest, to the industrialization of cities, and to the rise of modern capitalism. Street noise evoked past tumult associated with plebeian uprisings and revolution, whose clashing voices, threatening cries, and violent discord were comparatively recent memories, if not lived experience. As a cultural memory, however, the *Cris* promoted forgetting the association between street noise and charivari, plebeian sedition, or full-blown revolution. Memories of *vitriers* doing double duty as window breakers, of *oublayeurs* being thieves, of *marchandes d'habits* operating as defrauders faded and were replaced with reassuring and domesticated types who made the city feel familiar and charming. Representations of the *petits-métiers* also diverted attention from the rise of an industrial working class that had little in common with the small-scale tradespeople and street criers of yore. Street criers were remade into nostalgic symbols, revealing both a maladjustment with the present state of society and a longing for imagined better times. In opposition to a present filled with discord, the past was reimagined as more harmonious, as bygone days when all social classes lived in concert, each knowing their proper place, and elites and workers mutually enjoyed the volubility and verve of street performances or informal commerce. Street cries clung to the past like fallen royalty and childhood dreams. The writings of Gérard de Nerval, Auguste Challamel, and Victor Fournel take us to that time and place, and attempt to keep the sounds of the past alive by evoking them time and time again.

For the *Cris* to circulate as nostalgic symbols, they also had to erase peddlers' role in the rise of early modern merchant capitalism and the development of the local economy in nineteenth-century Paris. Peddlers' labor and exertion dropped out of the *Cris*' iconography and, at least before mid-century, little mention was made in the Paris panoramas of peddlers' economic impact on their home villages, let alone their contributions to the Parisian marketplace. Peddlers catered mostly to workers who needed items brought to them, because they could not travel to central markets, or sought items piece by piece at low cost. Because they provided needed goods and services to workers and income to migrants, we could say peddlers participated in the process of modernization that turned Paris into one of the largest European capitals of the nineteenth century. But this role was rarely, if ever, acknowledged by nineteenth-century commentators. Descriptions of street criers tended to equate them with beggars or with idlers, with little or no economic impact on modern life. They resisted rather than heralded modernization. In Houssaye's poem, no one responds to the glazier's cry; in Huysmans's prose poem and Raffaëlli's sketch inspired by it, passersby do not stop to purchase chestnuts. They existed at the margins of the marketplace at a bare subsistence level. Insofar as peddlers survived, some late-nineteenth-century poets refused the sentimentalism that denied the peddlers' economic potential and that saw their value only in their picturesque beauty. Instead, poems such as Mallarmé's "Chansons bas" celebrated peddlers' resiliency in countering the rise of print advertising and mass-market consumerism. These noisemakers were the heroes of the avant-garde because they resisted a silence that sounded like bourgeois apathy and complacency.

By domesticating tradespeoples' sounds and reducing them to prints and sounds that the middle class could buy and sell, the *Cris* effectively silenced the peddlers they represented. The sellers, ironically, became objects to be sold. Collecting *Cris* turned peddlers into commodities while denying them any economic activity. Collectors could contemplate *Cris* while remembering street noises at a safe, nostalgic remove. Edmond de Goncourt, for example, possessed a choice selection of *Cris* that brought back memories of street cries from within the protection of his museum-home. Bibliophiles and archivists such as Jacob, Alfred Franklin, and Jules Cousin reprinted luxurious collections of prints of the medieval *Cris*, while artists such as Raffaëlli or Bertall adapted traditional types in works such as *Types de Paris* or *La Comédie de notre temps*. Bertall's sketch of peddlers as collectibles preserved under glass aptly conveyed the process both of turning street criers into sound souvenirs and of muffling their cries. In different ways, the *dizains* of François Coppée and the photographs of Eugène Atget captured the picturesque quality of street criers while attenuating their vocalizations.

Scholarly interest in street cries mirrored the fascination of collectors. As this book illustrated, such artistic and commercial plenitude was the result of a powerful desire to collect and preserve street cries from disappearing. Journalists and flâneurs-writers such as J. B. Gouriet, Charles Yriarte, and Victor Fournel inventoried the celebrities of the streets in extensive detail, while musicians and composers such as Joseph Mainzer and Georges Kastner were especially keen on the musical classification and documentation of street cries. Mainzer and Kastner recorded their precise pitch and amplitude, tonality, syncopated rhythm, attack, and general musicality. They noted the linguistic features of cries in musical scores and in extensive annotations on criers' regional accents and diction. Some poets also sought to transpose street cries into their poetry. The range of attempts to record street cries in musical transcriptions and poems was part of the same impulse to document and preserve fading sound cultures that led to the development of sound recording (Martinville in the late 1850s) and sound reproduction (Cros and Edison in the 1880s). Sound archives by Ferdinand Brunot took the scholarly investigation to the next level. Today sonic archeology exploits the potential of multimedia to reconstitute soundscapes of the past.[2]

Following the lead of Mainzer and others, *City of Noise* attends to different ways of giving form to street cries in musical, visual, and verbal sketches. It is worth underscoring the continuities between the transmedial tradition of the *Cris de Paris*, from its beginnings with Guillaume de la Villeneuve's "Les Crieries de Paris," to its expression in a variety of media including print and music, and extending to avant-garde poetry and art representing the city and its peddlers. The kind of flâneur-writing in literary guidebooks, *tableaux*, and panoramas, which helped describe and circulate a common notion of how Paris looked, sounded, and felt, were directly indebted to the tradition of the *Cris de Paris*. The *Cris* harmonized a cacophony of vocalizations in polyphonic form. The polyphony of medieval and Renaissance texts gave way to the more serial presentation of checkerboard broadsheets, suites of prints, guidebook typologies, and sequences of poems in a collection. The polyphony of the Renaissance, Rabelaisian noisemaking, and Gallic spirit later inspired avant-garde poets' pursuit of dissonance and syncopation to upset poetic convention. Poets explored a range of means of recording street cries in various forms, from direct quotation in Richepin to enigmatic allusion in Mallarmé and from sentimental sound bite in Coppée to parodic spoof in Cros. Artists such as Raffaëlli and Atget chose to accentuate detail and humanize peddlers, whereas others, such as Toulouse-Lautrec, opted for a more detached representation. Throughout the book, an emphasis on word-image-sound relations is intended to show how printed forms borrowed from aural/oral forms and *vice versa*.

How the chosen form orchestrated and otherwise organized street noises into orderly compositions influenced whether peddlers' cries were perceived as reassuring or intrusive, harmonious or strident, plaintive or lively, mute or voluble. Fournel turned street cries into a pleasing "melopoeia" as he strolled through the streets orchestrating the city-as-concert. In other writings, he described the "plaintive cry" of Paris, subsuming the sounds of the entire old city with the *Cris de Paris*. In keeping with "flâneur-writing" on peddlers, poets such as Houssaye and Coppée attenuated the shrillness of the cries to harmonize the city streets. When Houssaye and Louisa Siefert similarly hear peddlers' "song full of tears" and "poem of misery," their aestheticized approach to poverty conditions their perception. The sentimental co-optation of street cries was another means of fostering amnesia of past working-class uprisings, riots, and revolutions (1789, 1830, 1848, 1870) and playing to bourgeois self-righteousness and complacency. Houssaye and Coppée performed in the realm of aesthetics what the prefects of police endeavored to achieve through city ordinances, namely tempering the noise of informal commerce. Even though a poet such as Richepin claimed in his preface to have heard the misery of the streets and to have recorded it directly in his poetry, readers today hear instead perceptions of street vendors mired in paternalism that tug at heartstrings but never rip them apart. The harmonization of street cries is in part a sociopolitical reordering along the lines of what Jacques Attali called the "political economy of music." People hear a hierarchical order that situates each note in relation to the norm.

City of Noise accentuated how modern poetry, as distinct from the journalism, caricature, or literary guidebooks to which chapters 4 and 5 show it is indebted, can be significant in any attempt at reconstructing soundscapes of the past. Baudelaire, for instance, aimed to capture what was inassimilable in the glazier's cry in a way that escaped Houssaye. Resisting the urge to transpose the cry into an aesthetic sound, he shocked the reader with its stridency and forced us to think about the latent violence in urban sonic relations. Baudelaire and Mallarmé exposed the hypocrisy of harmonization, the collusion of music and power. By identifying with the peddler, they questioned the immutable divide between the quiet and the noisy. Sonic relations in their poetry are far more ambiguous or ironic, as the poems force listeners to confront their response to the crier. Charles Cros, too, avoided the sentimentalism of Coppée by mocking the clichéd manner in which his predecessor turned street noises into familiar musical settings. Finally Georges Lorin celebrated the blaring city for its power to wrench us from our daily grind and make us dizzy with the noise.

Avant-garde poets often identified with the peddler, but these identifications raise many more questions about the functions of poetry and of peddling than they provide answers for. Acknowledging the formative role of urban encounters, Baudelaire and his followers adopted peddlers as kindred spirits, because of their similarities: they were both marginalized and disempowered by the bourgeois order, and yet they depended on the bourgeoisie for their livelihoods. Indeed, both poet and peddler aspired to independence from the marketplace, but nevertheless they were not immune to the effects of print advertising and the commercialization of the word. As both poets and peddlers exercise a vocal art and craft, they also share a vocation that links them to a rich artistic tradition. At the same time, however, the peddler can end up the Baudelairean poet's antagonist, at the very least because of the way the artist exploits the street for profit or fame. He speaks for the peddler, but about poetry's, rather than peddling's, meaning. Moroever, the identity of the peddler, both familiar and uncanny, both maker and breaker of windows, cannot easily be appropriated or pinned down. By comparing poetry and peddling, we face the question of what a "peddling poetry" is, or better, does: does it touch listeners and move them beyond complacency to act publicly and charitably? Or, does it force introspection, disorientation even, as we listen keenly and reflect intently on what goes on around us? This book shows the value of listening to poets call attention to the street noise, whether their peddling poetry brings people together in a harmonious scene, as in Houssaye and Coppée, or wrenches them apart in a dissonant confrontation, as in Baudelaire and Mallarmé.

Poets reconstruct for readers and listeners today a mediated experience of nineteenth-century street noise that can both reconcile and disquiet. In different ways, these poems argue for the resiliency of peddling, transforming peddlers into countercultural figures whose cries heroically rise up against the tide of modern (capitalist) progress. They intimate other ways to think about peddlers' relationship to the economy in the twenty-first century: street vendors cultivate resourcefulness and independence, and their garrulousness and attention-getting techniques have influenced sales strategies and advertising in the age of print. In the twentieth century, peddlers continued to inspire modernist artists, who were attracted either by the picturesque or by the resistant potential of the figure: Amadeo Modigliani, Marc Chagall, and Fernand Léger painted peddlers; George Brassaï and Eugène Atget photographed them; Georges Lacombe in the silent film *La Zone* (1928), René Clair in *Sous les toits de Paris* (1930), and Marcel Carné in *Les Enfants du Paradis* (1945) filmed them.

It is worth noting, however, that whether poets, journalists, composers, or bibliophiles discussed street cries, all these commentators came from non-working-class backgrounds. Though a few workers left autobiographies that provide a subaltern's perspective into everyday life, such as the mason Martin Nadaud, or the unskilled laborer and sometime peddler Norbert Truquin,[3] workers themselves were not as keen to record street cries and do not discuss the *Cris de Paris* as do their bourgeois contemporaries. Most of the sources available provide a bourgeois perspective on the transformation of the nineteenth-century urban soundscape. As Charles Virmaître succinctly states in *Paris qui s'efface*: "These street scenes are difficult to reconstruct, given that the poor devils who are their heroes have not left any traces other than in the memories of people one must seek out in slums and shelters, which are their tombs."[4] Any historical investigation into the sounds of the past has to work around the limited availability of firsthand accounts of sounds by people who did not think themselves significant enough to record and document, as well as the bias that motivated others to tune in with a mix of horror and fascination to the cries of those "poor devils" they heard in the streets.

The collective experience of sounds is what gives aurality meaning, even though, clearly, there is an element of idiosyncrasy in sound perception. The street cries of peddlers and hawkers were meaningful sounds that resonated as a shared cultural experience in the nineteenth century, even for those who rarely heard them, or chose not to write about them. Following the flâneur, which has been central to my discussion, has been instrumental because of the ways in which this figure hones sensual observation and introspection. Within these accounts of flânerie, each writer's reactions are different. Some writers are more sensitive to the sounds in their environment than others are, and their accounts of walking in the city offer richer, more detailed, and personal narratives of listening to street noises. Why, for instance, do Fournel and Baudelaire write so well about sound? It was a curious discovery to find that Fournel and Baudelaire, both dedicated flâneurs, shared an appreciation for the jerky harmony and intoxication of the senses produced by peddling sounds, albeit for entirely different reasons. Whereas Fournel was by all accounts a man of "rectitude"[5] and a conservative journalist who perceived the contemporary world filtered through the grandeur of the past, the iconoclast Baudelaire sought to "fathom the Unknown" as he states in *The Flowers of Evil*. Whereas Baudelaire shatters the peddler's windowpanes making an explosive sound, Fournel attempts to preserve peddlers' voices as acoustic rarities under glass. One makes noise, while the other silences it.

Another impediment can also close our ears to the sounds of the past: the unwitting deafness of scholarship. Given the long-standing association between sight and urban experience—traceable to Walter Benjamin's impact on cultural studies—scholars have sometimes scoped out the metropolitan spectacle but tune out the aural dimensions of their academic flânerie. Such toning down of city noise follows Georg Simmel's highly influential sociology of the senses, which privileged the eye over the ear. A practice of cultural studies and urban studies that is closely allied with visual culture developed in the late 1990s and early 2000s, in which scholars paid close attention to material changes to cities perceived by the scopophilic eye—such as arcades, boulevards, and department stores—and to protocinematic technologies such as the panoramas, without consideration of their other sensory dimensions.[6] *City of Noise* argues that vision did not dominate the other senses in the nineteenth century; rather, the era placed great emphasis on selective listening and sensitivity to intrusive noise grew. To account for these changes enriches our historical understanding of the nineteenth-century city, as well as helps us imagine the continuity between the ubiquity of street noise at that time and at present.

In the twenty-first century, peddlers still operate and vocalize in locations as diverse as New York City, Mexico City, Dakar, Port-au-Prince, Calcutta, Sidi Bouzid,[7] and even Paris. The *rempailleur* who mends old hardback chairs with straw seats and backs still seeks out customers at outdoor markets in Paris. The *plastificateur* on the street offers to put plastic on your business cards. A vendor sets up a temporary stall on the street and aggressively markets his wares. Fruit vendors and ambulant flower sellers call out their seasonal offerings. Food trucks are developing into an informal economy of their own. Buskers market their music on the metro, while others peddle candy or newspapers. Modern forms of peddling are alive and well, and the intrusiveness of street trade remains a point of contention in today's noise-conscious society.

Notes

Introduction

1. Sanderson, *Sketches of Paris*, 20–21.

2. King, *My Paris*, 268.

3. Jarves, *Parisian Sights*, 177.

4. This is all the more striking because the early decades of the twentieth century saw a marked increase in antinoise campaigns in America. See Smilor, "American Noise 1900–1930," 319–30. Vaillant, "Peddling Noise," 257–87.

5. Strong, *Sensations of Paris*, 327. Gilman, "Parisian Pedlars," *Cosmopolitan*, 327–35.

6. Martin, "Les Cris de Paris," 162. Martin was a journalist, historian, politician, and author of the fifteen volume *Histoire de France* (1833–1836). All translations are my own, unless otherwise noted.

7. Smith, *Sensing the Past*, 8–18. Mark Smith summarizes and critiques the theory of the great divide which postulates the modern emergence of vision as the dominant sense. See also Thompson, *The Soundscape of Modernity*.

8. Kahn, *Noise, Water, Meat*, 9.

9. I use the term "soundscape" as aural landscape in its broadest sense. The term was coined by Canadian composer Murray Schafer in his book *The Soundscape*. A succinct definition can be found in Thompson, *The Soundscape of Modernity*, 1–2.

10. I have limited this list to those whose work I personally found most influential. The *Auditory Culture Reader* and the *Sound Studies Reader* provide useful entry points into the range of research in "sound studies." Garrioch's "Sounds of the City" immerses the reader in the sounds of the past.

11. Thompson, *The Soundscape of Modernity*, 144–46.

12. Steven Connor's series of five programs on noise presented on BBC Radio February 24–28, 1997, is a useful resource for defining "noise." See http://www.stevenconnor .com/noise/, accessed June 30, 2011.

13. Attali, *Noise: The Political Economy of Music*, 29. Note that Attali understands noise exclusively within a musical framework: "music [is] the organization of noise" (4). In contrast to Attali, I broaden noise to include sounds such as cries, which overtly challenge definitions of music, harmony, and dissonance.

14. Attali, *Noise*, 19. The following sentences on harmony draw from Attali, 60–61.

15. Nora, ed. *Les Lieux de mémoire*. Assmann, "Canon and Archive," 97–107. Rigney, "The Dynamics of Remembrance," 345–53.

16. See Fontaine, *History of Pedlars*.

17. Here I follow John C. Cross's argument in *Informal Politics* where he suggests that rather than see street vendors as victims who have lost the struggle against the formal economy, we should stress their vitality and ability to break rules in order to avoid regulations (2–3). Cross uses the terms "formal" and "informal economy," the latter coined by Keith Hart in 1970 and 1973. Also useful is Jérôme Monnet's paradigmatic approach to types of street vendors, "Le Commerce de rue, ambulant ou informel et ses rapports avec la métropolisation: Une ébauche de modélisation," *Autrepart*, 93–109.

Chapter 1. Aural Flânerie

1. Benjamin, "The Paris of the Second Empire," in *The Writer of Modern Life*, 66–96.

2. Buck-Morss, *The Dialectics of Seeing*. Although I do not use the expression in this way, Susan Buck-Morss uses this term in relation to Theodor Adorno: "It was Adorno who pointed to the station-switching behavior of the radio listener as a kind of aural flânerie" (345).

3. Lauster, *Sketches of the Nineteenth Century*; Lauster, "Walter Benjamin's Myth of the Flâneur," 139–56; Rose, *Flâneurs & Idlers*. For a literary and sociological reading of the *physiologies*, see Preiss, *Les Physiologies en France*; Stiénon, *La Littérature des physiologies*. The genre of the *physiologies*, or verbal/visual sketches of contemporary types in the 1830s and 1840s, borrowed from the tradition of moralists' character types, and Lavater and Gall's physiognomy; however, their parodic playfulness also mocked these scientific and moralist discourses.

4. Tonkiss, "Aural Postcards," 303–310.

5. Richter, *Walter Benjamin*, 170.

6. Tonkiss, "Aural Postcards," 306.

7. Benjamin, *One Way Street*, 89.

8. Koepnick, "Benjamin's Silence," in *Sound Matters*, 119.

9. David Frisby draws attention to the flâneur's tactility in "The Flâneur in Social Theory," 81–110.

10. Simmel, *Simmel on Culture*, 110, 114.

11. Antinoise campaigns did not begin in earnest until the twentieth century; for more on the history of the perception of noise as nuisance, see Bijsterveld, *Mechanical Sound*,

57; Alain Corbin, *Time, Desire, Horror*, 156. For more on Lessing, see Baron, "Noise and Degeneration," 165–78.

12. On Simmel's and Lessing's conception of the bodily imaginary, see Cowan, "Imagining Modernity," 124–46. Hillel Schwartz has argued against the myth of the vulnerable ear in "The Indefensible Ear: A History," in *The Auditory Culture Reader*, 487–501.

13. Simmel, *Simmel on Culture*, 119, 178.

14. Benjamin, *The Arcades Project*. See entries M8a, 1 and M16a, 2.

15. Benjamin, *The Writer of Modern Life*, 191.

16. On Poe and the kaleidoscope, see Hayes, "The Flâneur in the Parlor," 103–19.

17. The kaleidoscope appears in writings on the flâneur before Baudelaire, such as "Le Flâneur à Paris," which uses the motif to describe the flâneur's erratic, changeable thoughts: "the playful movements of the kaleidoscope are no more indeterminate, no more capricious, no more multiplicitous than those of his mind." See Anonymous [Un Flâneur], "Le Flâneur à Paris," in *Paris ou Le Livre des Cent-et-un*, 104. One hundred and one writers allegedly contributed to the volume, hence the title.

18. Nesci, *Le Flâneur et les flâneuses*, 62–63.

19. Janin evokes both the *daguerréotype* and the *lanterne magique* to convey how flâneur-writing in *Les Français peints par eux-mêmes* captures contemporaneity. Janin, in *Les Français peints*, 1:19, 22. Fournel compares the flâneur to a mobile daguerreotype in *Ce qu'on voit*, 261. It is worth remembering, however, that some diorama spectacles had a sonic component. Walter Benjamin has many entries on the music performed in diorama, panorama, and the like, casting doubt on the uniquely visual experience of spectatorship in these spaces.

20. Schwartz, "Cinematic Spectatorship before the Apparatus," 298.

21. Janin, *Un hiver à Paris*, 195, cited in Burton, "The Unseen Seer," 50–68. Burton outlines the myth of detachment, but recently Lauster and Rose have shown that the myth of detachment is not grounded in a meticulous reading of the text and images.

22. Hans Jonas (1954) argues that spatial distance is a distinctive feature of sight; however, he does not consider that one can also hear people from a distance, often before they are in the line of sight. Jonas, "The Nobility of Sight," 507–19.

23. Crary, *Techniques of the Observer*.

24. *Physiologies* were cheap, illustrated books on urban character types, such as the flâneur or the *grisette*, that were popular during the 1830s and 1840s. Though similar in their attention to contemporary society, they are not to be confused with the collective, multivolume, and more expensive compilations such as *Les Français peints par eux-mêmes* or *Paris-Guide*. I borrow the catch-all term "literary guidebooks" to designate both the *physiologies* and the compilations, from Ferguson, *Paris as Revolution*, 58.

25. Huart, *Physiologie du flâneur*, 76. All translations are my own unless otherwise attributed in the notes.

26. Lacroix, "Le Flâneur," in *Les Français peints*, 2:151.

27. Jouy, "La Journée d'un flâneur," 283 ; "Le Flâneur Parisien," *Le Figaro*, November 13, 1831.

28. Anonymous [Un Flâneur], *Paris ou Le Livre des Cent-et-un*, 1831, 105.

29. Lacroix, "Le Flâneur," in *Les Français peints*, 2:154–55.

30. Huart, *Physiologie du flâneur*, 79–80. The relationship between hawkers and newspapers will be discussed further in the section titled "Mallarmé Sings Low, with Raffaëlli on Bass" in chapter 5.

31. Lacroix, "Le Flâneur," in *Les Français peints*, 2:155.

32. Huart, *Physiologie du flâneur*, 53.

33. Lacroix, "Le Flâneur," in *Les Français peints*, 2:153. On the badaud, see Huart, *Physiologie du flâneur*, chapter 13. The sharp flâneur/badaud distinction in the pre-1850s literature weakens in the second half of the century. By the time Victor Fournel defines the badaud, he has evolved into a more attentive and thoughtful figure (261); while the flâneur remains in full possession of his individuality, the badaud can lose himself in the crowd that intoxicates him (*Ce qu'on voit*, 261–63).

34. Balzac, *The Physiology of Marriage*, 32. Original in Balzac, *Physiologie du mariage*, 28.

35. Balzac's appeal to the senses, I believe, can be linked to his taste for François Rabelais. In addition to *Physiologie du mariage*, *La Peau de chagrin* and *Contes drolatiques* make reference to the sixteenth-century sensualist. After a period of unpopularity during the Classical era, Rabelais was revived by the French Romantics in the first half of the nineteenth century. He was also prized by avant-garde groups at the fin de siècle for his "Gallic spirit." See Voisin-Fougère, *Le Rire de Rabelais*.

36. Balzac's appeal to intersensoriality can be interpreted as a Rabelaisian gesture. Lucien Febvre and Robert Mandrou hypothesized that hearing and smelling were more developed in the sixteenth century than in the post-Cartesian period, although this argument has been challenged (among others) by Leigh Eric Schmidt in *The Auditory Culture Reader* (44). The Rabelaisian revival that Balzac launched suggests that the sensorium had fleshed out by the nineteenth century. In chapter 5, I evoke Rabelaisian sensibility again in terms of "l'esprit gaulois" or Gallic spirit.

37. Nesci, *Le Flâneur et les flâneuses*, 114.

38. Details of the life of Victor Fournel (1829–1894) can be found in Pierre Larousse's *Grand Dictionnaire universel du XIXe siècle*, 8:691. An obituary appeared in *Revue d'Art Dramatique* 35.7–9 (August 1, 1893): 152–58.

39. Fournel, *Ce qu'on voit*, 261. I use gender-biased language in my translations here and elsewhere to reflect the writer's gender-exclusive definition of the flâneur.

40. Ibid., 262.

41. The existence and identity of the *flâneuse* has been a subject of debate among scholars. For a discussion, see Nesci, *Le Flâneur et les flâneuses*.

42. Girardin, *Lettres parisiennes*, 230–31.

43. Hamon, *Imageries*, 54. See also Starobinski and Pevear, "Windows: From Rousseau to Baudelaire," 551–60.

44. For a discussion of Girardin's "Le Lorgnon," see Nesci, *Le Flâneur et les flâneuses*, 177–82.

45. Simmel, *Simmel on Culture*, 115.

46. The *badaud* listens to "Ma Normandie" for over an hour in Huart, *Physiologie du flâneur*, 96. The same song figures in *Mr Ledbury's Adventures at Home and Abroad* in Bent-

ley's Miscellany for 1842 and "Punch's Continental Tour, Stage the Third" in *Punch or the London Charivari for 1843–44* (see Rose, *Flâneurs & Idlers*, 31n129).

47. Bertall possibly quotes Carle Vernet's *Cris de Paris dessinés d'après nature*, no. 17, entitled "Ioup la Catarina." Savoyards travelled to the capital as seasonal migrants. They performed as street musicians and entertainers in the winter, leaving Savoy in October to return home at Easter. Some of these performers were children, apprenticed or enslaved by handlers, as John Zucchi documents in *The Little Slaves of the Harp*.

48. Leterrier, "Musique populaire et musique savante," *Revue d'Histoire du XIXe Siècle*, 19 (1999), modified August 26, 2008, accessed September 12, 2010, http://rh19.revues. org/index157.html, page 4 of 15. It is interesting to note with Hélène Landron in the exhibition catalog *Musiciens des rues de Paris* that the permitting process that regulated street musicians did not consider their talent but rather used exclusively administrative criteria such as nationality, address, and background checks (79).

49. Bertall, *La Comédie de notre temps*, 237.

50. Fournel, *Les Cris de Paris*, 76.

51. Fétis, "De la musique des rues," 288. Fétis comments on the speed with which street musicians appropriated pieces by established composers, sometimes to the composers' dismay. He adds however that the musical establishment ought to recognize that once on the streets the piece will be canonized (290).

52. For example, the *Ordonnance concernant les joueurs d'orgues dans les rues et places publiques du 10 septembre 1828*. The text of the ordinances can be found in tome 2 of *Collection officielle des ordonnances de police depuis 1800 jusqu'à 1844*.

53. See Corbin, *Village Bells*.

54. New levels of attentive behaviors and the engineered acoustics of the concert hall would later satisfy this desire. James H. Johnson describes the new expectation that audiences remain silent and listen, in *Listening in Paris*. For more on how modern acoustics changed how we listen, see Leterrier, "Musique populaire et musique savante," and Thompson, *The Soundscape of Modernity*.

55. Fournel, *Ce qu'on voit*, 4

56. Ibid., 16.

57. On blind musicians, see Fournel, *Ce qu'on voit*, 33. For more on "Solsirépifpan, premier homme-orchestre des boulevards," see Gétreau, "Concerts ambulants," and "Les Musiciens de rue sous l'autorité de la police parisienne," in *Musiciens des rues de Paris*, 41–47. For Fournel on the "homme-orchestre," *Ce qu'on voit*, 38.

58. Fournel, *Ce qu'on voit*, 45–46.

59. The Musard family was linked with public concerts on the Champs Élysées in the 1830s. Philippe Musard (1792–1859) was the artistic director of the Concerts-Musard and balls at the Opéra until 1854. His son Alfred was born in 1818. The author claims to be a grandson, but is it only coincidental that the (pseudonymous?) author capitalizes on the pun (a *musard* is a *flâneur* or idler)?

60. It is worth remembering however that Bernadille (a.k.a. Geronte and Fournel) found artists such as Édouard Manet and Edgar Degas crude. See Clark, *The Painter of Modern Life*, 97.

61. Fournel, *Ce qu'on voit*, 14–15.

62. Ibid., 24.

63. Johnson, *Listening in Paris*, 262.

64. Fournel, however, did not show the same appreciation for the café concert (Clark, *The Painter of Modern Life*, 230–33). The mockery and distaste are palpable in Bernadille's chapter on the café-concert written in July 1872: "Last night, Sunday, while strolling on the Champs-Élysées toward the Cours-la-Reine park, I heard the loud noise of an orchestra, dominated by the high-pitched squeals of an epileptic soprano. Turning my head, I saw a richly-illuminated façade. Five hundred curious faces with gaping mouths listened from outside, and were drinking the heart-rending ['déchirant'] harmony with a satisfaction as marked as if it were iced lemonade. It was one of the cafés-concerts on the Champs Élysées: the Clock Pavilion [at the Louvre] or the Alcazar in the summertime, no matter!" (*Esquisses et Croquis parisiens*, 34).

65. In Balzac's *Gambara*, the eponymous musician and his wife end up performing on the Champs-Élysées to make ends meet.

66. Fournel, *Ce qu'on voit*, 27, my emphasis.

67. Ibid., my emphasis.

68. Forgues and Grandville, *Petites Misères de la vie humaine*, 329–30.

69. Thompson, "Rough Music Reconsidered," 20.

70. Davis, "The Reasons of Misrule," 100. Tilly, "Charivaris, Repertoires, and Urban Politics," 79. The French charivari was frequently used to humiliate widows/widowers entering second marriages and other sexual offenses and, therefore, can be said to uphold conservative norms; in the nineteenth century, political figures such as *députés* are charivarized as an early form of political protest.

71. Traits that are disregarded by Old Nick and Grandville might include the assembly's location in front of a private house to right a specific offense, the collective nature of the ritual, and the outnumbering of the victims by their numerous adjudicators.

72. Maria d'Anspach also penned "La Modiste" and "La Religieuse" in *Les Français peints par eux-mêmes*. Whereas Pierre Bouttier, the editor of the Omnibus edition of *Les Français* identifies her as a relation of the Margravine d'Anspach and of Milady Cravens, J. M. Quérard claims that Maria d'Anspach was a pseudonym of Julie Bordier, a milliner. See *Les Auteurs déguisés de la littérature*.

73. Anspach, *Le Prisme*, 184.

74. Balzac, "Paris en 1831," in *À Paris*, 37. We can find a similar complaint in Amaury Duval, "Une journée de flâneur," in *Paris ou Le Livre des Cent-et-un*, Collection électronique de la Médiathèque André Malraux de Lisieux (May 16, 2008), accesssed July 26, 2012, http://www.bmlisieux.com/curiosa/duval001.htm.

75. Anspach, *Le Prisme*, 185.

76. The December 1831 ordinance ordered the expulsion of *saltimbanques* from Paris, an order that would be renewed in subsequent decades. For an overview, see Burton, *The Flâneur and His City*, 55–60. Cubero, *Histoire du vagabondage*, 254.

77. Robert Darnton examines the link between street performers and salacious ru-

mors in France during the eighteenth century in *Poetry and the Police*. Though I have not examined this relationship here, controlling sonic street culture in order to crack down on antigovernment communication networks remained a priority in the nineteenth century.

78. The "Ordonnance concernant les joueurs d'orgue dans les places publiques" of 1816, the first of its kind, demanded that street musicians obtain permits, which included a printed visa form to be regularly renewed and a medallion that they wore to identify themselves. Permits were issued based on *bonnes moeurs* rather than musical talent. Itinerant tradesmen and performers (perceived as uncontrollable and disorderly) were equated with vagabonds and were the target of legislation enacted to encourage sedentary professions that could be subject to quality control, price monitoring, and fiscal regulation. For the details of the permitting process, see Landron, *Musiciens des rues de Paris*, 74–79.

79. Ibid., 76.

80. Cubero, *Histoire du vagabondage*, 230–32, 238; Landron, *Musiciens des rues de Paris*, 78; Olwen Hufton, "Begging, Vagrancy, Vagabondage and the Law," 97–123.

81. Picker, *Victorian Soundscapes*, 58–59. John M. Picker discusses the anti-street-music campaign in 1850s–60s Britain in his *Victorian Soundscapes*. In London, as in Paris, resentment for street musicians, particularly organ grinders, was linked to xenophobia and anti-immigration sentiment. The "Act for the Better Regulation of Street Music in the Metropolis," drafted by avid anti-street-music politician MP Michael T. Bass, sought to make it easier for householders to lodge complaints against street musicians who could then be assessed a fine or taken into custody. Picker shows how efforts such as Bass's reveal the formation of a new group identity of urban intellectuals who demand the right to silence for the sake of their professional livelihoods.

82. Anspach, *Le Prisme*, 186.

83. Fournel, *Ce qu'on voit*, 344.

84. Fournel, *Ce qu'on voit*, 320. A very similar statement is put forth by Jules Janin in *Un hiver à Paris* in 1845: "In Paris there are places, frightful *passages*, labyrinths, ruins, courtyards inhabited by all the thieves in the city. . . . These footsteps that you hear softly echoing on the muddy pavement, they are those of the *patrouille grise* or night-time patrol that is beginning its relentless chase . . . in the hideous recesses that Paris conceals behind its palaces and museums" (201, my translation). The slang Fournel refers to could be Yiddish, a language alluded to in James McCabe's description of Le Temple secondhand clothes market, in *Paris by Sunlight and Gaslight*, 617.

85. Rieger, "'Ce qu'on voit,'" 19.

86. Fournel, *Ce qu'on voit*, 21, 127, 8. Fournel uses the word "bizarre" at least six times.

87. Ibid., 294.

88. Ibid., 302.

89. The replacement of the *pavé* with *bitume* or asphalt in the newer neighborhoods would reduce the traffic noise. Balzac rails against *bitume* in "Monographie du rentier," in *Les Français peints*, 2:69.

Chapter 2. Blason Sonore

1. French custom considered wholesale trade "honest" and "noble," whereas retail sales were "lowly" or "servile" according to Jacques Savary, "Du commerce en gros et de son excellence," book 1, chapter 3 in *Le Parfait Négociant* quoted in *Retailers and Consumer Changes*, 16. For more historical detail about the relationship between the colporteurs and the guilds, see Vissière, "La Bouche et le Ventre de Paris," 71–89.

2. *COLPORTEUR* "describes small-scale ambulant tradesmen who carry their merchandise on their back or in front of them, in baskets or cases, etc. . . . They travel from town to town. Also describes those who cry out and sell bulletins, judgments, etc. . . . in the streets, with the approbation of authorities." *Dictionnaire de l'Académie française*, 6th edition (1835), s.v. "colporteur," 1:344, my translation.

3. Kastner and Thierry, *Les Voix de Paris*, 68–69.

4. Strong, *Sensations of Paris*, 206–9. Jarves, *Parisian Sights*, 179. Born in Boston, Jarves (1818–88) was an American expatriate, art writer, and collector.

5. Gilman, "Parisian Pedlars," 327.

6. John C. Cross argues convincingly that the "formal" economy never successfully squashes the "informal" economy in *Informal Politics*. I return to this observation in the conclusion.

7. Diaz, "Visions balzaciennes," 77. Baudelaire, *Œuvres complètes*, 85. Baudelaire, *The Flowers of Evil*, 175.

8. I borrow this evocative expression from Karin Bijsterveld and José Van Dijck, eds., *Sound Souvenirs*.

9. My reference to "cultural memory" draws less from Pierre Nora's "sites of memory" than from Ann Rigney's "dynamics of remembrance." She shifts the emphasis in memory studies from sites to process and circulation in "The Dynamics of Remembrance," 345–53.

10. Crapelet, ed., *Proverbes et Dictons populaires*; Franklin, *Les Rues et les Cris*.

11. Vissière, "Des cris pour rire?" 85–106. When Vissière refers to *gauloiserie* (99), he usefully but anachronistically applies a concept coined in the nineteenth century (*l'esprit gaulois* or Gallic spirit) to the medieval Cries. See Trotter, "L'Esprit Gaulois," 70–83. The bibliophile Jacob titled an anthology of seventeenth-century works on street noise, *Paris ridicule et burlesque,* accessed August 10, 2012, http://www.textesrares.com/paris000.php.

12. Dillon, *The Sense of Sound*, 77–91.

13. Ibid., 87–90.

14. For example, as Katherine Ellis documents, in the space of fourteen concerts in the winter of 1829–30, Janequin's *Les Cris de Paris* was performed four times. See *Interpreting the Musical Past*, 157–58.

15. Kastner and Thierry, *Les Voix de Paris*. Some of the music is included in the compact disc *L'Écrit du cri* by the Ensemble Clément Janequin with Dominique Visse. "Ethnographie" is included for the first time in the sixth edition of the *Dictionnaire de l'Académie française* (1835).

16. Among the more well-known works listed by Kastner are *La Muette de Portici* by Daniel-François Auber, *Les Cris de Paris, grande valse imitative* by Victor Parisot, *Voilà l'plaisir* by Edmond Lhuillier, and *Les Cris populaires de la Provence* by Félicien David. Many more are discussed by musicologist Jean-Rémy Julien in *Musique et Publicité*.

17. The pantomime's plot is retold by Théophile Gautier in "Shakespeare aux Funambules," 75–84, and later immortalized in Carné's film *Les Enfants du paradis*. For details, see Lansac, "'Chand d'habits!," 49–60.

18. Lauster, *Sketches of the Nineteenth Century*, 155. Lauster makes the connection between the Cries and various dramatic traditions (pantomime, commedia dell'arte, the trope of *theatrum mundi*). She cites for instance the juxtaposition of criers and popular theaters on the boulevards as described by Balzac in "Histoire et physiologie des boulevards de Paris," in *Le Diable à Paris*.

19. Charpentier, from Erato, *Louise*, complete recording introductory notes, quoted in Rifkin, *Street Noises*, 132.

20. Julien, *Musique et Publicité*, 134–36.

21. For a more extensive discussion, see Boutin, "Sound Memory," 67–78.

22. Balzac, *Old Goriot*, trans. Ellen Marriage, 195–99. *Le Père Goriot*, 3:201–2.

23. Julien, *Musique et Publicité*, 112–13.

24. Massin's *Les Cris de la ville* is an invaluable resource for whoever wishes to survey or research the repertoire of images of street cries. Beall's *Kaufrufe und Strassenhändler* extends Massin's catalog to inventory Cries in other European countries (plus China, North America, and Latin America) and analyzes how images of street criers mediate cultural issues and cross national borders. She remarks on the popularity of French print (20). More recently, Vincent Milliot's *Les Cris de Paris*, Sheila McTigue's "Perfect Deformity, Ideal Beauty," Sean Shesgreen's *Images of the Outcast* and Katie Scott's "Edme Bouchardon's 'Cris de Paris'" have significantly advanced the research on Cries, though McTigue and Shesgreen do not discuss French Cries. Scott's interpretations of rhythms and of sounds "pitched, ordered and arranged" (73) in Bouchardon's "Cris de Paris" is especially relevant to the present discussion. She also touches on the policing of watercarriers in ways that resonate with chapter 3.

25. This image is part of a series of eighteen woodcuts in the Bibliothèque de l'Arsenal collection. Beall, *Kaufrufe und Strassenhändler*, 210. On the history of the *oublie* pastry, see Bonnain, "D'une pâtisserie cérémonielle," 542–61.

26. For example, see the series by Louis-Edmé Bouchardon, *Études prises dans le bas peuple ou les Cris de Paris*, 1737–46 (sixty plates]); François Boucher, *Les Cris de Paris*, 1737 (twelve etched drawings); J. B. Marie Poisson, *Cris de Paris dessinés d'après nature*, 1769 (twelve suites of six plates); Joseph Watteau de Lille, *Cris et Costumes de Paris*, 1786; and Carle Vernet, *Cris de Paris, dessinés d'après nature par C. Vernet à Paris*, 1822 (series of one hundred color lithographs). For a brief overview, see the Stanford Art Gallery exhibition catalog by Miller, *Street Criers*.

27. Milliot adds that iconographies of street cries disappeared during the French Revolution, but resurged under the Restoration; see *Les Cris de Paris*, 317–18.

28. Ibid., 104.

29. McTigue examines how Annibale Carracci's *Arti di Bologna* appealed to a diverse class of buyers from collectors, antiquarians, librarians, and personal secretaries to working-class artisans.

30. Milliot makes note of an advertisement for engravings of the *Cris* based on Boucher in the *Mercure de France*, an elite periodical.

31. Pilinski and Cousin, *Cris de Paris.*

32. Milliot discusses the tendency to conceive of the Cries as a transparent reflection of life in *Les Cris de Paris*, 47.

33. Goncourt, *La Maison d'un artiste*, 2:110. See also his catalog entry on Bouchardon in Goncourt, 1:50.

34. For a related analysis, see Higonnet, "Real Fashion," 145.

35. Milliot, *Les Cris de Paris*, 207. Milliot refers to the erasure of the manual laborer's exertion and exhaustion as a travesty (*"travestissement"*) in *Les Cris de Paris.*

36. Gavarni produced a series of *Cris de Paris* (Rittner, c. 1828) according to the Goncourt brothers (*Gavarni l'homme*, 41). Armelhault and Bocher, however, specify that this type is a "physionomie anglaise" made in England, but printed in Paris by Imprimeur Bertauts (*Gavarni: Catalogue Raisonné*, no. 2074, 491). Gavarni visited England and published several sketches of street types during his stay (1847–51). *Marchand de casseroles* is one of them.

37. The following notable works are related to Cries iconography: Gustave Courbet, *The Knife Grinders*, 1848–50, Columbus Museum of Art, Ohio. Edouard Manet, *The Street Singer*, 1862, New York Public Library; *The Street Singer*, 1862, Museum of Fine Arts, Boston; *The Old Musician*, 1862, National Gallery of Art, Washington; *The Ragpicker*, 1865–70, The Norton Simon Foundation. Street types are also the focus of *Knife Grinder, rue Mosnier*, 1878, oil on canvas, Philadelphia Museum of Art. Henri de Toulouse-Lautrec, *Le Marchand de marrons*, 1897, Smith College Museum of Art. Eugène Atget, *Les Petits Métiers de rue*, 1899–99 and *Les Zoniers* 1899–1913, Bibliothèque nationale de France, Eastman House. Beyond the artistic avant-garde, Shesgreen identifies further transformations of the Cries tradition in documentary or institutional photographs of prostitutes, criminals, and lunatics (192). Meyer Schapiro and Linda Nochlin were among the first to draw attention to the importance of popular imagery, especially *images d'Épinal* but also the *petits métiers* (Schapiro, 168–69), in Gustave Courbet's art and by extension in modern art. See Schapiro, "Courbet and Popular Imagery," 164–91; Nochlin, "Gustave Courbet's *Meeting*," 209–22.

38. Shesgreen, *Images of the Outcast*, 110.

39. See Scott, "Edme Bouchardon's 'Cris de Paris'" for a discussion of rhythm in his suite (81–82).

40. Goncourt, *La Maison d'un artiste*, 2:110. The Cries refer to specific prints in Bouchardon's suite *Études prises dans le bas peuple ou les Cris de Paris*. Original emphasis.

41. Anne Leonard has explored how images can capture sonic experience, specifically listening to music in late-nineteenth-century art. She argues that the new status of attentive listening in the nineteenth century meant that painters turned to musical attentiveness in their pictorial works. I am suggesting we extend her theory to encom-

pass works that do not explicitly represent listeners, but that elicit the experience of attentive listening in the viewer. See "Picturing Listening," 266–86.

42. Among the most original depictions of street criers is Otto Dix's (1891–1969) *Le Marchand d'allumettes* [The Match Seller] (oil and collage on canvas, 1920, Staatsgalerie, Stuttgart, Germany). The German expressionist painter goes so far as to write out the cry on his canvas. The street seller is a war veteran and amputee who cries out "Matches, genuine Swedish matches," which are written in chalky oil paint on the canvas.

43. The expression is Priscilla Ferguson's from *Paris as Revolution*.

44. Julien, Klein, and Mongrédien, *Orphée Phrygien*, 39.

45. Janin, introduction to *Les Français*, 1:13, 21.

46. Le Men and Abélès, *Les Français peints par eux-mêmes*, 6–7.

47. Ibid., 7, 38–39. See also Lauster, *Sketches of the Nineteenth Century*, 153.

48. Le Men and Abélès, *Les Français peints par eux-mêmes*, 40, 43.

49. Ibid., 39.

50. Mainzer in *Les Français peints*, 2:793. References to Mainzer's essays in this edition will follow in the text. Henry Martin, recalling his arrival in Paris from the provinces, makes a similar remark in "Les Cris de Paris," 162.

51. *Grove Music Online*, s.v. "Mainzer, Joseph," by Bernarr Rainbow, accessed September 24, 2010, http://www.oxfordmusiconline.com.proxy.lib.fsu.edu/subscriber/article/grove/music/17487. Murphy, "Joseph Mainzer's 'Sacred and Beautiful Mission,'" 33–46.

52. Murphy, "Joseph Mainzer's 'Sacred and Beautiful Mission,'" 38.

53. Curmer's need to secure wealthy subscribers to finance his project explains the shift from a predominant emphasis on elegant circles to a more inclusive portrayal of the popular classes (see Le Men and Abélès, *Les Français peints par eux-mêmes*, 33–34).

54. Le Men goes so far as to suggest that *Les Français* heralded the Republic of 1848 (Le Men and Abélès, 33). Although militant advocacy is palpable in volumes 4 and 5, it is worth remarking however that Émile de la Bédollierre's portrait of the law student in volume 1 can be read as a tacit response to concurrent parliamentary debates about the overcrowding of Parisian law schools and underemployment of jurists. See Boutin, "The Title of Lawyer Leads Nowhere," 57–80.

55. The character types in these sections of *Les Francais peints par eux-mêmes* have an ironic or playful tone that is absent in sketches that treat the working classes. See Sieburth, "Une idéologie du lisible," 48n15.

56. Janin, "Les Petits Métiers," 141, 154.

57. Martin, "Le Cris de Paris," 158–59.

58. Kastner and Thierry, *Les Voix de Paris*, v.

59. In *The Soundscape of Modernity*, Emily Thompson argues that sound and space were divorced once acoustical and sound-proofing technologies eliminated reverberations and made different spaces (concert halls for instance) sound similar.

60. Cited in Murphy, "Joseph Mainzer's 'Sacred and Beautiful Mission,'" 42. On the collection of folkloric songs, see Fabre, "Proverbes, contes et chansons," 3555–81. See also Brix, "Une renaissance romantique," 31–40.

61. Gouriet is the first to include a score in a narrative about street criers; whereas

Vathier or Wattier is among the first to include the score in a print. Vathier is reproduced in Beall, *Kaufrufe und Strassenhändler*, 213, 263, and discussed in Julien, *Musique et Publicité*.

62. *Revue et Gazette Musicale*, September 20, 1835, cited in Murphy, "Joseph Mainzer's 'Sacred and Beautiful Mission,'" 307.

63. Ortigue, *Introduction à l'étude comparée des tonalités*, 168.

64. Ibid., 219–20.

65. *Grove Music Online*, s.v. "Plainchant," by Kenneth Levy, et al., accessed May 25, 2012, http://www.oxfordmusiconline.com.proxy.lib.fsu.edu/subscriber/article/grove/music/40099pg11.

66. Bergeron, *Decadent Enchantments*, 18–19. I thank Helen Abbott for her remarks on this section.

67. Genlis, *Mémoires inédits*, 112–13, cited in Fournel, *Les Cris de Paris*, 68. Genlis explains that since the criers could not sing cheerfully during the Terror, they never lost the tone of lamentation they acquired during the Revolution.

68. Fournel, *Les Cris de Paris*, 66–67.

69. Saint-Saëns, "A Note on Rameau," 92. I thank Marcia Porter for help with this source. Saint-Saëns was himself an interpreter of Rameau's music and edited the incomplete *Oeuvres complètes* from 1895 to 1905.

70. Proust, *À la recherche*, 3:623–36, *In Search of Lost Time*, 5:147–63. References to these editions will follow in the text. For a literary commentary on the passage, see Gantrel, "Albertine ou l'Étrangère," 3–25. For a musical interpretation, see Spitzer, "Étymologie d'un cri de Paris," 474–81. Julien, "L'Influence des crieurs," 147–57. LeBlanc, "De Charpentier à Wagner," 903–21.

71. Contemporaries also compared Debussy's recitative to Gregorian chant and to Rameau, who praised the natural musical abilities of street criers in *Code de la musique* (see Milliot, *Les Cris de Paris*, 283). The word "natural" may best be understood in opposition to the screaming voice in French eighteenth-century opera as discussed in Kastner and Thierry (referring to the street crier turned countertenor Etienne Lainez): "From his manner of stressing the words separately, the voice was emitted in fits and with effort; as a result, sounds would only be produced as cries that were most often disagreeable" (19, my translation).

Chapter 3. Sonic Classifications in Haussmann's Paris

1. For a comprehensive overview of Haussmann's plan, see Jordan, *Transforming Paris*, 188.

2. Fournel, *Les Cris de Paris*, 70. "Je suis le cri plaintif et impuissant de Paris qui s'en va contre Paris qui vient." Fournel, *Paris nouveau et Paris futur*, 2.

3. See Augoyard and Torgue, eds. *À l'écoute de l'environnement*. For an overview on spatial acoustics, auditory spatial awareness, and cultural acoustics, see the introduction to Blesser and Salter, *Spaces Speak*. The architect and historian of sound Olivier Balaÿ provides a detailed interpretation of nineteenth-century spatial acoustics in Lyon, in *L'Espace sonore*.

4. Mainzer, in *Les Français peints*, 2:788, 821.

5. Marchand, *Paris, histoire*, 85.

6. Luchet, "Les Passages," 6:97–113.

7. See Mainzer, in *Les Français peints*, 2:836, 851, 868, 870. Fétis, "De la musique des rues," 288–93.

8. Musset, "Parisiens et Parisiennes," 445. Paul was the older brother of Alfred, the poet and author of *La Confession d'un enfant du siècle*.

9. Martin, "Les Cris de Paris," 3:164.

10. Pallasmaa, *The Eyes of the Skin*, 25, 46. For another, pointed discussion of architecture and acoustical effects, see Balaÿ, "The 19th Century Transformation," 1–10, accessed June 8, 2012, http://doc.cresson.grenoble.archi.fr/opac/doc_num.php?explnum_id=279.

11. Yriarte, "Les Types parisiens," 929.

12. Sand, "La Rêverie à Paris," 1196.

13. In *Apartment Stories*, Sharon Marcus discusses the apartment building as a sanctuary from the noise from the street and the neighbors. According to Jean-Pierre Gutton, the search for quietude as part of the pursuit of intimacy dates back to the mid-eighteenth century (*Bruits et sons*, 84–94).

14. Vincent, "Les Dernières Échoppes," 972–80.

15. Frébault, *Les Industriels du macadam*, 54–55.

16. Ibid., 95, 102–4.

17. Mainzer, in *Les Français peints*, 2:811, 842. Trollope, *Paris and the Parisians*, 1:125.

18. Balzac, "Histoire et physiologie," 1:101.

19. Challamel, *Les Amuseurs de la rue*, 5. Nerval, "Le Boulevard du Temple," 70–71.

20. Énault, "Au bord de l'eau," 229. Edmond Texier also comments on the *petits industriels* on the Pont Neuf in the chapter titled "Le Pont Neuf" (*Tableau de Paris*, 244). Even types not encountered on the Pont Neuf are treated in this catchall chapter.

21. Texier, *Tableau de Paris*, 1:67. Texier also contributes to *Paris Guide* a chapter on hawkers based on his own *Tableau de Paris*.

22. Frébault, *Les Industriels du macadam*, 34, 44.

23. Amicis, *Studies of Paris*, 16, 18.

24. King, *My Paris*, 268.

25. Hahn, *Scenes of Parisian Modernity*, 138. Shouting the news was prohibited in 1889.

26. As Bijsterveld explains in *Mechanical Sound*, restrictions on the noisemaking of unincorporated trades are long-standing in Europe (56–57). Throughout the eighteenth century, legislation was passed to regulate *petits métiers*. The continuities between ancien regime and the post-Revolutionary regulation would be worth further study. In "Edme Bouchardon's 'Cris de Paris,'" Scott addresses the legislation on health pertaining to water-carriers cited by Nicolas Delamare's *Traité de la police* (60). In different ways, eighteenth-century French historians Laura Mason and Dean T. Ferguson argue that restrictions on where petty tradesmen and street entertainers could practice their livelihoods, prescriptions as to good conduct, and permitting (through the wearing of

a medallion), are evidence of a new approach to disturbances of the peace that aim to control dissenting bodies and movement. See Mason, *Singing the French Revolution*, 169–70; Ferguson, "The Body, the Corporate Idiom," 569–72.

27. Gisquet, *Mémoires de M. Gisquet*, 273, 325–37.

28. Vigier, *Paris pendant la monarchie*, 271.

29. Martin, "Les Cris de Paris," 165.

30. Janin, "Les Petits Métiers," 151–75.

31. Baruch-Gourden, "La Police et le commerce ambulant," 251–67. My discussion of the ordinances on street vendors is indebted to Baruch-Gourden. Also, Du Camp, "Les Halles centrales," 191–92. See articles 2881, 3551, 3983, and 4103 in volume 6 of *Collection officielle des ordonnances de police depuis 1851 jusqu'à 1861*.

32. Landron, *Musiciens des rues de Paris*, 78. Many literary guidebooks also refer to police surveillance. See *Paris Guide*, 964, 978.

33. *Ordonnances sur les marchés publics*, 1865, articles 56–58. See Thompson, *The Virtuous Marketplace*, 116, 203n100.

34. See Baruch-Gourden, "La Police et le commerce ambulant," 251–69.

35. A 1902 municipal police report cited in Baruch-Gourden, "La Police et le commerce ambulant," 262.

36. Haussmann, *Mémoire sur les eaux de Paris*, 1:53.

37. Corbin, *Time, Desire, and Horror*, 156. He details the concerns of pre-Haussmannian hygienists in this chapter but does not provide further information (or sources) about hygienists' perceptions of street cries.

38. *Collection officielle des ordonnances de police depuis 1851*, vol. 6, articles 2336, 2417, 3035, 3070, 4093. On thresholds of intolerance, see Corbin, "Bruits, excès," 13–23. Geneviève Massard-Guilbaud also discusses the existence of complaints against noise in the early part of the nineteenth century, but argues that they lacked legitimacy because unlike stench, noise was not considered a health threat. See *Histoire de la pollution industrielle*, 72.

39. Nadar, *Le Cas de cloches*, 21. On bells as nuisance, see Corbin, *Village Bells*, 303–4.

40. Trollope, *Paris and the Parisians*, 118.

41. Ṣaffār, *Disorienting Encounters*, 131.

42. *L'Illustration* cited in Ṣaffār, *Disorienting Encounters*, 131n.13.

43. Jordan, *Transforming Paris*, 221.

44. Balzac, "Monographie du rentier," 2:69. Balzac's *rentier* first praises asphalt then desists when he realizes it cannot stand up to "the countless wheels that circulate in all directions in Paris." On paving and circulation, see chapter 6 on urban circulation in Fonssagrives, *Hygiène et assainissement des villes*, 119, 203, 219.

45. Hahn, *Scenes of Parisian Modernity*, 134–35.

46. On the health effects of traffic noise, see Fonssagrives, *La Maison: Étude d'hygiène et de bien-être domestiques* (1871), 347, quoted in *Hygiène et assainissement des villes*, 200.

47. Bijsterveld, *Mechanical Sound*. Karen Bijsterveld examines noise abatement campaigns in the United States and Europe, though in the case of the latter the emphasis is

on Britain, Germany, Holland, and less on France. According to Bijsterveld, the Society for the Suppression of Noise was established in France in 1928.

48. Gutton, *Bruits et sons*, 145.

49. Fournel, *Ce qu'on voit*, 262.

50. Here I follow Aleida Assmann's emphasis on the interrelation of remembrance and forgetting in the workings of cultural memory.

51. The entry for "colporteurs" in Diderot and d'Alembert's *Encyclopédie* (1753) reads: "in former times they were people of bad faith who roamed from town to town, selling and buying merchandise that was to be sold exclusively at markets" (3:659–60, my translation). Alfred Franklin, in his late-nineteenth-century *Dictionnaire historique des arts, métiers et professions*, also underscored the shady nature of peddlers who trafficked in defective merchandise.

52. Fournel, *Les Cris de Paris*, 59–60; Mainzer, in *Les Français peints*, 2:804; Beall, *Kaufrufe und Strassenhändler*, 19. Fétis, "De la musique des rues," 290.

53. Mercier, *Tableau de Paris*, 1:1050–51.

54. Mercier's description of the *Cris de Paris* recalls an engraving by Hogarth (1697–1764) titled *The Cries of London*, depicting an aristocrat's negative reaction to a band of street musicians outside his window, with the notable exception that Mercier seeks to separate the bourgeois, not the aristocratic, observer from the populace. Mercier also discusses street cries in chapters 60 "Les Colporteurs" (1:158–60) and 516 "Falots" (1:1414–17) of *Tableau de Paris*.

55. Mercier, *L'An 2440*, 36. Translation in Vidler, "Reading the City," 239.

56. For more discussion, see Milliot, *Les Cris de Paris*, chapter 9.

57. Mercier, *Le Nouveau Paris*, 212.

58. Fournel, *Les Cris de Paris*, 220.

59. Milliot, *Les Cris de Paris*, 342.

60. Kroen, *Politics and Theater*, 183; see also Darnton, *Poetry and the Police*; and Mason, *Singing the French Revolution*.

61. Goncourt cited in Kastner and Thierry, *Les Voix de Paris*, 73.

62. On the construction of reassuring images of peddlers in the nineteenth century, see Milliot, *Le Cris de Paris*, 355–56. My discussion of cultural memory as actively circulated memory that keeps the past present draws heavily from Aleida Assmann's distinction between "canon" as active, selective remembering and "archive" as passive, cumulative storage, as well as Ann Rigney's dual emphasis on how cultural memories are (i) constructed in the present rather than resurrected from the past and (ii) repeatedly circulated in a variety of media ("remediation"). See Assmann, "Canon and Archive," 97–107. Rigney, "Plenitude, Scarcity," 11–28.

63. Mainzer, in *Les Français peints*, 2:790.

64. Nadar, "Daguerréotype acoustique."

65. In 2008, the First Sounds Project has made it possible to listen to Scott's 1860 recordings. Consult http://www.firstsounds.org/sounds/scott.php to listen to "the earliest clearly recognizable record of the human voice yet recovered." Accessed July 26, 2013.

66. Mainzer, in *Les Français peints*, 2:790, 887.

67. Classen, *The Deepest Sense*, 145.

68. The premise of *Le Diable à Paris* is that Satan sends his attendant, Flammèche, to Paris to record everything there is to know about the city, as P. J. Stahl explains in the volume's prologue. The miniatures the Devil examines could also be Messein porcelain statuettes of peddlers, which were, and still are, sold.

69. Brunot, "Le Musée de la parole." "Les Archives de la parole" were inaugurated on June 3, 1911; this collection is now part of the Audiovisual department at the Bibliothèque nationale de France. More information about "Les Archives de la parole" can be found on the Gallica—BNF website, at http://gallicadossiers.bnf.fr/ArchivesParole/, accessed March 29, 2001.

70. Péheu's recording, which is not part of the "Archives de la parole," is not an ethnographic document, but rather an "imitation," suggesting that it is closer to a cabaret performance piece wherein the actor imitates various cries and dialogues with merchants. *Les Cris parisiens: Scène d'imitations; Ressemblance: monologue,* spoken by Jean Péheu, audio recording, Bibliothèque nationale de France, Audiovisual department, SD 78 25–11567, 78 rpm disc, doi: ark:/12148/bpt6k127305d.

71. Beraldi, *Paris qui crie*. An influential French bibliophile, Beraldi was the president of Société des Amis des livres.

72. Dufour, *Lettres d'un Sicilien*, 77–79. The Sicilian Jean-Paul Marana (1642–93) resided in Paris in 1692 and wrote a travel journal in Italian that was translated in the eighteenth century and reedited in the nineteenth century.

73. See Le Men, Abélès and Preiss, *Les Français peints par eux-mêmes*, 46. See also Hamon, "Littérature et réclame," 5–10.

74. Fournel, *Ce qu'on voit*, 302.

75. The March 19, 1889, law restricts the right of newsprint vendors to impose their product on the public's ear. Only the title, not the content can be advertised through shouting out. Postering after 1881 was unrestricted except for limited access to public buildings and colored paper reserved for official use. Prior restrictions included visas, approval procedures, and regulatory stamps. Le Poittevin, *Traité de la presse*, part 3.

76. Hamon, *Imageries*, 310.

Chapter 4. Listening to the Glazier's Cry

1. Several scholars, including Pierre Citron in *La Poésie de Paris* and Karlheinz Stierle in *La Capitale des signes*, identify the 1830s as a turning point in the history of Paris, the moment when the city acquired a modern sense of place.

2. Benjamin, *The Writer of Modern Life*, 54, 108–9. As a member of the criminal underworld, "the apache," explains Benjamin, "abjures virtue and laws; he terminates the *contrat social* forever" (107).

3. After the trial of *Les Fleurs du mal* in 1857, Baudelaire produced a second edition (1861) that included a new section, "Tableaux parisiens." On the significance of the word "tableaux," see Stierle, *La Capitale des signes*, 88–90, 451–53.

4. See my earlier discussions of Mainzer's contributions to *Les Français peints par eux-mêmes*, of Yriarte's *Paris grotesque*, and Fournel's *Ce qu'on voit*.

5. Baudelaire, *The Painter of Modern Life*, 184–85. Original French in Baudelaire, *Œuvres complètes*, 2:562. References to Baudelaire's poetry and prose will be to the two-volume Pléiade edition, abbreviated O.C. when clarification is needed.

6. Baudelaire, O.C., 1:200–201, 216, 221. These juvenilia are not included in the Oxford World Classics translation of *The Flowers of Evil*. Other English titles in parentheses can be found in this Oxford University Press edition translated by James McGowan.

7. The red-haired singer was renowned on the streets. She was painted by Emile Deroy and also inspired a poem by Banville, "Colombine à la rue. À une petite chanteuse des rues," from *Les Stalactites*.

8. Berger's close reading of "À une mendiante rousse" explores changes to the traditional economy of giving and their impact on the function of poetic language. See *Scènes d'aumône*, 208–23. For another interpretation of the significance of beggars in the period, see Greaney, *Untimely Beggar*.

9. Indeed a ragpicker known as "the General" was a soapbox orator in Paris in the 1840s. See Pichois's comments in Baudelaire, O.C., 1:1048.

10. The discordant shouts in "Le Crépuscule du soir" (1:311; "Twilight" [50]) are those of the insane in an asylum atop Mount Fourvière, in Lyon, where Baudelaire lived as a teenager, according to Baudelaire's editor, Claude Pichois, O.C., 1:1328; however, without this biographical and bibliographical information, the cries could be any cacophonous human voices. The first quote is from "Le Tir et le Cimetière" (1:351; "The Shooting Range and the Cemetery" [111]). English translations of the prose poems refer to *The Parisian Prowler*, trans. Edward Kaplan.

11. *Le Peintre* in O.C., 2:692; *The Painter*, 10. "M. G." is Baudelaire's designation for the sketch artist Monsieur Constantin Guys.

12. It is worth recalling a similar point made in an influential article by Ross Chambers about Baudelaire's incorporation of noise as entropy into poetic beauty in *Les Fleurs du mal*: "Baudelaire then does not present noise as an impediment to communication so much as he sees noise-traversed communication as the only mode available to modern poetic speech." Chambers relies on a model borrowed from information theory to argue that noise is a significant feature of Baudelaire's street poetry, because it generates entropy and thus impedes communication. The result, continues Chambers, is that meaning and language are questioned at every turn. Chambers, "Baudelaire's Street Poetry," 253.

13. O.C., 1:276; *Parisian Prowler*, 129–30.

14. Ross Chambers and Sonya Stephens provide classic interpretations of this homage. See Chambers, "Baudelaire's Dedicatory Practice," 5–17; and Stephens, *Baudelaire's Prose Poems*.

15. Chambers, "Baudelaire's Dedicatory Practice," 5–17.

16. Houssaye, *Œuvres poétiques*, 287–90. The poem, "La Chanson du vitrier," is also reproduced in Baudelaire, O.C., 1:1309–11. It was first published in *Poésies complètes* (Paris: Charpentier, 1850) now available online on Gallica.

17. Murphy, *Logiques*, 336. My interpretation of "La Chanson du vitrier" and "Le Mauvais Vitrier" are indebted to Murphy's insightful and far-reaching reading of Baudelaire.

18. Berger, *Scènes d'aumône*, 178–79.

19. It would be worth comparing Houssaye's poem with "À une mendiante rousse"; in Baudelaire's poem, the red-haired beggar-woman is deprived of the kind of backstory that Houssaye provides in his poem. The emphasis is placed instead on the speaker's fantasies and the gesture of giving alms never is completed in the traditional sense. See Berger's analysis in *Scènes d'aumône*.

20. See Murphy, *Logiques*, 342.

21. Girardin, *Lettres parisiennes*, 1:189; my translation.

22. Mainzer, "Le Vitrier Peintre," 2:915. La Bédollierre, "Le Vitrier ambulant," 92.

23. Baudelaire reminisces about his loitering in "boutiques de vitrier" (glazier's shops) in the *Salon of 1846* (O.C., 2:443).

24. Burton, "Destruction as Creation," 302. Burton's remarks on the glazier's cry as embodiment of the "swan-song . . . of a dying street trade . . . [and] superseded socioeconomic order" are integral to my argument.

25. Mainzer, in *Les Français*, 2:913. La Bédollierre, "Le Vitrier ambulant," 91–93.

26. Murphy, *Logiques*, and Burton, "Destruction as Creation" document these connotations.

27. Houssaye, in Baudelaire, O.C., 1:1310.

28. Murphy, *Logiques*, 357–58.

29. These tensions in the text lead Steve Murphy to claim rightly that Houssaye is not able to control the intentional directions of his own text (*Logiques*, 385).

30. Houssaye, in Baudelaire, O.C., 1:1310.

31. Burton, "Destruction as Creation," 303n15.

32. "Ohé le vitrier" appears in a musical play by Dinaux, Sue, and Pilati, *Les Mystères de Paris: roman en cinq parties et onze tableaux*, presented at the Théâtre de la Porte Saint-Martin (1844), and "ô vitrier" is found in J. K. Huysmans's *En ménage*. Kastner cites "oh! vitri!" in *Les Voix de Paris*, 79.

33. Kastner and Thierry, *Les Voix de Paris*, 79; my translation.

34. Kastner and Thierry, *Les Voix de Paris*, 112; Kastner quoted in Planté, "Ce qu'on entend dans la voix," 103. It may well be that Grétry used conventional diction in the lines of noble characters while he omitted the silent 'e' mainly in the dialogue of lower-class characters. I wish to thank Adeline Heck and Richard Rath for their help interpreting Mainzer's and Bertall's scores.

35. La Bédollierre, *Les Industriels*, 89–90. I use the International Phonetic Alphabet in this paragraph.

36. Mainzer, *Les Français*, 2:913–14; my translation.

37. See chapter 2, section "The Tonality of Street Cries."

38. Hector Berlioz, "*Louise Miller* opéra de M. Alaffre. Académie impériale de musique," *Revue de Paris* 3 (1853): 242, repr., *À travers chants: Études musicales, adorations, boutades et critiques*, 92, quoted in Planté, "Ce qu'on entend dans la voix," 103.

39. Culler, *The Pursuit of Signs*, 135–55.

40. "oh, int. and n.1." OED Online. Last updated OED Third Edition, March 2004. Oxford University Press. Accessed August 31, 2012.

41. See Murphy, *Logiques*, 346–48.

42. Houssaye, *Les Confessions*, 3:193.

43. See Houssaye, *Le Violon de Franjolé,* 270–75.

44. On the circulation of tears, see Vincent-Buffault, *Histoire des larmes*. Or David J. Denby, *Sentimental Narrative*.

45. Murphy, *Logiques*, 345–49.

46. Stephens, *Baudelaire's Prose Poems*, 75. Stephens who astutely elucidates the duplicitous forms of irony in "Le Mauvais Vitrier," argues that Baudelaire both critiques bourgeois commercialism and strives to reproduce, perhaps parodically, its search for novelty and singularity (85).

47. Houssaye, *Poésies complètes*, 168. The essay states it was first published in *L'Artiste* in 1848.

48. Gautier, *La Presse*, 4:321–22, quoted in Bénichou, *Nerval*, 349. See also Banville, "Musique populaire et poésie," 121. For a general overview of the influence of song on nineteenth-century French poetry, see Buffard-Moret, *La Chanson poétique*. I thank Helen Abbott for the reference to this book.

49. Rimbaud, *Œuvres complètes*, 263; *Complete Works, Selected Letters*, 284–85.

50. Désaugiers, *Chansons et poésies diverses*, 1855, accessed June 26, 2012, http://www .miscellanees.com/d/paris01.htm. I thank Catherine Nesci for pointing this reference out to me. Désaugiers was as famous as Béranger in his lifetime. The Désaugiers poem was translated by John Oxenford, and included in Longfellow, *Poems of Places: An Anthology in 31 volumes* (1876–79).

51. Béranger uses the dramatic persona of the old-clothes–man to mock political instability and criticize the opportunism of the elites who change clothes as they change political affiliations. Desbordes-Valmore's sentimental elegy uses a refrain that repeats the night-crier's cry "Éveillez-vous gens qui dormez . . ." in a story of two lovers' nocturnal encounter (conveniently prolonged when the fiancé bribes the crier to stretch out his call). Bénichou examines Nerval's and more broadly nineteenth-century French poetry's appropriations of folkloric songs in *Nerval et la chanson folklorique*. Because his focus is primarily on rural folklore, he does not consider street cries and urban popular aural culture.

52. Bertrand, *Œuvres complètes*, 241. The translation is mine. Poggenburg remarks that the night crier's cry "Réveillez-vous gens qui dormez" used by Bertrand in "Le Clair de lune" (43) and Desbordes-Valmore in "Le Crieur de nuit" is cited in Langlé, "Le Clocheteur des trépassés."

53. Siefert, *Rayons perdus*, 116.

54. Bénichou, *Nerval*, 350.

55. Murphy, *Logiques*, 351.

56. O.C., 2:175; my translation.

57. Baudelaire, "Marceline Desbordes-Valmore," O.C., 2:147. For more on Baudelaire's essay on Desbordes-Valmore, see Lloyd, "Baudelaire, Marceline Desbordes-Valmore,"

65–74; Boutin, "Desbordes-Valmore, Lamartine and Poetic Motherhood," 315–30. Desbordes-Valmore's poetry was widely associated with songs and cries, notably by Barbey d'Aurevilly who coined the expression "la poésie du Cri," but careful analysis shows that her poetry of the cry has less to do with gender stereotypes than with class and her lack of formal education; for a discussion, see Planté, "Ce qu'on entend dans la voix."

58. On the impact of popular song on Baudelaire's formative years, see Robb, *La Poésie de Baudelaire*, 243–78.

59. Commentators often mention that "À une mendiante rousse" appropriates the heptasyllabic form of Ronsard's "Ode à la Fontaine Bellerie," but following Robb, we should note that this poem also exactly replicates the form of Banville's "À Gavarni" (*Poésie de Baudelaire*, 261). As Robb documents, the red-haired street musician inspired several song-like poems, including Banville's "À une petite chanteuse des rues," Dupont's (1851) "La Joueuse de guitare," and Esquiros's (1849) "Une petite chanteuse des rues."

60. See Abbott, "Baudelaire's 'Le Jet d'eau,'" 37–56.

61. Abbott, *Parisian Intersections*.

62. Baudelaire, *Correspondance*, 2:208.

63. Nodier, *Dictionnaire des onomatopées*, 168.

64. The *Trésor de la Langue française* (TLFi) online dictionary provides information on the relative literary frequency of a word, or the number of times a word occurs in a given corpus divided by the total number of words in the same corpus. This data is a measure of the word's importance in a given corpus or historical period. In the TLFi, the relative literary frequency for *strident* referring to a sound is 94 (http://www.cnrtl.fr/definition/strident, consulted September 8, 2012). By comparison, the same dictionary scores the relative literary frequency of *harmonieux* at 1,813 (http://www.cnrtl.fr/definition/harmonieux). I conducted textual mining searches using the ARTFL database and found similar results: the literary frequency rises steadily throughout the century and is greatest between 1850 and 1899 (frequency of 123). The word is used by Rabelais, but then is not recorded until Voltaire (a single occurrence). Often the adjective describes instruments or birds, occasionally the human voice as in *Les Misérables*. Finally, textual mining using Google Ngram Viewer shows similar results, with a steady rise of usage beginning in 1840 and continuing throughout the nineteenth century, reaching a high in our period and its greatest peak in 1920 after World War I. A comparative analysis of the Google Ngram of *harmonieux* (http://goo.gl/OApOAz) and that of *strident* (http://goo.gl/P6mtTq) shows that the rate of occurrence in French of the former term stays relatively stable between 1800 and 1900, whereas the latter rises steadily throughout the century.

65. Murphy, *Logiques*, 367. Burt, *Poetry's Appeal*, 27–28.

66. On frustrating hermeneutics, see Krueger, "Telling Stories in Baudelaire's *Spleen de Paris*," 281–99.

67. Murphy, *Logiques*, 357.

68. Johnson discusses Niccolò Paganini's association with the devil in *Listening in Paris*, 265–75, 336n8, 341–42n44.

69. Music from both the Kastner and the Lebeau pieces can be sampled on the CD *L'Écrit du cri* by Ensemble Clément Janequin with Dominique Visse.

70. Mainzer, in *Les Français*, 2:913–14; my translation.

71. The Baudelairean reader cannot help but make the connection between Mainzer's description of this glazier's cry and the shrill whistle blast that interrupted Fancioulle in "Une mort héroïque" (1:322; "A Heroic Death" [66]).

72. Kaplan translates "une action d'éclat" by "brilliant action" (*The Parisian Prowler*, 14). We should note that the French words "*éclat*" and "*éclatant*" contain both aural and visual connotations, and that "brilliant" characterizes intense bright light and high frequency sound.

73. Jonathan Culler, whose analysis emphasizes the self-reflexivity of the poem, refers to the poem as "calembour en action" using an expression Baudelaire coined, in "Baudelaire and Poe," 61–73.

74. Lloyd, *Baudelaire's World*, 157. Lloyd clarifies the irony in the poem earlier in her book when she states that the narrative voice shatters the glass panels to liberate art from "representational limitations" (67). Baudelaire as an artist wants it both ways: to reveal the world as it is *and* to embellish it.

75. For a succinct overview, see Jackson, "Bruit et musique," 48–51, repr., in *Baudelaire sans fin*, 63–74.

76. Burton, "Bonding and Breaking," 65. As Burton writes, "It is difficult to imagine a better description of the *Petits poèmes en prose* themselves: a 'symphonie en sourdine' continually broken by explosive, disjunctive sounds, voices, and actions, a unique interweaving of the concordant and discordant, the lyric and the counter-lyric."

77. For a discussion of harmony in Baudelaire, see Evans, *Baudelaire and Intertextuality*, 133, Prendergast, *Paris and the Nineteenth Century*. Evans usefully discusses the interrelation between "harmony," "uniformity and consonance," "discordance," and "dissonance" in Baudelaire in terms of Wagnerian music and with broad reference to his other critical works. Prendergast concludes that the only way for Baudelaire to "stay poetically in the city" is for him to "forsa[ke] or modi[fy] the ideal of harmony" (131).

78. Prendergast emphasizes that dissonance can take the form of irony (151–52).

79. *Fusées*, O.C., 1:661; my translation.

80. Michael Cowan insightfully comments on Baudelaire's "effort to incorporate noise and its scattering function into literary aesthetics." See "Imagining Modernity through the Ear," 133–34.

Chapter 5. "Cry Louder, Street Crier"

1. Mortelette, "Francois Coppée," 542–53.

2. A *dizain* is a ten-line stanza that was popular in the Renaissance (in the poetry of Maurice de Scève). It was resurrected by Coppée in a simplified form that blurs the boundaries between lyric poetry and prose. Wafa Abid examines Coppée's prosaic style and emulation of Émile Zola in "Les Enjeux du prosaïsme," 348–62.

3. One can find such clichés in *Les Français peints par eux-mêmes* and *Physiologie de la grisette*. Other famous grisettes appear in Victor Hugo's *Les Misérables*, Henry Murger's

Scènes de la vie de Bohème, George Sand's *Horace*, and Alfred de Musset's *Mimi Pinson*. The grisette, a mythic figure of the 1830s, was a poorly paid young woman employed in the garment or millinery trade. Sometimes identified as a female bohemian, she often lived with a law or medical student who abandoned her upon graduation. Abid discusses Coppée's predilection for cliché and stock images in "Les Enjeux du prosaïsme," 360.

4. *Poésies de François Coppée*, 116; my translation.

5. See Murphy, *Stratégies de Rimbaud*, 205. See also, Murphy, "'Pauvre Coppée,'" 55–78.

6. Arthur Rimbaud, "Conneries II: Paris," *Œuvres complètes*, 174. Philippe Hamon discusses the use of posters and advertisements in Rimbaud's "Paris" in *Imageries*, 157–60, and *Expositions*, 132–33. Steve Murphy, who provides a thorough analysis of the poem, suggests the non sequitur form recalls the *Cris de Paris* in *Stratégies de Rimbaud*, 241. See also Reboul, *Rimbaud dans son temps*, 265–87; and Saint-Clair, "'Soyons chrétiens!'?"

7. Syncopated language, popular references, repetition, and song are used most notably in "Le Hareng Saur," Cros's most famous monologue-poem, as well as "Chanson des sculpteurs," and "Brave Homme."

8. Lorin, *Paris rose*, 57–62. The poem is quoted at the beginning and end of this chapter.

9. Cros drafted and submitted his scientific proposal for the *paléophone* independently from Thomas Edison in April 1877, but it was Edison who first succeeded in realizing a working phonograph, getting a patent, and marketing his device. Due to Cros's inability (because of lack of interest or of funding) to bring his invention to the market, Edison is usually credited with the invention of sound recording in 1878. Cros also had a hand in inventing color photography. See Cros, *Œuvres complètes . . . et textes scientifiques*, 579–80.

10. Cros, *Œuvres complètes*, collection Pléiade, 148; my translation.

11. See chapter 3.

12. Mercier, *Tableau de Paris*, chapter 464, 1:1285–86.

13. Mainzer, in *Les Français peints*, 2:838.

14. André Breton includes the *fumistes* as precursors to the surrealists in *Anthologie de l'humour noir*. Daniel Grojnowski provides a definition in English of *fumisme* as an avant-garde philosophy that announces twentieth-century humor in "Hydropathes and Company," in Cate and Shaw, *The Spirit of Montmartre*, 95–109.

15. As David Trotter explains, *l'esprit gaulois* is an anachronistic term that describes the coarse humor widely associated with the Middle Ages (especially medieval *fabliaux*) in the nineteenth century. "L'Esprit Gaulois," in Cameron, *Humour and History*, 70–83. Olga Anna Dull discusses the appeal of Rabelais and *l'esprit gaulois* among the artistic avant-garde and cabaret culture of Montmartre in the 1890s in "From Rabelais to the Avant-Garde," in Cate and Shaw, *The Spirit of Montmartre*, 199–241.

16. A different line of investigation might lead the reader of Cros's poem back to Baudelaire's "Paysage" in *The Flowers of Evil* where the speaker also looks out his garret window and hears the carillon and the workshop.

17. See my discussion in the section "The Multimodal Genres of the *Cris de Paris*: Musical, Graphic, Textual" in chapter 2.

18. Cros, *Œuvres complètes*, collection Pléiade, 150; my translation.

19. Musset, "Parisiens et Parisiennes," 449.

20. Frébault, *Les Industriels du macadam*, 82.

21. The verbs in the poem, all in the infinitive, situate the action outside of time, as in a dream.

22. A nonlexical onomatopoeia, according to Attridge in *Peculiar Language*, involves "the use of the phonetic characteristics of the language to imitate a sound without attempting to produce recognizable verbal structures" (136). I should note that "tin tin" is a standard French onomatopoeia, linked to the verb "tinter" (to clank).

23. Baudelaire, O.C., 1:661; my translation.

24. On the changing meaning of poverty in nineteenth-century France and poets' reactions to pauperism, see Berger, *Scènes d'aumône*.

25. *La Chanson des gueux* was a sensation when it was published, catapulting its author to celebrity. A transitional figure between the Parnassians and the symbolists, Richepin is largely overshadowed today by the sustained innovation of the poets who came after him. For more on Richepin's reception, see Sutton, *The Life and Work of Jean Richepin*. Richepin, *La Chanson des Gueux*, 99–100, 101–3, 106–9, 115, 124–27. Alissa Le Blanc provides an insightful reading of *La Chanson des Gueux* in "Parler au nom des Gueux?," 141–77.

26. Frébault refers to Montmartre in *Les Industriels du macadam* (100–102). Richepin mentions Sceaux and Clamart in "Du mouron pour les p'tits oiseaux." Fernand Pelez immortalized the destitution of the violet seller in "Un martyr ou le marchand de violettes," representing a poor boy in rags who has fallen asleep on the job.

27. That is not to say that the type was not discussed earlier. In "Ce qui disparaît de Paris" (1845), Balzac wrote nostalgically that soon "a coco-vendor will be an insoluble problem when one sees his original portrait, his bells, beautiful silver tympani, the footless goblet of our ancestors, the goldsmith's carved lilies, the pride of the bourgeois, and his water-tower, all dolled up, covered in silks and plumes, some of which were silver" (16, my translation; un marchand de coco sera comme un problème insoluble quand on verra sa portraiture originale, ses sonnettes, des belles timbales d'argent, le hanap sans pied de nos ancêtres, ces lis de l'orfèvrerie, de l'orgueil des bourgeois, et son château d'eau pomponné, cramoisi de soieries, à panaches, dont plusieurs étaient d'argent).

28. Maupassant, *Contes et Nouvelles*, 1:70–73.

29. Édouard Deransart wrote a musical composition on street cries in 1881, *Les Cris de la rue (Saynète-Panorama)*. An excerpt is available on the CD *L'Écrit du cri* performed by Ensemble Clément Janequin with Dominique Visse.

30. Mallarmé, *Œuvres complètes*, 2:84–85, 88. Mallarmé, *Collected Poems*, 95.

31. See Abbott, *Between Baudelaire and Mallarmé* for a different reading of "Pauvre Enfant pâle" (83–85). See also Klein, "D'un Post-scriptum à 'Pauvre enfant pâle' . . .," 175–90. We might see in Jacques Prévert's poem "L'Orgue de Barbarie" another instance of pairing criminality and street music.

32. Although the World's Fair celebrated modernity, one of the most successful exhibits was an attraction recreating Old Paris by Albert Robida. As Elizabeth Emery

explains, this attraction struck a chord with France's nascent conservation movement; French conservation law dates from 1887 and a Commission du Vieux Paris was tasked in 1897 with documenting and preserving Old Paris. See "Protecting the Past," 65–85.

33. Raffaëlli uses the term in "Conférence faite par M. Raffaëlli au Palais des Beaux-Arts de Bruxelles au Salon annuel des XX, le 7 février 1885," quoted in Delafond and Genet-Bondeville, *Jean-François Raffaëlli*, 37.

34. Alexandre, *Jean-François Raffaëlli*, 9. See also Delafond, and Genet-Bondeville *Jean-François Raffaëlli*, 34, 39.

35. Barbara S. Fields, author of a 1979 Columbia University dissertation on the artist, argues that Raffaëlli "depart[s] from the traditional picturesque image of the ragpicker" in her entry in Grove Art Online. Oxford Art Online, accessed July 17, 2012, http://www.oxfordartonline.com.proxy.lib.fsu.edu/subscriber/article/grove/art/T070550. My subsequent analysis of the image of the old-clothes–woman does not bear this interpretation out.

36. Berson, *The New Painting*, 1:287. Raffaëlli contributed four etchings to Huysmans's *Croquis parisiens* (1880).

37. M. de Thémines, "Causerie: Beaux-Arts: Les Artistes indépendants," *La Patrie* April 7, 1880, in Berson, *The New Painting*, 1:310.

38. As Charles S. Moffet suggests in "The Fifth Exhibition: Disarray and Disappointment," Raffaëlli was successful because he offered "apparent stability during a period of instability and stylistic floundering" (304).

39. Austin, *Poetic Principles*, 142. See also the exhibition catalog *A Painter's Poet: Stéphane Mallarmé and His Impressionist Circle*. The work provides a useful overview of Mallarmé's relationship with Raffaëlli as well as Manet, Whistler, Degas, and Berthe Morisot, among others.

40. The bulldog also appears in the lithograph *At the Souris Madame Palmyre* (1897; Wittrock, 184, Delteil, 210), in which the dog is on a leash held by a woman (presumably Madame Palmyre, owner of the lesbian café The Souris in Montmartre) in a large feather hat, much like the one in "The Chestnut Vendor." *Divan Japonais* (Delteil, 341, Wittrock, P11); *Marchand de marrons* (Delteil, 335, Wittrock, 232, Adhémar, 254). See Wittrock, *Toulouse-Lautrec*; Delteil, *Henri de Toulouse-Lautrec*; Adhémar, *Toulouse-Lautrec*.

41. Armand Silvestre, "Le Monde des arts, Exposition de la rue des Pyramides (suite et fin)," *La Vie Moderne*, May 1, 1880, in Berson, *The New Painting*, 1:307.

42. The two sonnets ("La Marchande d'herbes aromatiques" and "Le Savetier") under the title "Chansons bas" were included in the Deman edition in 1899, and the five quatrains poems under the title "Les Types de la rue" can today be found in the section "Poèmes non recueillis."

43. Mallarmé, *Correspondance*, 3:250n2; my emphasis.

44. The collaboration went both ways: Mallarmé sent Raffaëlli "La Petite Marchande de lavande," which the artist had not included in his initial series of illustrated types; Raffaëlli sent the poet a sketch of a stonebreaker after which Mallarmé wrote "Le Savetier." See Austin, *Poetic Principles*; and Pearson, *Mallarmé and Circumstance*, 227.

45. Mallarmé, *Correspondance*, 3:250n2; emphasis in the original. Raffaëlli's letter

contains a list of the seven sketches sent to the poet. Mallarmé's letter has been lost. He discusses the Raffaëlli project again in letters dated February and March 1889 (286, 296).

46. Pearson aptly uses the term "bathos" in *Mallarmé and Circumstance*.

47. Delafond and Genet-Bondeville, *Jean-François Raffaëlli*, 69.

48. See Pearson, *Mallarmé and Circumstance*, 227.

49. *Les Français peints*, 2:846.

50. There is no umbrella in Meissonier's type.

51. *Œuvres complètes*, 1:58. Weinfield, trans., *Collected Poems*, 61.

52. Mainzer, in *Les Français peints*, 2:847–55; Frémy, in *Les Français peints*, 1:499–507; Balzac, "Une marchande à la toilette ou Madame la Ressource en 1844," in *Le Diable à Paris*, vol. 2 (*Le Tiroir du Diable*), 271–77. Balzac's type was immortalized in his novel *Splendeurs et misères des courtisanes*.

53. Thompson argues that the regulation of commerce involved controlling women's relationship to commerce and domesticating merchant women, especially the *poissarde* at les Halles. See *The Virtuous Marketplace*. In this example, as in others such as the orange seller in Edward King's *My Paris (268)*, mentioned in chapter 3, the female voice is perceived as especially noxious.

54. Charpy, "Formes et échelles du commerce d'occasion," paragraph 54, consulted June 30, 2012, rh19.revues.org/index373.html.

55. More recently, Claude Ballif (*Chansons bas. Opus 3*, 1956) and Barbara Kolb (*Figments, Chansons bas, Three Place Settings*, 1972) have adapted Mallarmé's sonnets for voice and piano.

56. See Catani, *The Poet in Society*, 9–10.

57. Shaw, "Mallarmé, Pre-Postmodern, Proto Dada," 47–56.

58. *Œuvres complètes*, 1:58. Weinfield, trans., *Collected Poems*, 60. Peter Hambly locates a possible source of "Le Cantonnier," other "Chansons bas," and their humor in Banville. See Hambly, "Lecture de quelques 'Chansons bas,'" 397–411.

59. *Œuvres complètes*, 1:33; Weinfield, trans., *Collected Poems*, 59.

60. The series was published in 1880 in *Croquis parisiens*, illustrated by Raffaëlli (and Forain), and is not to be confused with Raffaëlli's *Types de Paris* (1889) to which Huysmans also contributed "Les Habitués de café."

61. Huysmans, *Croquis parisiens*, ed. Delvaille, 115. *Parisian Sketches*, 86.

62. Fisher, "Paris 'prose blanche,'" 271–83. Fisher reminds us that the *complainte* is an oral genre from the Renaissance; she argues that Laforgue transforms the poet into a "crier" (her word) who hassles passersby trying to get their attention, but the content of the message is not much more than white noise. Fisher also argues that his poetry reduces language to the order of the cry by relying on juxtaposition, interjections, nominal phrases, and phonic resonance. As Christopher Prendergast shows, "the text generates a network of commercial terms and images—wholesale, retail, real estate, lease, cash register, rent, credit, mortgages, interest, stocks, balance-sheet—variously, randomly, yet relatedly clustered around the idea of Paris for sale or rent." See his expert, close reading of the commercial and literary references, "semantic derailment," and nonsen-

sical "verbal circularity" of the "Grande Complainte" in *Paris and the Nineteenth Century*, 196. Translated titles refer to *Poems of Jules Laforgue* translated by Peter Dale. It is worth stating that there are no traditional street cries in Laforgue's poem.

63. Zachmann suggests that Mallarmé was hawking in these essays on the London Annual International exhibition in *Frameworks for Mallarmé*, 165–70. See also, Catani, *The Poet in Society*. Mallarmé, *Œuvres complètes*, 2:218–23, 224–28.

64. A similar irony emerges from the incongruity of publishing Baudelaire's "Le Mauvais Vitrier" in *La Presse* in 1862.

65. Blanc, "Mallarmé on the Press," 417.

66. Mallarmé, *Œuvres complètes*, 2:221; Rosemary Lloyd translation, in *Mallarmé in prose*, 27–28.

67. "Étalages" in Mallarmé, *Œuvres complètes* 2:223. Lloyd translation in *Mallarmé in prose*, 30.

68. To further the comparison with Huysmans, see Nunley, "Huysmans and the Aesthetics," 187–206.

69. Austin draws attention to the poet's resentment toward the cobbler who would bind the poet's wanderlust and toward the lavender vendor whose raised eyebrow signifies her effrontery (*Poetic Principles*, 146, 154). Female vendors were especially known for their audacity and aggressive selling practices, as Émile Zola exploits in *Le Ventre de Paris*.

Conclusion

1. I heard the knife-sharpener in Montreal in August 2013. The reporter Stéphane Leclair documented the story of Tony l'Aiguiseur in a radio program in 2008. "Aiguiseur de métal: sur les traces des derniers camions ambulants," Radio Canada broadcast, aired June 7, 2008, on the *Madacam Tribus* program, 14 minutes 15 seconds, accessed August 13, 2013, http://www.radio-canada.ca/audio-video/pop.shtml#urlMedia=http://www .radio-canada.ca/Medianet/2008/CBF/MacadamTribus200806072205_2.asx. Parisians have had similar experiences today. See "Paris, maman et moi" blog, May 8, 2013, by Sheily Parisienne, accessed August 13, 2013, http://parismamanetmoi. com/2013/05/08/remouleur-un-des-derniers-petits-metiers-parisiens/. See also Philogène Gagne-Petit, "Les Rémouleurs histoire, actualité," blog, accessed August 13, 2013, http://remouleurs.wordpress.com/category/le-remouleur-dans-lart/. In another vein, the Musée Carnavalet has recently brought this material into the public eye in the exhibition *Eugène Atget, Paris* held April 25 to July 29, 2012.

2. Recreating the sounds of Parisian street commerce is one of the goals of Projet Bretez directed by Mylène Pardoen and Bertrand Merlier at Université Lumière Lyon 2 in France. The researchers aim to reconstitute the sounds of eighteenth-century Paris by developing interactive visual and audible three-dimensional maps based on the "Plan Turgot" by cartographer Louis Bretez (1734–39) and selected works of art from the period. See Projet Bretez, accessed August 9, 2014, *http://www.maaav.fr/bretez/index.html.*

3. Nadaud and Truquin are among the autobiographies excerpted in Mark Traugott's edition of *The French Worker: Autobiographies from the Early Industrial Era*.

4. Virmaître, *Paris qui s'efface*, 314.

5. The word is used in Fournel's obituary in the *Revue d'art dramatique*, 154.

6. Schwartz and Jay are two prominent scholars whose research significantly developed the field of visual culture.

7. A vegetable seller, who set himself on fire after police confiscated his unlicensed cart in Sidi Bouzid, launched the revolution in Tunisia in 2011.

Works Cited

Audio Material

Les Cris parisiens: Scène d'imitations; Ressemblance: Monologue, spoken by Jean Péheu. Audio recording, ca. 1910s. Bibliothèque nationale de France, Audiovisual department, SD 78 25–11567. 78 rpm disc. Online since December 2008. DOI: ark:/12148/bpt6k127305d.

Ensemble Clément Janequin, with Dominique Visse. *L'Écrit du cri. Renaissance and 19th to 21st-Century Songs*. Harmonia Mundi, HMC 902028, 2009, compact disc. Recorded in August 2008. Includes music by Janequin, Kastner and Servin.

Books and Periodicals

Abbott, Helen. "Baudelaire's 'Le Jet d'eau' and the Politics of Performance." *Dix-Neuf* 17.1 (2013): 37–56.

———. *Between Baudelaire and Mallarmé: Voice, Conversation and Music*. Burlington: Ashgate, 2009.

———. *Parisian Intersections: Baudelaire's Legacy to Composers*. Oxford: Peter Lang, 2012.

Abid, Wafa. "Les Enjeux du prosaïsme et les influences de Zola et du naturalisme sur la poésie réaliste de François Coppée." *Excavatio* 18.1–2 (2003): 348–62.

Adhémar, Jean. *Toulouse-Lautrec: His Complete Lithographs and Drypoints*. New York: Harry N. Abrams, 1965.

Alexandre, Arsène. *Jean-François Raffaëlli, peintre, graveur, sculpteur*. Paris: H. Floury, 1909.

Alter, Nora M., and Lutz Koepnick. *Sound Matters: Essays on the Acoustics of German Culture*. New York: Berghahn, 2005.

Amicis, Edmondo de. *Studies of Paris*. Translated by W. W. Cady. 3rd ed. New York: Putman's Sons, 1882.

Anonymous [Un Flâneur]. "Le Flâneur à Paris." In *Paris ou Le Livre des Cent-et-un*. Vol. 6. Paris: Ladvocat, 1831. 95–110.

Anspach, Maria d.' "Les Musiciens ambulants." *Le Prisme*. Supplement to *Les Français peints par eux-mêmes: Encyclopédie morale du XIXe siècle*. Edited by L. Curmer. Paris: L. Curmer, 1842. 183–86.

Armelhault, J., and E. Bocher. *Gavarni: Catalogue Raisonné of the Graphic Work*. San Francisco: Alan Wofsy Fine Arts, 2004.

Assmann, Aleida. "Canon and Archive." In Erll and Nünning, *Cultural Memory Studies*, 97–107.

Attali, Jacques. *Noise: The Political Economy of Music*. Minneapolis: University of Minnesota Press, 1985.

Attridge, Derek. *Peculiar Language: Literature as Difference from the Renaissance to James Joyce*. Ithaca: Cornell University Press, 1988.

Augoyard, Jean-François, and Henry Torgue, eds. *À l'écoute de l'environnement: Répertoires des effets sonores*. Marseilles: Editions Parenthèses, 1995. Translated by Andrea McCartney and David Paquette as *Sonic Experience: A Guide to Everyday Sounds*. Montreal, Ithaca: McGill-Queen's University Press, 2006.

Austin, Lloyd James. *Poetic Principles and Practice: Occasional Papers on Baudelaire, Mallarmé, and Valéry*. Cambridge: Cambridge University Press, 1987.

Balaÿ, Olivier. "The 19th Century Transformation of the Urban Soundscape." *Internoise 2007: The 36th International Congress and Exhibition on Noise Control Engineering: Global Approaches to Noise Control*. Istanbul, August 28–31, 2007. Istanbul: Internoise, 2007. 1–10. Accessed June 8, 2012. http://doc.cresson.grenoble.archi.fr/opac/doc_num. php?explnum_id=279.

———. *L'Espace sonore de la ville au XIXe siècle*. Bernin, Isère, France: À la Croisée, 2003.

Balzac, Honoré de. "Ce qui disparaît de Paris." In Hetzel, *Le Diable à Paris*, 1:11–19.

———. "Histoire et physiologie des boulevards de Paris de la Madeleine à la Bastille." In Hetzel, *Le Diable à Paris*, 1:89–102.

———. "Une marchande à la toilette ou Madame la Ressource en 1844." In Hetzel, *Le Diable à Paris*, 2:271–77.

———. "Monographie du rentier." In Curmer, *Les Français peints par eux-mêmes*. 2:65–86.

———. *Old Goriot*. Translated by Ellen Marriage. London: J. M. Dent and Sons, 1913.

———. *À Paris*. Prefaced by Roger Caillois. Paris: Éditions Complexe, 1993.

———. *Le Père Goriot*. Vol. 3 of *La Comédie humaine*. Edited by Pierre-Georges Castex. Bibliothèque de la Pléiade. Paris: Gallimard, 1976–81.

———. *Physiologie du mariage*. Paris: Calmann-Lévy, 1868.

———. *The Physiology of Marriage*. Introduced by Sharon Marcus. Baltimore: Johns Hopkins University Press, 1997.

Banville, Théodore de. "Musique populaire et poésie. Juste Olivier, *Les Chansons lointaines*. Le Corsaire-Satan, le 4 mars 1847." In *Critique littéraire, artistique, et musicale choisie.* Edited by Peter J. Edwards and S. Hambly. Paris: Éditions Honoré Champion, 2003.

———. *Œuvres poétiques complètes: Odes funambulesques.* Paris: Éditions Honoré Champion, 1995.

Baron, Lawrence. "Noise and Degeneration: Theodor Lessing's Crusade for Quiet." *Journal of Contemporary History* 17.1 (1982): 165–78.

Baruch-Gourden, Jean-Michel. "La Police et le commerce ambulant à Paris au XIXe siècle." In *Maintien de l'ordre et polices en France et en Europe au XIXe siècle.* Edited by Philippe Vigier. Paris: Créaphis, 2002.

Baudelaire, Charles. *Correspondance.* Edited by Claude Pichois and Jean Ziegler. 2 vols. Paris: Gallimard, 1973.

———. *The Flowers of Evil.* Translated by James McGowan. Oxford World's Classics. Oxford: Oxford University Press, 1993.

———. *Œuvres complètes.* Edited by Claude Pichois. 2 vols. Bibliothèque de la Pléaide. Paris: Gallimard, 1975.

———. *The Painter of Modern Life and Other Essays.* Translated by Jonathan Mayne. London: Phaidon, 1995.

———. *The Parisian Prowler.* Translated by Edward Kaplan. Athens: University of Georgia Press, 1997.

Beall, Karen F. *Kaufrufe und Strassenhändler: Eine Bibliographie. Cries and Itinerant Trades: A Bibliography.* Hamburg: Hauswedell, 1975.

Bénichou, Paul. *Nerval et la chanson folklorique.* Paris: J. Corti, 1970.

Benjamin, Walter. *The Arcades Project.* Translated by Howard Eiland and Kevin McLaughlin. Cambridge: Belknap Press of Harvard University Press, 1999.

———. *One Way Street and Other Writings.* Translated by J. A. Underwood. London: Penguin, 2009.

———. *The Writer of Modern Life: Essays on Charles Baudelaire.* Edited by Michael W. Jennings. Cambridge: Belknap Press of Harvard University Press, 2006.

Beraldi, Henri. "Préface." *Paris qui crie, petits métiers.* Edited by Albert Arnal. Paris: Pour les Amis du livre par Georges Chamerot, 1890.

Berger, Anne Emmanuelle. *Scènes d'aumône: Misère et Poésie au XIXe siècle.* Romantisme et Modernités 90. Paris: Éditions Honoré Champion, 2004.

Bergeron, Katherine. *Decadent Enchantments: The Revival of Gregorian Chant at Solesmes.* California Studies in 19th Century Music. Berkeley: University of California Press, 1998.

Bernadille. *Esquisses et Croquis parisiens. See* Fournel, Victor.

Berson, Ruth. *The New Painting Impressionism 1874–1886: Documentation.* 2 vols. Seattle: Fine Arts Museums of San Francisco, University of Washington Press, 1996.

Bertall [Charles Albert d'Arnoux]. *La Comédie de notre temps.* Paris: Plon et Nourrit, 1874.

Bertrand, Aloysius. *Œuvres complètes.* Edited by Helen Hart Poggenburg. Paris: Éditions Honoré Champion, 2000.

Bijsterveld, Karin. *Mechanical Sound: Technology, Culture, and Public Problems of Noise in the Twentieth Century.* Cambridge: MIT Press, 2008.

Bijsterveld, Karin, and José Van Dijck, eds. *Sound Souvenirs: Audio Technologies, Memory and Cultural Practices*. Amsterdam: Amsterdam University Press, 2009.

Blanc, Dina. "Mallarmé on the Press and Literature: 'Étalages' and 'Le Livre, instrument spirituel.'" *French Review* 71.3 (1998): 414–24.

Blesser, Barry, and Linda-Ruth Salter. *Spaces Speak, Are You Listening? Experiencing Aural Architecture*. Cambridge: MIT Press, 2006.

Blondé, Bruno, and Natacha Coquery. *Retailers and Consumer Changes in Early Modern Europe: England, France, Italy and the Low Countries*. Tours: Presses universitaires Francois-Rabelais, Maison des sciences de l'homme, Villes et territoires, 2005.

Bonnain, Rolande. "D'une pâtisserie cérémonielle: Usage de l'oublie." *Ethnologie française,* nouvelle série, 23.4 (1993), 542–61. Accessed September 15, 2011. http://www.jstor.org/stable/40989498.

Boutin, Aimée. "Desbordes-Valmore, Lamartine and Poetic Motherhood." *French Forum* 24.3 (1999): 315–30.

———. "Sound Memory: Paris Street Cries in Balzac's *Père Goriot*." *French Forum* 30.2 (2005): 67–78.

———. "'The Title of Lawyer Leads Nowhere!': The Physiology of the Law Student in Paul Gavarni, Émile de la Bédollierre and George Sand." *Nineteenth-Century French Studies* 40.1–2 (2011–12): 57–80.

Brix, Michel. "Une renaissance romantique: Les Chansons populaires." *Voix du peuple dans la littérature des XIXe et XXe siècles: Actes du colloque de Strasbourg 12, 13, 14 mai 2005*. Strasbourg: Université de Strasbourg, 2006. 31–40.

Brunot, Ferdinand. "Le Musée de la parole." *Paris-Journal*, March 21, 1910.

Buck-Morss, Susan. *The Dialectics of Seeing: Walter Benjamin and the Arcades Project*. Cambridge: MIT Press, 1989.

Buffard-Moret, Brigitte. *La Chanson poétique au XIXe siècle*. Rennes, France: Presses universitaires de Rennes, 2007.

Bull, Michael, and Les Back, eds. *The Auditory Culture Reader*. Sensory Formations Series. Oxford: Berg, 2003.

Burt, Ellen S. *Poetry's Appeal: Nineteenth-Century French Lyric and the Political Space*. Stanford: Stanford University Press, 1999.

Burton, Richard D. E. "Bonding and Breaking in Baudelaire's 'Petits poèmes en prose.'" *Modern Language Review* 88.1 (1993): 58–73.

———. "Destruction as Creation: 'Le Mauvais Vitrier' and the Poetics and Politics of Violence." *Romanic Review* 83.3 (1992): 297–322.

———. *The Flâneur and His City: Patterns of Daily Life in Paris, 1815–1851*. Durham, England: University of Durham, 1994.

———. "The Unseen Seer, or Proteus in the City: Aspects of a Nineteenth-Century Parisian Myth." *French Studies* 62.1 (1998): 50–68.

Catani, Damian. *The Poet in Society: Art, Consumerism, and Politics in Mallarmé*. New York: P. Lang, 2003.

Cate, Phillip, and Mary Shaw, eds. *The Spirit of Montmartre: Cabarets, Humor and the Avant-*

garde 1875–1905. New Brunswick, N.J.: Jane Voorhees Zimmerli Art Museum, 1996. 95–109.

Challamel, Augustin. *Les Amuseurs de la rue.* Paris: Ducrocq, 1875.

Chambers, Ross. "Baudelaire's Dedicatory Practice." *SubStance* 17.56 (1988): 5–17.

———. "Baudelaire's Street Poetry." *Nineteenth-Century French Studies* 13.4 (1985): 244–59.

Charpy, Manuel. "Formes et échelles du commerce d'occasion au XIXe siècle: L'exemple du vêtement à Paris." *Revue d'Histoire du XIXe Siècle* 24 (2002): 125–50. Accessed June 30, 2012. rh19.revues.org/index373.html.

Citron, Pierre. *La Poésie de Paris dans la littérature française: De Rousseau à Baudelaire.* Paris: Éditions de Minuit, 1961.

Clark, T. J. *The Painter of Modern Life: Paris in the Art of Manet and His Followers.* Rev. ed. Princeton: Princeton University Press, 1999.

Classen, Constance. *The Deepest Sense: A Cultural History of Touch.* Studies in Sensory History. Urbana: University of Illinois Press, 2012.

Collection officielle des ordonnances de police depuis 1800 jusqu'à 1844, imprimée par ordre de M. Gabriel Delessert, Pair de France, Conseiller d'État, Préfet de Police. Vol. 2. Paris: Librairie administrative de Pierre Dupont, 1844.

Collection officielle des ordonnances de police depuis 1851 jusqu'à 1861, imprimé par ordre de M. Boittelle, préfet de police. Vol. 6. Paris: Librairie administrative de Paul Dupont, 1865.

Connor, Steven. *Noise: A Series of 5 Radio Programs.* Radio broadcast transmitted on BBC Radio 3 on February 24–28, 1997. Accessed June 30, 2011. www.stevenconnor.com/noise/.

Coppée, François. *Poésies de François Coppée 1869–1874: Les Humbles—Écrit pendant le siège. Plus de sang—Promenades et Intérieurs; Le Cahier Rouge.* Paris: Alphonse Lemerre, 1878.

Corbin, Alain. "Bruits, excès, sensations, discipline: Tolérable et intolérable. entretien avec Alain Corbin." *Equinoxes. Revue Romane de Sciences Humaines* 11 (1994): 13–23.

———. *Time, Desire, and Horror: Towards a History of the Senses.* Cambridge: Polity Press, 1995.

———. *Village Bells: Sound and Meaning in the Nineteenth-Century French Countryside.* Translated by Martin Thom. New York: Columbia University Press, 1998.

Cowan, Michael. "Imagining Modernity through the Ear: Rilke's Aufzeichnungen Des Malte Laurids Brigge and the Noise of Modern Life." *Arcadia* 46.1 (2006): 124–46.

Crapelet, Georges-Adrien, ed. *Proverbes et Dictons populaires: Avec les dits du mercier et des marchands, et les Crieries de Paris, aux XIIIe et XIVe siècles.* Paris: Impr. de Crapelet, 1831.

Crary, Jonathan. *Techniques of the Observer: On Vision and Modernity in the Nineteenth Century.* Cambridge: MIT Press, 1990.

Cros, Charles. *Œuvres complètes.* Edited by Louis Forestier and Pierre Olivier Walzer. Bibliothèque de la Pléiade. Paris: Gallimard, 1970.

———. *Œuvres complètes: Poèmes, contes, monologues, et textes scientifiques avec de nombreux inédits, des variantes, des notes, et illustrés de portraits, dessins et manuscrits en fac-similé.* Edited by Louis Forestier and Pascal Pia. Paris: J.-J. Pauvert, 1964.

Cross, John C. *Informal Politics: Street Vendors and the State in Mexico City.* Stanford: Stanford University Press, 1998.

Cubero, José. *Histoire du vagabondage du Moyen Age à nos jours*. Paris: Editions Imago, 1998.

Culler, Jonathan. "Baudelaire and Poe." *Zeitschrift für Französische Sprache und Literatur* 100 (1990): 61–73.

——. *The Pursuit of Signs*. Rev. ed. Ithaca: Cornell University Press, 2002 [1983].

Curmer, Léon, ed. *Les Français peints par eux-mêmes: Encyclopédie morale du XIXe siècle*. 9 vols. Paris: Curmer, 1840–42. Reprinted with preface and notes by Pierre Bouttier. 2 vols. Paris: Omnibus, 2003. Page references are to the 2003 edition.

Darnton, Robert. *Poetry and the Police: Communication Networks in Eighteenth-Century Paris*. Cambridge: Harvard University Press, 2010.

Davis, Nathalie Zemon. "The Reasons of Misrule." *Society and Culture in Early Modern France: Eight Essays*. Stanford: Stanford University Press, 1975. 97–123.

Delafond, Marianne, and Caroline Genet-Bondeville. *Jean-François Raffaëlli*. Paris: Bibliothèque des arts, 1999.

Delteil, Loÿs. *Henri de Toulouse-Lautrec: Le Peintre graveur illustré*. Vol. 10 and 11. Paris: Chez l'auteur, 1920.

Denby, David J. *Sentimental Narrative and the Social Order in France 1760–1820*. Cambridge: Cambridge University Press, 2006.

Désaugiers, Marc Antoine. "Tableau de Paris à cinq heures du matin." In Le Roux de Lincy, M. Dumersan, Hippolyte Raymond Colet, Maurice Ourry, Charles François Daubigny, Louis Joseph Trimolet, and L. C. A. Steinheil, contribs., *Chants et chansons populaires de la France*. Paris: H. L. Delloye, 1843. Accessed June 26, 2012. http://www.miscellanees.com/d/paris01.htm.

Desbordes-Valmore, Marceline. "Le Crieur de nuit." *Revue des Deux Mondes* 2 (May 1833): 319.

Diaz, Brigitte. "Visions balzaciennes de Paris: Au-delà du panorama." *Revue des Sciences Humaines* 294 (2009): 73–89.

Diderot, Denis, and Jean d'Alembert, eds. *Encyclopédie, Dictionnaire raisonné des sciences, des arts et des métiers, par une Société de Gens de lettres*. Vol. 3. Edited by Robert Morrissey. Chicago: University of Chicago ARTFL Encyclopédie Project. Accessed August 8, 2002. http://encyclopedie.uchicago.edu/.

Dillon, Emma. *The Sense of Sound: Musical Meaning in France, 1260–1330*. New York: Oxford University Press, 2012.

Du Camp, Maxime. "Les Halles centrales. Le marché ambulant." *Paris: Ses organes, ses fonctions et sa vie dans la seconde moitié du XIXe siècle*. Vol. 2. Paris: Hachette, 1870. 190–210.

Dufour, Valentin. Preface to *Lettres d'un Sicilien à un de ses amis*. By Giovanni Paolo Marana. Edited by V. Dufour. Paris: A. Quantin, 1883.

Dull, Olga Anna. "From Rabelais to the Avant-Garde." In Cate and Shaw, *The Spirit of Montmartre*, 199–241.

Duval, Amaury. "Une journée de flâneur sur les boulevards du Nord." *Paris ou Le Livre des Cent-et-un*. Vol. 12. Paris: Ladvocat, 1833. Accessed July 26, 2012. http://www.bmlisieux.com/curiosa/duval001.htm.

Ellis, Katherine. *Interpreting the Musical Past: Early Music in Nineteenth-Century France*. Oxford: Oxford University Press, 2005.

Emery, Elizabeth. "Protecting the Past: Albert Robida and the Vieux Paris Exhibit at the 1900 World's Fair." *Journal of European Studies* 35.1 (2005): 65–85.

Énault, Louis. "Au bord de l'eau." *Paris et les Parisiens au XIXe siècle: Mœurs, arts et monuments*. Edited by Eugène Lami. Paris: Morizot, 1856. 207–37.

Erll, Astrid, and Ansgar Nünning, eds. *Cultural Memory Studies: An International and Interdisciplinary Handbook*. Berlin: De Gruyter, 2008.

Evans, Margery. *Baudelaire and Intertextuality: Poetry at the Crossroads*. New York: Cambridge University Press, 1993.

Fabre, Daniel. "Proverbes, contes et chansons." In Nora, *Les Lieux de mémoire*, 3:3555–81.

Fauquet, Joël-Marie, ed. *Dictionnaire de la musique en France au XIXe siècle*. Paris: Fayard, 2003.

Ferguson, Dean T. "The Body, the Corporate Idiom, and the Police of the Unincorporated Worker in Early Modern Lyons." *French Historical Studies* 23.4 (Fall 2000): 545–75.

Ferguson, Priscilla Parkhurst. *Paris as Revolution: Writing the Nineteenth-Century City*. Berkeley: University of California Press, 1994.

Fétis, Édouard. "De la musique des rues" [Étude sur la musique populaire des rues de Paris et son influence sur les mœurs au dix-neuvième siècle]. *Revue Musicale* 9.37 (1835): 288–93.

Fields, Barbara S. Grove Art Online. Oxford Art Online. Accessed July 17, 2012. http://www.oxfordartonline.com.proxy.lib.fsu.edu/subscriber/article/grove/art/T070550.

Fisher, Dominique D. "Paris 'prose blanche': Complainte, 'spleenuosité' et écritures de la modernité chez Laforgue." In *Repression and Expression: Literary and Social Coding in Nineteenth-Century France*. Edited by Carrol F. Coates and Marilyn Gaddis Rose. New York: Peter Lang, 1996. 271–83.

"Le Flâneur Parisien." *Le Figaro*, November 13, 1831.

Fonssagrives, Jean-Baptiste. *Hygiène et assainissement des villes*. Paris: J.-B. Baillière, 1874.

Fontaine, Laurence. *History of Pedlars in Europe*. Translated by Vicki Whittaker. Durham, N.C.: Duke University Press, 1996.

Forgues, Paul-Émile Daurand, and J. J. Grandville. *Petites Misères de la vie humaine*. Paris: H. Fournier, 1846.

Fournel, Victor [Bernadille]. *Esquisses et Croquis parisiens: Petite chronique du temps présent*. Paris: Plon, 1876.

Fournel, Victor. *Ce qu'on voit dans les rues de Paris*. Paris: Delahays, 1858.

——. *Les Cris de Paris: Types et Physionomies d'autrefois*. Paris: Les Éditions de Paris, 1887. Reprint, Paris: Les Éditions de Paris Max Chaleil, 2003.

——. *Paris nouveau et Paris futur*. Paris: Jacques Lecoffre, 1865.

Franklin, Alfred. *Dictionnaire historique des arts, métiers et professions*. Paris: Welter, 1906.

——. *Les Rues et les Cris de Paris au XIIIe siècle*. Paris: L. Willem, 1874.

Frébault, Élie. *Les Industriels du macadam*. 2nd ed. Paris: A. Le Chevalier, 1868.

Frémy, Arnould. "La Revendeuse à la toilette." In Curmer, *Les Français peints*, 1:499–507.

Frisby, David. "The Flâneur in Social Theory." In *The Flâneur*. Edited by Keith Tester. London: Routledge, 1994. 81–110.

Gantrel, Martine. "Albertine ou l'Étrangère: Une nouvelle interprétation des 'Cris de Paris' dans *La Prisonnière*." *Revue d'Histoire Littéraire de la France* 100.1 (2000): 3–25.

Garrioch, David. "Sounds of the City: The Soundscape of Early Modern European Towns." *Urban History* 30.1 (2003): 5–25.

Gauthier, Laure, and Mélanie Traversier. *Mélodies urbaines: La Musique dans les villes d'Europe (XVIe–XIXe siècles)*. Paris: Presses de l'université Paris-Sorbonne, 2008.

Gautier, Théophile. "Shakespeare aux Funambules." *Revue de Paris*, September 4, 1842, 75–84.

Genlis, Stéphanie Félicité de. *Mémoires inédits de madame la comtesse de Genlis: Pour servir à l'histoire des dix-huitième et dix-neuvième siècles*. Vol. 7. Paris: Colburn, 1826.

Gétreau, Florence. "Concerts ambulants: Portraits de quelques célébrités en plein vent." "Les Musiciens de rue sous l'autorité de la police parisienne." In Landron, *Musiciens des rues de Paris*, 41–47.

Gilman, Bradley. "Parisian Pedlars and Their Musical Cries." *Cosmopolitan, a Monthly Illustrated Magazine* 38.3 (Jan. 1905): 327–35.

Girardin, Delphine de. *Lettres parisiennes du Vicomte de Launay*. Paris: Mercure de France, 2004.

Gisquet, Henri. *Mémoires de M. Gisquet, ancien préfet de police*. Vol. 1. 4 vols. Paris: Marchand, 1840.

Goncourt, Edmond de. *La Maison d'un artiste*. 2 vols. Paris: Charpentier, 1881.

Goncourt, Edmond, and Jules de. *Gavarni l'homme et l'œuvre*. Paris: E. Fasquelle, 1926.

Gouriet, J.-B. *Personnages célèbres dans les rues de Paris depuis une haute antiquité jusqu'à nos jours*. Vol. 2. Paris: Lerouge, 1811.

Greaney, Patrick. *Untimely Beggar: Poverty and Power from Baudelaire to Benjamin*. Minneapolis: University of Minnesota Press, 2008.

Grojnowski, Daniel. "Hydropathes and Company." In Cate and Shaw, *The Spirit of Montmartre*, 95–109.

Gutton, Jean-Pierre. *Bruits et sons dans notre histoire*. Paris: Presses universitaires de France, 2000.

Hahn, H. Hazel. *Scenes of Parisian Modernity: Culture and Consumption in the Nineteenth Century*. New York: Palgrave Macmillan, 2009.

Hambly, Peter. "Lecture de quelques 'Chansons bas' de Mallarmé." *Nineteenth-Century French Studies* 20 (1991–92): 397–411.

Hamon, Philippe. *Expositions: Literature and Architecture in Nineteenth-Century France*. Translated by Katia Sainson-Frank and Lisa Maguire. Introduction by Richard Sieburth. Berkeley: University of California Press, 1992.

———. *Imageries: Littérature et image au XIXe siècle*. Paris: José Corti, 2007.

———. "Littérature et réclame: Le cru et le cri." *Romantisme* 155 (2012): 5–10.

Haussmann, Georges-Eugène. *Mémoire sur les eaux de Paris présenté à la commission municipale*. Paris: Vinchon, 1854.

Hayes, Kevin. "The Flâneur in the Parlor: Poe's Philosophy of Furniture." *Prospects* 27 (2002): 103–19.

Hetzel, Pierre-Jules, ed. *Le Diable à Paris. Paris et les Parisiens. Mœurs et Coutumes, Caractères et Portraits des habitants de Paris [etc.] Texte par MM. George Sand, P.-J. Stahl . . . [et autres] . . . précédé d'une histoire de Paris par Théophile Lavallée; illustrations, les gens de Paris, séries de gravures avec légendes, par Gavarni; Paris comique, vignettes par Bertall; vues, monuments édifices particuliers, lieux célèbres et principaux aspects de Paris par Champin, Bertrand, d'Aubigny, Français.* 2 vols. Paris: J. Hetzel, 1845–46. (Volume 2 also published under the alternate title, *Le Tiroir du diable.*)

Higonnet, Anne. "Real Fashion: Clothes Unmake the Working Woman." *Spectacles of Realism: Body, Gender and Genre.* Edited by Margaret Cohen and Christopher Prendergast. Minneapolis: University of Minnesota Press, 1995. 137–62.

Houssaye, Arsène. *Les Confessions: Souvenirs d'un demi-siècle, 1830–1880.* Paris: s.n., 1885.

——. *Œuvres poétiques: L'amour, l'art, la vie; Histoire d'Arsène Houssaye par Théodore de Banville.* Paris: Hachette, 1857.

——. *Poésies complètes de Arsène Houssaye.* Paris: Charpentier, 1850.

——. *Le Violon de Franjolé, Le Domino rose et le domino noir, etc. . . .* 6th ed. Paris: Hachette, 1859.

Howes, David. *Sensual Relations: Engaging the Senses in Culture and Social Theory.* Ann Harbor: University of Michigan Press, 2003.

Huart, Louis. *Physiologie du flâneur.* Paris: Aubert-Lavigne, 1841.

Hufton, Olwen. "Begging, Vagrancy, Vagabondage and the Law: An Aspect of the Problem of Poverty in Eighteenth-Century France." *European History Quarterly* 2 (1972): 97–123.

Huysmans, J.-K. *Croquis parisiens.* Paris: Henri Vaton, 1880.

——. *Croquis parisiens.* Edited by Bernard Delvaille. Geneva: Slatkine, 1996.

——. *Parisian Sketches.* Translated by Brendan King. Cambs, U.K.: Dedalus, Dedalus European Classics, 2004.

Jackson, John E. "Bruit et musique." *Magazine littéraire* 418 (Jan. 2003): 48–51. Reprinted in *Baudelaire sans fin: Essais sur* Les Fleurs du mal. Paris: Corti, 2005. 63–74.

Jacob. *Paris ridicule et burlesque au XVIIe siècle.* Paris: Adolphe Delahays, 1859.

Janin, Jules. *Un hiver à Paris.* Paris: Aubert et Curmer, 1843.

——. "Introduction." In Curmer, *Les Français peints par eux-mêmes,* 1:9–22.

——. "Les Petits Métiers." *Les Catacombes.* Vol. 3. Paris: Werdet, 1839. 139–75.

Jarves, James Jackson. *Parisian Sights and French Principles, Seen through American Spectacles.* New York: Harper and Brothers, 1855.

Johnson, James H. *Listening in Paris: A Cultural History.* Berkeley: University of California Press, 1996.

Jonas, Hans. "The Nobility of Sight." *Philosophy and Phenomenological Research* 14.4 (1954): 507–19.

Jordan, David. *Transforming Paris: The Life and Labors of Baron Haussmann.* Chicago: University of Chicago Press, 2005.

Jouy, Étienne de. "La Journée d'un flâneur." *Nouveaux Tableaux de Paris ou Observations sur les mœurs et usages des Parisiens au commencement du XIXe siècle.* Vol. 2. Paris: Ainé, 1828. 274–91.

Julien, Jean-Rémy. "L'Influence des crieurs de rue de Paris sur le récitatif debussyste: Une hypothèse." *International Review of the Aesthetics and Sociology of Music* 152 (1984): 147–57.

———. *Musique et Publicité: Du cri de Paris aux messages publicitaires radiophoniques et télévisés.* Paris: Flammarion, 1989.

Julien, Jean-Rémy, Jean-Claude Klein, and Jean Mongrédien. *Orphée Phrygien: Les Musiques de la Révolution.* Paris: Éditions du May, 1989.

Kahn, Douglas. *Noise, Water, Meat: A History of Sound in the Arts.* Cambridge: MIT Press, 1999.

Kastner, [Jean-]Georges, and Edouard Thierry. *Les Voix de Paris: Essai d'une histoire littéraire et musicale des cris populaires de la capitale, depuis le moyen âge jusqu'à nos jours, précédé de considérations sur l'origine et le caractère du cri en général, et suivi de les Cris de Paris, grande symphonie humoristique vocale et instrumentale.* Paris: G. Brandus, Dufour, 1857.

King, Edward. *My Paris: French Character Sketches.* Boston: Loring, 1868.

Klein, Raoul. "D'un Post-scriptum à 'Pauvre enfant pâle' . . ." *La Pensée du paradoxe: Approches du romantisme, Hommage à Michel Crouzet.* Edited by Didier Philippot and Fabienne Bercegol. Paris: Presses de l'université Paris-Sorbonne, 2006. 175–90.

Kroen, Sheryl. *Politics and Theater: The Crisis of Legitimacy in Restoration France, 1815–1830.* Berkeley: University of California Press, 2000.

Krueger, Cheryl. "Telling Stories in Baudelaire's *Spleen de Paris.*" *Nineteenth-Century French Studies* 30.3 (2002): 281–99.

La Bédollierre, Émile de. *Les Industriels: Métiers et professions en France.* Paris: Janet, 1842.

Lacroix, Auguste de. "Le Flâneur." In Curmer, *Les Français peints par eux-mêmes,* 2:151–62.

Laforgue, Jules. *Poems of Jules Laforgue.* Translated by Peter Dale. Greenwick, U.K.: Anvil Press Poetry, 2001.

Landron, Hélène. *Musiciens des rues de Paris: Musée national des arts et traditions populaires 18 novembre 1997–27 avril 1998.* Paris: Réunion des Musées Nationaux, 1997.

Langlé, Ferdinand. "Le Clocheteur des trépassés." *Les Contes du gay scavoir: Ballades, fabliaux et tradition du Moyen-âge.* Paris: Firmin Didot, n.d. (1828?).

Lansac, Frédéric. "'Chand d'habits! De 1832 à 1922, une pantomime spectrale?" *Pantomime et théâtre du corps: Transparence et opacité du hors-texte.* Edited by Arnaud Rykner. Rennes, France: Presses universitaires de Rennes, 2009. 49–60.

Larousse, Pierre. *Grand Dictionnaire universel du XIXe siècle.* 17 vols.

Lauster, Martina. *Sketches of the Nineteenth Century: European Journalism and Its Physiologies, 1830–50.* Basingstoke, England: Palgrave Macmillan, 2007.

———. "Walter Benjamin's Myth of the Flâneur." *Modern Language Review* 102.1 (2007): 139–56.

Le Blanc, Alissa. "Parler au nom des Gueux? Remarques sur *La Chansons des Gueux* (1876) de Jean Richepin." In *En quel nom parler?* Edited by Dominique Rabaté. Modernités 31. Bordeaux: Presses universitaires de Bordeaux, 2010. 141–77.

Leblanc, Cécile. "De Charpentier à Wagner: Transfigurations musicales dans les cris de Paris chez Proust." *Revue d'Histoire de la France* 4 (2007): 903–21.

Le Men, Ségolène, Luce Abélès, and Nathalie Preiss. *Les Français peints par eux-mêmes: Panorama social du XIXe siècle.* Paris: Éditions de la Réunion des musées nationaux, 1993.

Le Poittevin, Gustave. *Traité de la presse.* Vol. 1. Paris: Larose, 1902.

Leonard, Anne. "Picturing Listening in the Late Nineteenth Century." *Art Bulletin* 89.2 (2007): 266–86.

Leterrier, Sophie-Anne. "Musique populaire et musique savante au XIXe siècle: Du 'peuple' au 'public.'" *Revue d'Histoire du XIXe Siècle* 19 (1999). Last modified August 26, 2008. Accessed September 12, 2010. http://rh19.revues.org/index157.html.

Levy, Kenneth, et al. "Plainchant." Grove Music Online. Oxford Music Online. Accessed May 25, 2012. http://www.oxfordmusiconline.com.proxy.lib.fsu.edu/subscriber/article/grove/music/40099pg11.

Lloyd, Rosemary. "Baudelaire, Marceline Desbordes-Valmore et la fraternité des poètes." *Bulletin baudelairien* 26.2 (1991): 65–74.

——. *Baudelaire's World.* Ithaca: Cornell University Press, 2002.

Longfellow, H. W., ed. *Poems of Places: An Anthology in 31 Volumes.* Boston: James Osgood and Co., 1876–79.

Lorin, Georges. *Paris rose, illustré par Luigi Loir & Cabriol.* Paris: Paul Ollendorff, editeur, 1884.

Luchet, Auguste. "Les Passages." *Nouveau Tableau de Paris au XIXe siècle.* Vol. 6. Paris: Mme Charles-Béchet, 1834–35. 97–113.

Mainzer, Joseph. "Les Cris de Paris." "Le Pâtissier." "Le Porteur d'eau." "La Laitière." "Le Marchand de coco." "Le Marchand d'habits." "Le Marchand de mottes." "Le Raccommodeur de faïence." "Le Marchand de parapluies." "Le Marchand de peaux de lapins." "Le Cafetier." "Le Vitrier Peintre." In *Les Français peints*, 2:785–918.

Mallarmé, Stéphane. *Collected Poems.* Translated by Henry Weinfield. Berkeley: University of California Press, 1994.

——. *Correspondance.* Edited by Lloyd J. Austin and Henri Mondor. Paris: Gallimard, Coll. Pléaide, 1969.

——. *Mallarmé in prose.* Edited by Mary Ann Caws. New York: New Directions, 2001.

——. *Œuvres complètes.* Edited by Bertrand Marchal. 2 vols. Bibliothèque de la Pléiade. Paris: Gallimard, 1998–2003.

Marchand, Bertrand. *Paris, histoire d'une ville: XIXe–XXe siècle.* Paris: Éditions du Seuil, 1993.

Marcus, Sharon. *Apartment Stories: City and Home in Nineteenth-Century Paris and London.* Berkeley: University of California Press, 1999.

Martin, Henry. "Les Cris de Paris." *Nouveau Tableau de Paris au XIXe siècle.* Vol. 3. Paris: Mme Charles-Béchet, 1834–35. 157–71.

Mason, Laura. *Singing the French Revolution: Popular Culture and Politics, 1787–1799.* Ithaca: Cornell University Press, 1996.

Massard-Guilbaud, Geneviève. *Histoire de la pollution industrielle: France, 1789–1914.* Collection en Temps & Lieux. 17. Paris: École des hautes études en sciences sociales (EHESS), 2010.

Massin, Robert. *Les Cris de la ville: Commerces ambulants et petits métiers de la rue*. Paris: Gallimard, 1978.

Maupassant, Guy de. *Contes et Nouvelles*. Edited by Louis Forestier. Bibliothèque de la Pléaide. Paris: Gallimard, 1974.

McCabe, James. *Paris by Sunlight and Gaslight*. Philadelphia: National Publishing Company, 1869.

McTigue, Sheila. "Perfect Deformity, Ideal Beauty, and the Imaginaire of Work: The Reception of Annibale Carraci's *Arti di Bologna* in 1646." *Oxford Art Journal* 16.1 (1993): 75–91.

Mercier, Louis-Sébastien. *L'An 2440: Rêve s'il en fut jamais*. Edited by C. Cave and C. Marcandier-Colard. Paris: La Découverte, 1999.

———. *Le Nouveau Paris*. Edited by Jean-Claude Bonnet. Paris: Mercure de France, 1994.

———. *Tableau de Paris*. Edited by Jean-Claude Bonnet. Paris: Mercure de France, 1994.

Meyer Schapiro, Meyer. "Courbet and Popular Imagery: An Essay on Realism and Naïveté." *Journal of the Warburg and Courtauld Institutes* 4.3/4 (April 1941–July 1942): 164–91.

Miller, Dwight. *Street Criers and Itinerant Tradesmen in European Prints*. Stanford: Department of Art, Stanford University, 2007.

Milliot, Vincent. *Les Cris de Paris ou le Peuple travesti: Les Représentations des petits métiers parisiens XVIe -XVIIIe siècles*. Paris: Publications de la Sorbonne, 1995.

Moffett, Charles. "The Fifth Exhibition: Disarray and Disappointment." *The New Painting, Impressionism, 1874–1886*. Geneva: University of Washington Press, 1986. 293–369.

Monnet, Jérôme. "Le Commerce de rue, ambulant ou informel et ses rapports avec la métropolisation: Une ébauche de modélisation." *Autrepart* 39.3 (2006): 93–109.

Mortelette, Yann. "Francois Coppée et la poétique de l'horizon: De la promenade en banlieue au voyage imaginaire." *Studi Francese* 45 (2001): 542–53.

Murphy, Kerry. "Joseph Mainzer's 'Sacred and Beautiful Mission': An Aspect of Parisian Musical Life of the 1830s." *Music and Letters* 75.1 (1994): 33–46.

Murphy, Steve. *Logiques du dernier Baudelaire: Lectures du* Spleen de Paris. Champion Classiques. Série "Essais." Vol. 7. Paris: Éditions Honoré Champion, 2007.

———. "'Pauvre Coppée,' naturaliste et poète béni." *Cahiers naturalistes* 81 (2007): 55–78.

———. *Stratégies de Rimbaud*. Paris: Éditions Honoré Champion, 2004.

Musset, Paul de. "Parisiens et Parisiennes." *Paris et les Parisiens au XIXe siècle: Mœurs, arts et monuments*. Edited by Eugène Lami. Paris: Morizot, 1856. 403–57.

Muzard. *Voyage d'un flâneur dans les rues de Paris, album biographique grotesque contenant les portraits en miniature de toutes les célébrités en plein vent recueillis et saisis à la volée par le petit fils de M. Muzard*. Paris: Chez les marchands de nouveauté, 1839. In: *Société des amis des arts de la Moselle. Exposition de 1869: Catalogue*. Metz: F. Blanc, 1869. Accessed June 23, 2011. http://gallica.bnf.fr/ark:/12148/bpt6k5493743j.

Nadar. *Le Cas de cloches*. Chambéry, France: Ménard, 1883.

———. "Les Histoires du mois: Le Daguérréotype acoustique." *Musée français-anglais*, December 24, 1856.

Nerval, Gérard de. "Le Boulevard du Temple." *Paris et ses alentours.* Edited by Michel Laporte. Paris: Encre Éditions, 1980. 63–84.

Nesci, Catherine. *Le Flâneur et les flâneuses: Les Femmes et la ville à l'époque romantique.* Grenoble: Éditions littéraires et linguistiques de l'Université de Grenoble (ELLUG), 2007.

Nochlin, Linda. "Gustave Courbet's *Meeting*: A Portrait of the Artist as a Wandering Jew." *Art Bulletin* 49,3 (1967): 209–22.

Nodier, Charles. *Dictionnaire des onomatopées.* Paris: Demonville, imprimeur-libraire, 1808. DOI: ark:/12148/bpt6k123239j.

Nora, Pierre. *Les Lieux de mémoire.* Paris: Gallimard, Quarto, 1997.

Nunley, Charles. "Huysmans and the Aesthetics of Solitude in *Croquis parisiens.*" *French Forum* 21.2 (1996): 187–206.

Ortigue, Joseph-Louis de. *Introduction à l'étude comparée des tonalités et principalement du chant grégorien et de la musique moderne.* Paris: Potier, 1853.

Pallasmaa, Juhani. *The Eyes of the Skin: Architecture and the Senses.* Chichester, England: Wiley and Sons, 2005.

Paris Guide par les principaux écrivains et artistes de la France: Deuxième Partie; La vie. Paris: Librairie Internationale, 1867.

Pearson, Roger. *Mallarmé and Circumstance: The Translation of Silence.* Oxford: Oxford University Press, 2004.

Picker, John M. *Victorian Soundscapes.* Oxford: Oxford University Press, 2003.

Pilinski, Adam, and Jules Cousin. *Cris de Paris au seizième siècle.* Paris: Veuve Labitte, 1885.

Planté, Christine. "Ce qu'on entend dans la voix: Notes à partir de Marceline Desbordes-Valmore." In *Penser la voix.* Edited by Gérard Dessons. Special issue of *La Licorne* 41 (1997): 87–106.

Preiss, Nathalie. *Les Physiologies en France au XIXe siècle: Étude historique, littéraire et stylistique.* Paris: Editions InterUniversitaires, 1999.

Prendergast, Christopher. *Paris and the Nineteenth Century.* Cambridge: Blackwell, 1992 [1996].

Proust, Marcel. *À la recherche du temps perdu. La Prisonnière.* Edited by J.-Y. Tadié, Antoine Compagnon and Pierre-Edmond Robert. Vol. 3. Bibliothèque de la Pléiade. Paris: Gallimard, 1988.

———. *In Search of Lost Time: The Captive; The Fugitive.* Translated by C. K. Scott Moncrieff and Terence Kilmartin. Vol. 5. New York: Modern Library, 1993.

Quérard, J. M. *Les Auteurs déguisés de la littérature française au XIXe siècle.* Paris: Au Bureau du bibliothécaire, 1845.

Raffaëlli, Jean-François. *Types de Paris.* Paris: Plon-Nourrit, 1889.

Rainbow, Bernarr. "Mainzer, Joseph." Grove Music Online. Oxford Music Online. Accessed September 24, 2010. http://www.oxfordmusiconline.com.proxy.lib.fsu.edu/subscriber/article/grove/music/17487.

Reboul, Yves. *Rimbaud dans son temps.* Études rimbaldiennes 3. Paris: Classiques Garnier, 2009.

Richepin, Jean. *La Chanson des Gueux, édition définitive.* Paris: Maurice Dreyfous, 1881.

Richter, Gerhard. *Walter Benjamin and the Corpus of Autobiography*. Detroit: Wayne State University Press, 2000.

Rieger, Dietmar. "'Ce qu'on voit dans les rues de Paris': Marginalités sociales et regards bourgeois." *Romantisme* 59 (1988): 19–29.

Rifkin, Adrian. *Street Noises: Parisian Pleasures 1900–1940*. Manchester: Manchester University Press, 1993.

Rigney, Ann. "The Dynamics of Remembrance." In Erll and Nünning, *Cultural Memory Studies*, 345–53.

——. "Plenitude, Scarcity and the Circulation of Cultural Memory." *Journal of European Studies* 35.1 (2005): 11–28.

Rimbaud, Arthur. *Complete Works, Selected Letters: A Bilingual Edition*. Translated by Wallace Fowlie. Foreword by Seth Whidden. Chicago: Chicago University Press, 2005.

——. *Œuvres complètes*. Edited by André Guyaux and Aurélia Cervoni. Bibliothèque de la Pléaide. Paris: Gallimard, 2009.

Robb, Graham. *La Poésie de Baudelaire et la poésie française 1838–1852*. Paris: Aubier, 1993.

Roos, Jane Mayo, ed. *A Painter's Poet: Stéphane Mallarmé and His Impressionist Circle*. New York: The Bertha and Karl Leubsdorf Art Gallery, Hunter College of the City of New York in conjunction with the Bibliothèque littéraire Jacques Doucet, Paris, 1999.

Rose, Margaret. Preface to *Flâneurs & Idlers: Louis Huart: Physiologie du flâneur 1841 & Albert Smith: The National History of the Idler upon Town 1848*. By Louis Huart and Albert Smith. Edited by Margaret Rose. Vol. 8. Bielefeld, Germany: Aisthesis Verlag, 2007.

Ṣaffār, Muḥammad. *Disorienting Encounters: Travels of a Moroccan Scholar in France in 1845–1846: The Voyage of Muḥammad as-Ṣaffār*. Translated and edited by Susan Gilson Miller. Berkeley: University of California Press, 1992.

Saint-Clair, Robert. "'Soyons chrétiens!'? Mémoire, anticapitalisme et communauté dans *Paris*." *La Poésie jubilatoire: Rimbaud, Verlaine et l'Album zutique*. Edited by Seth Whidden. Paris: Classiques Garnier, 2010.

Saint-Saëns, Camille. "A Note on Rameau." *Outspoken Essays on Music*. Translated by Fred Rothwell. London: Kegan Pual, Trench, Trubner and Co; New York: E. Dutton, 1922. 89–96.

Sand, George. "La Rêverie à Paris." In *Paris Guide par les principaux écrivains et artistes de la France: Deuxième Partie: La vie*. Paris: Librairie Internationale; Bruxelles: Lacroix, Verbroeckhoven et Cie, 1867. 1196–203.

Sanderson, John. *Sketches of Paris: Letters to His Friends*. Philadelphia: E. L. Carey & Hart, 1838.

Schafer, Murray R. *The Soundscape: Our Sonic Environment and the Tuning of the World*. Rochester, N.Y.: Destiny Books, 1994.

Schmidt, Leigh Eric. "Hearing Loss." In Bull and Black, *The Auditory Culture Reader*, 41–61.

Schwartz, Hillel. "The Indefensible Ear: A History." In Bull and Black, *The Auditory Culture Reader*, 487–501.

Schwartz, Vanessa R. "Cinematic Spectatorship before the Apparatus." *Cinema and the Invention of Modern Life*. Edited by Leo Charney and Vanessa Schwartz. Berkeley: University of California Press, 1995. 297–319.

Scott, Katie. "Edme Bouchardon's 'Cris de Paris': Crying Food in Early Modern Paris." *Word & Image: A Journal of Verbal/Visual Enquiry* 29:1 (2013): 59–91. Accessed July 15, 2014. DOI: 10.1080/02666286.2012.738081.

Shaw, Mary. "Mallarmé, Pre-Postmodern, Proto Dada." *Dalhousie French Studies* 25 (1993): 47–56.

Shesgreen, Sean. *Images of the Outcast: The Urban Poor in the Cries of London.* New Brunswick, N.J.: Rutgers University Press, 2002.

Sieburth, Richard. "Une idéologie du lisible: Le phénomène des 'Physiologies.'" *Romantisme* 47 (1985): 39–60.

Siefert, Louisa. *Rayons perdus.* Paris: Lemerre, 1868.

Simmel, Georg. *Simmel on Culture: Selected Writings.* Edited by David Frisby and Mike Featherstone. London: Sage Publications, 1997.

Smilor, Raymond W. "American Noise 1900–1930." *Hearing History: A Reader.* Edited by Mark M. Smith. Athens: University of Georgia Press, 2004. 319–30.

Smith, Mark M. *Sensing the Past: Seeing, Hearing, Smelling, Tasting, and Touching in History.* Berkeley: University of California Press, 2007.

Spitzer, Léo. "Étymologie d'un cri de Paris." *Études de style* (1970): 474–81.

Starobinski, Jean, and Richard Pevear. "Windows: From Rousseau to Baudelaire." *Hudson Review* 40.4 (1988): 551–60.

Stephens, Sonya. *Baudelaire's Prose Poems.* Oxford: Oxford University Press, 1999.

Stiénon, Valérie. *La Littérature des physiologies: Sociopoétique d'un genre panoramique (1830–1845).* Paris: Classiques Garnier, 2012.

Stierle, Karlheinz. *La Capitale des signes: Paris et son discours.* Paris: Éditions de la Maison de l'homme, 2001.

Strong, Rowland. *Sensations of Paris.* London: J. Long, 1912.

Sutton, Howard. *The Life and Work of Jean Richepin.* Geneva: Droz; Paris: Minard, 1961.

Tester, Keith, ed. *The Flâneur.* London: Routledge, 1994.

Texier, Edmond. "Le Pont Neuf." In *Tableau de Paris.* 2 vols. Paris: Paulin et Le Chevalier, 1852–53.

Thompson, Edward P. "Rough Music Reconsidered." *Folklore* 103.1 (1992): 3–26.

Thompson, Emily Ann. *The Soundscape of Modernity: Architectural Acoustics and the Culture of Listening in America, 1900–1933.* Cambridge: MIT Press, 2002.

Thompson, Victoria. *The Virtuous Marketplace: Women, Men, Money and Politics in Paris, 1830–1870.* Baltimore: Johns Hopkins University Press, 2000.

Tilly, Charles. "Charivaris, Repertoires, and Urban Politics." In *French Cities in the Nineteenth-Century.* Edited by John Merriman. London: Hutchinson, 1982. 73–91.

Tonkiss, Fran. "Aural Postcards: Sound, Memory, and the City. In Bull and Black, *The Auditory Culture Reader*, 303–310.

Traugott, Mark, ed. *The French Worker: Autobiographies from the Early Industrial Era.* Berkeley: University of California Press, 1993.

Trollope, Frances Milton. *Paris and the Parisians in 1835.* London: Bentley, 1836.

Trotter, David. "L'Esprit Gaulois: Humour and National Mythology." In *Humour and History.* Edited by Keith Cameron. Oxford: Intellect Books, 1993. 70–83.

Vaillant, Derek. "Peddling Noise: Contesting the Civic Soundscape of Chicago, 1890–1913." *Journal of the Illinois State Historical Society* 96.3 (Autumn 2003): 257–87.

Vidler, Anthony. "Reading the City: The Urban Book from Mercier to Mittérand." *PMLA* 122.1 (Jan. 2007): 235–51.

Vigier, Philippe. *Paris pendant la monarchie de Juillet (1830–1848)*. Paris: Hachette, 1991.

Vincent, Charles. "Les Dernières Échoppes." In *Paris Guide par les principaux écrivains et artistes de la France: Deuxième Partie: La vie*. Paris: Librairie Internationale; Bruxelles: Lacroix, Verbroeckhoven et Cie, 1867. 972–80.

Vincent-Buffault, Anne. *Histoire des larmes: XVIIIe–XIXe siècles*. Paris: Payot, 2001. Translation of *The History of Tears: Sensibility and Sentimentality in France*. New York: St. Martin's 1991.

Virmaître, Charles. *Paris qui s'efface*. 2nd ed. Paris: A. Savine, 1887.

Vissière, Laurent. "La Bouche et le Ventre de Paris." *Histoire Urbaine* 16.2 (2006): 71–89.

———. "Des cris pour rire? Dérision et autodérision dans les Cris de Paris XIIe–XVIe siècles." *La Dérision au Moyen Âge: De la pratique sociale au rituel politique*. Edited by Élisabeth Crouzet-Pavan and Jacques Verger. Paris: Presses de l'Université de Paris-Sorbonne, 2007. 85–106.

Voisin-Fougère, Marie-Ange. *Le Rire de Rabelais au XIXe siècle: Histoire d'un malentendu*. Dijon, France: Éditions universitaires de Dijon, 2009.

Wittrock, Wolfgang. *Toulouse-Lautrec: The Complete Prints*. London: Sotherby's Publications by P. Wilson Publishers, 1985.

Yriarte, Charles. *Paris grotesque: Les Célébrités de la rue Paris (1815–1863)*. Paris: Librairie parisienne Dupray de la Mahérie éditeur, 1864.

———. "Les Types parisiens. Les Clubs." In *Paris Guide par les principaux écrivains et artistes de la France. Deuxième Partie: La Vie*. Paris: Librairie Internationale; Bruxelles: Lacroix, Verbroeckhoven et Cie, 1867. 929–37.

Zachmann, Gayle. *Frameworks for Mallarmé: The Photo and the Graphic of an Interdisciplinary Aesthetic*. Albany: SUNY, 2008.

Zucchi, John E. *The Little Slaves of the Harp: Italian Child Street Musicians in Nineteenth-Century Paris, London and New York*. Buffalo: McGill-Queen's University Press, 1992.

Index

AIMÉE BOUTIN teaches French literature and culture in the Department of Modern Languages and Linguistics at Florida State University. She is the author of *Maternal Echoes: The Poetry of Marceline Desbordes-Valmore and Alphonse de Lamartine*.

STUDIES IN SENSORY HISTORY

The University of Illinois Press
is a founding member of the
Association of American University Presses.

Composed in 10.5/13 Marat Pro
with Trade Gothic Condensed display
by Jim Proefrock
at the University of Illinois Press
Manufactured by Sheridan Books, Inc.

University of Illinois Press
1325 South Oak Street
Champaign, IL 61820-6903
www.press.uillinois.edu